The Civil War Tourist

Visiting Civil War Battlefields and Historical Sites

By Lenny Flank

Red and Black Publishers, Florida

Contents

Introduction

The Civil War could truly be thought of as the single defining event in American history. Nearly all of our domestic history for the preceding 100 years was a prelude that led up to it, and nearly all of our domestic history for the following 100 years was a reaction that resulted from it. The United States is the nation it is today, it could be argued, largely because of the Civil War. The War's social and political effects are still with us today and can be seen all around us.

Since then, although "race" has continued to play an often-unspoken role in American society, most people have shunned the racism of the past and have now embraced the goals of cultural diversity and racial equality. This was brought home to me by a docent who worked at a museum in Vicksburg MS that I visited while researching this book, who remarked, "We recognize here that the Civil War is over."

Sadly, though, there is still a small but thriving political movement in the United States today which not only does *not* recognize that the Civil War is over, but thinks that the wrong side won. They have adopted the same Confederate political arguments (and many times the same Confederate symbols) that led the nation to disaster back in 1861. And so, as the politics of racism and demagoguery once again attempts to divide us, the lessons of the Civil War are more relevant today than ever—so we do not repeat the mistakes of the past.

Those lessons can be found in the battlefields that we commemorate and memorialize. When one thinks of the American Civil War, one is apt to think of battles in Virginia, Tennessee, or Georgia. But in reality the Civil War was fought on a huge scale, with land battles as far north as Ohio and Vermont and as far west as Kansas, Arizona, and New Mexico. On sea, the war ranged across the Atlantic and Pacific, from the American coasts to the shores of Africa and Asia. In geography, as in social effects, the Civil War was wide-ranging.

But sadly, our Civil War history is slowly disappearing. The suburban sprawl produced by America's rapid growth in the 20th century overran and destroyed many historic sites before they could be preserved, and many significant battlefields are now lost under a layer of shopping malls and residential neighborhoods. Some sites were neglected because their history was not something that the local citizens particularly wanted to remember—nobody likes to memorialize a battle or war that they *lost*. And even today many Civil War sites, including such famous landmarks as Gettysburg, are threatened with encroaching commercial development. Working together with the National Park Service and state governments, private nonprofit organizations like the Civil War Trust and the National Trust for Historic Preservation have been raising money (and also raising awareness) in order to protect, obtain, and preserve our nation's historical sites and battlefields. Their admirable goal is, as they put it, to "Save Our History".

On the surface, this book is a history travelogue. Civil War battlefields such as Gettysburg and Antietam are some of the most popular tourist destinations in the US. So this is a narrative of the many Civil War sites, large and small, that I have visited over the years. It includes famous battlefields that are run by the National Park Service, and smaller unknown or forgotten places that are preserved as state or county historical parks, or which are not preserved at all but have miraculously managed to survive for a century and a half.

(A note about names: many of the battles in the US Civil War actually have two different names, since the North tended to name its fights after nearby rivers and the South preferred to name them after nearby towns. Thus, the Battle of Antietam is also known as the Battle of Sharpsburg, and the Battles of First and Second Manassas are also known as First and Second Bull Run. In this account, I will apply the name that has been officially used by the federal or state historical park which preserves the battlefield.)

But this travelogue is also a journey into America, into the history and culture which, for better or worse, have made us what we are today as a nation. The roots of 21st century America can be found in the fields of Gettysburg, the walls of Fort Sumter, the earthworks of Fort Pillow, and the cottage at Appomattox. The ghosts of the Civil War have never left us.

Slavery

A total of 13 British colonies were originally established by Royal Charter in American territory. They were tightly controlled by the British government. Under the mercantile colonial system, colonies were viewed as simply ways of siphoning wealth from foreign territories and sending it back to the homeland. Many of the colonial charters spelled out how trade was to be conducted in the colonies, with England having special privileges (including, in some cases, the right that all colonial trade had to be with, or at least go through, England). A series of laws known as the Navigation Acts formalized these restrictions, limiting the amount of manufacturing that the colonists could do (forbidding them outright from making their own iron cooking pots, for example), and essentially turning the colonies into a source of raw materials for British industry and a captive market for the finished products.

Almost from the beginning, however, the Thirteen American Colonies were differentiated from North to South. In the Southern colonies, the warm wet climate and rich soil was best-suited for large-scale agriculture, and most of the population was involved with the "plantation" system in which cash crops like tobacco, sugar, rice or indigo were grown on large farms and then shipped to England. In the Northern colonies, however, where large-scale plantations were not practical, most of the population either lived on small single-family subsistence farms, or were involved in the industrial trades (iron-working, leather-making, printing, etc) or with commercial shipping or fishing.

They were two very different economies, and they led to two very different cultures. In the North, most commercial shops were small and the owners usually did much of the work themselves. To help them, many proprietors took on "indentured servants": these were people from Europe (usually England) who agreed to work in the tradesman's shop for a set period (around seven years) in exchange for having their passage to America paid for by the proprietor. Later, as immigration proved too low to meet the demand for labor, workshops began to take in young boys as "apprentices", who would be housed and fed by the proprietor in exchange for learning the trade on the job, until the apprentice was ready to set up a shop of his own.

In the South, an entirely different social structure appeared. Here, it was most economical to have large plantation farms that could be worked with great numbers of the cheapest unskilled labor possible. In the first years of the American colonies, much of this cheap labor came from beggars, criminals, and other "undesirables" who were rounded up in London and sent to the colonies in lieu of a jail sentence. In 1619, however, a new source of cheap labor opened up when a Dutch trader sold a cargo of 20 African slaves to a plantation owner in Jamestown VA. By the time of the American Revolution in 1775, the import of enslaved people from Africa had been legalized in all 13 colonies, though by far the heaviest concentration was in the Southern plantation states. (A significant number of African-Americans in the North were freemen, and some 5,000 of them served in the Continental Army during the Revolutionary War.)

By the end of the 18th century, however, just after the United States won its independence from Britain, the plantation economy faced a crisis. The large tobacco, sugar, rice, and indigo plantations were losing productivity as the soil became exhausted, and new global sources of these products (especially in the Caribbean) were cutting into American exports and weakening the South's economy. Just in time, a new product appeared: cotton. England was beginning its Industrial Revolution and would soon become the textile capitol of the world, as mechanized looms and spinning jennies churned out finished cloth at a stupendous rate. To feed their insatiable demand for raw materials, the British imported cotton from all over the world—and this was a crop that was suitable for slave labor on the Southern plantations.

But it was an invention in 1793 that changed the Southern cotton industry and inadvertently set the country on the path that eventually led to Civil War. Although cotton was a profitable plantation crop, it was very labor-intensive: before the cotton could be spun, the large seeds had to be painstakingly cleaned out of the fibers by hand.

In 1793, a young man named Eli Whitney had just graduated from Yale and taken a job in South Carolina to work as a tutor for several plantation owners. In casual conversations, they mentioned the difficulty of separating cotton seeds from the fibers, and Whitney had a flash of insight. Later, the story would be told that he had gotten the basic idea for his seed-separating machine by the memory of watching a cat trying to attack a caged chicken: the cat's claws pulled the feathers through the wire cage, leaving the chicken behind.

Over the next few weeks, tinkering in his spare time, Eli Whitney invented his "cotton gin". Although its social effect would be huge, the machine itself was simple: the operator would pour freshly-picked cotton balls into a hopper and turn a handle. This would rotate a wire drum covered with hooks that passed between the teeth of a metal comb. The teeth of the comb were wide enough for the hooks to pass through, but too narrow for the cotton seeds. So as the drum turned, the cotton fibers would be caught by the hooks and pulled through the comb, while the seeds would be stripped off by the comb's teeth and fall away. A second drum, spinning more rapidly and covered with brushes, would then rub the seed-free cotton fibers off the first drum and collect them inside. The seeds would drop out of one side of the machine, and the clean cotton fibers would pile out the other side. The cotton seeds could now be gathered and pressed to make oil, meal, and animal feed, while the clean cotton fibers could be sold to the English textile mills.

Using a cotton gin, a slave labor force could now more than triple its output. It transformed the Southern economy. In 1830, the US had produced 750,000 bales of cotton: by 1850, when Eli Whitney's invention had become widespread across the South, production soared to 2,850,000 bales.

As the cotton economy grew, so too did the need for enslaved people to run it. From 1800 to 1850, the number of slaves in the South increased by 500%, and by 1860 the Southern plantation states were producing two-thirds of the world's entire cotton crop. The cotton plantations became fabulously wealthy, the English market seemed limitless, and "King Cotton" reigned supreme. The entire Southern economy was utterly dependent upon cotton and the slave labor which produced it. And that led to political discord.

In the North, while slavery was legal, it never became a large part of the economy, and there was always some tension over the institution. When Thomas Jefferson wrote his first draft of the Declaration of Independence, one of the grievances he charged King George with was allowing the slave trade in the colonies. The Southern colonies, who were completely dependent economically upon their enslaved labor, objected to this, fearing that it would lead to restrictions on slave-keeping, and the Continental Congress struck out this portion of Jefferson's draft. (Ironically, Jefferson himself was a plantation slave-owner, as were many of the Founding Fathers.)

When the US Constitution was being debated in 1788, the subject of slavery came up again. Since the number of political delegates each state had in the House of Representatives was dependent upon its population, the Southern states argued that its huge numbers of slaves should be counted towards its population, while the Northern states countered that under the Southern states' own laws their enslaved people were "property" and not residents. Eventually the argument was settled with the "Three-Fifths Compromise", in which it was agreed to count 60% of the slave numbers as "population". (The words "slave" and "slavery" do not appear anywhere in the Constitution—it instead refers euphemistically to "servants" who are "bound to labor".)

Slave auction, a contemporary illustration

At about this time, a new political movement appeared in the US—the "abolitionists". Based mostly in the North and made up at first of religious groups, they held the then-radical idea that African-Americans were people, that slavery as an institution was wrong and un-Christian, and that enslaved people should be freed and made equal citizens with full rights to vote and hold property.

At first the Southern slave states looked upon the abolitionists as just a kooky lunatic fringe—but as the movement grew and began to gain political power, they viewed them as a deadly threat to the whole slavery-based "Southern way of life". Southern states passed a number of "slave codes" which made it illegal for any African-American slave to be taught how to read and write or to possess a weapon. These repressive laws won sympathy for the abolitionist viewpoint, and escaped or freed slaves like Frederick Douglass became celebrities in the North.

By 1804, every Northern state had already abolished slavery within its borders. In 1808 Congress formally banned the African slave trade—it now became illegal to import enslaved people from overseas. Those slaves already inside the US, however, were unaffected by this law, and the population of enslaved people, concentrated mostly in the South, continued to grow. By 1860 there were at least 4 million African-American slaves in the US, making up about one-third of the South's entire population and constituting the majority of people in many areas.

The abolitionist movement meanwhile also continued to grow. In 1852, Harriet Beecher Stowe wrote *Uncle Tom's Cabin*, a novel that depicted the life of a slave in a Southern plantation. It became one of the highest-selling books ever printed in the US to that time. (According to legend, when President Abraham Lincoln met Stowe years later, he is reported to have said to her, "So *you* are the little woman who wrote the book that started this big war.") Abolitionist newspapers began to appear throughout the North and, with great risk, in some of the South.

No longer confined to religious groups, the abolitionists also began to frame their argument in economic terms: the economic ideology in the "Yankee-trader" North was free-market capitalism, of which "free labor" that could be bought for market wage rates (and which could use those wages to purchase commodities) was a crucial pillar. Slavery was, they argued, economically inefficient and was holding back the development of the American economy.

With words, came action. An entire illegal network known as the "Underground Railroad" appeared, dedicated solely to helping escaped slaves from the South reach freedom in Canada. Estimates of the number of "railroad passengers" range from 40,000 to over 100,000.

And soon abolitionist "action" led directly to bloodshed.

Bleeding Kansas
1854
Kansas

One could make a good argument that the Civil War didn't really start in 1861 at Fort Sumter, but in 1854 in Kansas.

In 1818, the Territory of Missouri applied for US statehood, but was refused because the Northern states did not want to admit another slave state. When Maine applied for statehood in 1819, the slavery issue came to the fore again. In 1820, the "Missouri Compromise" was reached—Maine would be admitted as a free state, Missouri would be admitted as a slave state, and a line was set at latitude 36' 30", above which any future US states would be free states, and below which they would be slave states. In 1850, another compromise was reached regarding the spread of slavery into the new territories that had been acquired through the war with Mexico: Texas would be slave, California would be free, and the rest would be allowed to vote on the matter—a procedure referred to as "Popular Sovereignty".

The Missouri Compromise ended the political contention over the slavery issue, but only for a while. In

1854, Nebraska Territory applied for statehood. Under the terms of the Missouri Compromise, it would be admitted as a free state. But then Senator Stephen A Douglas of Illinois (who would soon become famous as Abraham Lincoln's campaign debate opponent) introduced a bill to fund a transcontinental railroad which, coincidentally, would pass through Chicago. To pass his railroad bill, Douglas needed support from Southern Senators, and he got it by introducing a bill to split the Nebraska Territory into two separate states (Nebraska and Kansas), and allow each of their state legislatures to vote whether they wanted slavery or not. This effectively ended the Missouri Compromise. The Nebraska-Kansas Act and its "Popular Sovereignty" policy sounded nice and democratic, but in reality its major effect was to fan the flames of sectarian conflict and bring the tensions between North and South to the boiling point.

Two elections were scheduled in Kansas: in November 1854 voters would elect an "observer" representative to Congress, then in March 1855 they would elect a Territorial Legislature which would write a state constitution—and, significantly, in the process decide whether the state would be "free" or "slave". Both the pro-slavery faction, known as "bushwhackers", and the anti-slavery side, known as "jayhawkers", called for outside help. The elections quickly became wars. In Boston a group was formed called the "Emigrant Aid Society" which helped abolitionists travel to Kansas, founding the cities of Lawrence and Topeka. In Missouri, thousands of people crossed the border to vote illegally in the Kansas elections.

Things escalated out of control. Missouri Senator David Atchison called on the bushwhackers to "kill every God-damned abolitionist in the district". Back east, abolitionist leader Rev Henry Ward Beecher began smuggling Sharps rifles to jayhawker forces in Kansas (the guns became known as "Beecher's Bibles"). In one incident, a load of rifles was found aboard the steamship *Arabia*, hidden in a chest labeled "carpenter's tools".

Everywhere in the US, people chose up sides, as the slavery issue divided the country. In the North, abolitionists held "Free Kansas" rallies: in the South, guns and money flowed to pro-slavery militias.

When the elections were held, the pro-slavery forces won by large majorities through illegal votes from non-residents. The hastily-convened Territorial Legislature met in Lecompton and passed a Slavery Code, not only legalizing slavery but making it illegal to speak out in favor of abolition. They became known in the North as "The Bogus Laws". In response, the anti-slavery faction declared the election illegitimate and formed its own "territorial government" in Topeka. President Franklin Pierce now feared that an actual civil war would break out within the state, and declaring that the pro-slavery Lecompton legislature had won the elections, he recognized it as the only legal authority and ordered troops to close down the rival government in Topeka. Congress sent its own delegation to Kansas to investigate, which concluded that the elections had been fraudulent and that the vast majority of the residents were anti-slavery (though most of them were not abolitionist—they were "Free Soil" homesteading farmers who simply didn't want large slave-holding plantations to come in and buy up all the farming lands). President Pierce continued to uphold the pro-slavery legislature as the territory's legitimate government.

The violence now grew, as armed private armies roamed the territory attacking each other. On May 21, 1856, a unit of bushwhacker "militia" rode into the anti-slavery stronghold of Lawrence and began shooting and burning. Two abolitionist newspaper presses were destroyed, several buildings were burned down, and dozens of stores looted; one of the raiders was killed when a burning building fell on him. In retaliation for the raid, abolitionist leader John Brown and his "militia", armed mostly with pikes and farm tools, attacked the settlement along the Pottawatomie Creek on May 24, dragging five pro-slavery activists (two of them territorial government officials) out of their beds and executing them. On August 30, 1856, seven men were killed in another armed clash involving John Brown and his followers in Osawatomie: in turn, two years later in May 1858, at Marais des Cynges near Kansas City, "Border Ruffians" from Missouri shot five abolitionists. In all, at least 56 people are known to have been killed in armed confrontations between pro- and anti-slavery forces. The newspapers labeled it "Bleeding Kansas".

The political process was just as skewed. In 1857 the territorial legislature drew up a constitution that was a virtual copy of slave-state Missouri's and, supported by now-President James Buchanan, applied for Statehood, but Congress refused to accept it and ordered new elections. This time the anti-slavery faction won, and in 1859 they wrote a "free" constitution and again applied for admission as a state. Now it was the Southerners who blocked it in Congress. It wasn't until after the slave states seceded in 1861 that Kansas was admitted to the Union.

John Brown in Kansas—with Bible in one hand and gun in another

Today, the Kansas History Museum in Topeka has a number of exhibits presenting artifacts that interpret the "Bleeding Kansas" period. In Missouri, Kansas City's "Steamboat *Arabia* Museum" has a display of Sharps rifles that were confiscated during the "*Arabia* Incident".

Dred Scott Case
1859
Missouri

The violence of "Bleeding Kansas" brought the whole
slavery issue to a head. It destroyed one political party
and created another—and then a Supreme Court ruling
removed any possible reconciliation.

In the period before the Civil War, there were two
political parties in the US. The "Democrats" were the
party that grew out of the election of Andrew Jackson.
Before then, decision-making power had always been
with Congress and the President's job was to carry it
out. But Jackson had transformed the office of the
President: he made his own policies and browbeat
Congress into accepting them, and made many of his
policy decisions unilaterally and without Congressional
input. In effect, Jackson created the modern Presidency.

Jackson's political takeover did not go unopposed.
The "Nationalist Republican" party was made up of
Southern "states' rights" supporters who feared a
centralized government, and Northerners who favored a
strong Federal Government but did not like Jackson's
domination of it. But mostly, their entire political
platform was simple opposition to Andrew Jackson and

his Democrats. Mocking Jackson as a "King" and his supporters as "Tories", the Nationalist Republicans took the nickname "Whigs", adopted from the anti-royalist faction in England. But the American Whigs suffered from internal ideological schisms: the only glue that held them together was their common opposition to the Jacksonian Democrats. Only two Whig candidates were ever elected President—William Henry Harrison and Zachary Taylor—and both of them died in office.

It was the slavery issue in the 1850s (and particularly the Nebraska-Kansas Act) that finally killed the Whigs: an uneasy coalition of both pro- and anti-slavery groups, the Whig Party was unable to decide between the two factions and therefore lost them both, splitting itself down the middle. The pro-slavery Southerners left and joined the Democratic Party: the Northern abolitionists left and joined the new Republican Party. After 1854 the Whigs no longer ran any candidates for office.

As the Whigs weakened and collapsed, a call went out for a new political party, which would be openly anti-slavery. In March 1854, a convention of delegates, some of them former Whigs and some of them abolitionist Democrats, met in Wisconsin and formed the "Republican Party". Its growth was rapid: in the 1854 elections the new party won control of the Michigan State Legislature, and in 1856 it won a majority of the US House of Representatives—and its first Presidential candidate, John Fremont, carried 11 states.

Meanwhile, in St Louis, another storm was about to be unleashed. Dred Scott was an African-American who had been born into slavery in Virginia in 1795, and after a time was sold in St Louis to an Army doctor named John Emerson. Emerson in turn was assigned to various Army posts in Illinois and Wisconsin, both of which were, under the Missouri Compromise, "free" states, and during this time Scott married a fellow slave named Harriett. When Emerson died in 1843, both of these enslaved people became the inherited property of his widow Irene. In 1846, Dred Scott tried to purchase freedom for both he and his wife by paying Irene the ordinary purchase price for two slaves, but she refused.

Scott and a group of abolitionist lawyers then filed a lawsuit, arguing that during his residency in those "free" states where slavery had been illegal he had in effect been emancipated and was no longer a slave. The case, filed in St Louis, went all the way to the Supreme Court.

Dred Scott, a contemporary photograph

In March 1857, Supreme Court Chief Justice Roger Taney wrote the majority opinion. By a 7-2 vote, the Court concluded that as the son of two slaves, Scott was, legally, "property" and was not a citizen of the US or of any state. He therefore had no ability to sue in court, and his suit was dismissed. Further, the Missouri Compromise was itself unconstitutional because it improperly interfered with the ordinary property rights of slave-owners. As a result, the Compromise could no longer be enforced, and slaveholders were legally entitled to take their property (their slaves) with them any place in the United States. Slavery could not be banned or restricted anywhere in the country.

Taney hoped that this decision would be the definitive word on the matter and would settle the slavery issue once and for all. He could not have been more wrong. Instead, the effect was immediate and explosive: Northern abolitionists condemned the decision and swore to use any means to oppose it, while pro-slavery Southerners declared that it allowed the spread of slavery into every Northern state.

The path to war was now set.

Today, the Federal Courtroom in St Louis where the *Dred Scott* case was first argued is located on the grounds of the Jefferson National Expansion Memorial, near the St Louis Arch. The Courthouse was built in 1828 and remodeled in 1851, with a new dome later constructed during the Civil War. As with all Southern courthouses, the building was used as an auction-house to sell off enslaved people whose legal owners had died without a will, as part of their estate.

In 1930, the City of St Louis built another courthouse and the Old Courthouse sat empty. The family who had originally donated the land for the building now sued to regain the deed, since it had been specified that the land be used only for a courthouse. In 1940, the Old Courthouse became part of the current National Memorial. There is a display of historical documents and exhibits interpreting the case and the Court rulings.

John Brown's Raid

October 16, 1859
West Virginia

One of the northern abolitionists who had come to prominence in "Bleeding Kansas" was John Brown. Born in Connecticut, his family had moved to Ohio when he was young. Always in debt, Brown had failed in a number of business ventures before joining the abolitionist movement in the 1840s. When the conflict broke out in Kansas, Brown moved there with five of his sons. After pro-slavery militia raided the town of Lawrence in May 1856, Brown retaliated by leading a band of 22 followers on a raid at Pottawatomie Creek, killing five pro-slavery settlers (one of Brown's sons was also killed during the raid). He became notorious across the country for this and other ruthless attacks.

In 1857, Brown and his followers left Kansas and returned back east, where, convinced that only a violent uprising would be able to defeat slavery, he now laid grandiose plans to spark a cataclysmic slave rebellion that would sweep across the South. After two years of preaching and recruiting, he had 22 men, including three of his sons and five former slaves, ready to follow him.

By 1859 they were prepared to start their rebellion. Believing that thousands of enslaved people throughout the South would follow his example and rise in revolt, Brown concluded that he would need weapons to arm them all. So his first target was the Federal Arsenal at Harpers Ferry. Located in what was then a part of Virginia, Harpers Ferry was an important industrial center, with dozens of water-powered mills and factories strung out along the banks of the Shenandoah River. Among these was the Harpers Ferry Armory, which manufactured firearms for the US Army. One of the people to which Brown confided his plans was former slave and abolitionist icon Frederick Douglass, who viewed him as a crazy madman and told him simply, "You'll never get out alive".

John Brown's Fort

Just after dark on October 16, Brown made his move, though he had no real strategy, had made no plans for the large-scale distribution of weapons, and had no escape route if things failed. His small "army" entered the Arsenal and took control of four buildings: the firehouse, the master-at-arms cottage, and the two storehouses where the weapons were kept. Brown also gathered up several dozen hostages. A few local citizens were killed when they tried to intervene.

Federal troops were then dispatched to the scene, and the next morning Brown and his followers (holed up inside the firehouse, which became known as "John Brown's Fort") were surrounded by a company of US troops commanded by Lt Col Robert E Lee. Two days later, Lee ended the standoff by storming the building. In the firefight, ten of Brown's followers, including two of his sons, were killed, and Brown himself was wounded and captured.

His trial on charges of treason and murder caused a nationwide sensation and galvanized the public. Southern slave-holders considered Brown to be a mere criminal, while Northern abolitionists praised him as a hero. Even the pacifist writer Henry David Thoreau wrote, "I think that for once the Sharps rifles and the revolvers were employed in a righteous cause." When Brown was hanged on December 2, 1859, the abolitionist movement gained a powerful symbolic martyr—one of the most famous songs of the coming Civil War would be titled "John Brown's Body".

After the Civil War, Storer's College was built in the town of Harper's Ferry. One of the first racially integrated colleges in the US, it remained open until 1954. In 1944, the area around Harper's Ferry, including the College, was designated as a National Monument.

Today, the Harper's Ferry Arsenal is a National Historic Site which has grown to around 4000 acres. The master-at-arms cottage still exists and houses a museum, while only the foundations of the two armory buildings remain. The firehouse that served as "John Brown's Fort" has been reconstructed. Most of the buildings along the main streets have been restored to their 1850's appearance, and contain museums and interpretive displays with re-enactors.

Fort Sumter
April 12, 1861
South Carolina

In his death, John Brown did more to end slavery in the US than he did in his life. His trial and execution deepened the rift that had always existed between North and South, and the subsequent election of Abraham Lincoln and the anti-slavery Republican Party in 1860 made the gap unbridgeable. Secession was now inevitable.

South Carolina was first to act. Even before Lincoln had assumed office, the state legislature passed a motion of secession which was confirmed soon after by referendum. On December 20, South Carolina formally announced her withdrawal from the United States. In Congress, the Crittenden Compromise was proposed, which in essence resurrected the old Missouri Compromise, drawing a line across the continent to divide slave states from free. But it was far too late. By February 1861, Mississippi, Florida, Alabama, Georgia, Louisiana and Texas had all seceded, and others followed later.

All of these states issued statements of secession, and all of them cited "slavery" as their reason for seceding. "For the last ten years we have had numerous and serious causes of complaint against our non-slave-holding confederate States with reference to the subject of African slavery.... A brief history of the rise, progress, and policy of anti-slavery and the political organization into whose hands the administration of the Federal Government has been committed will fully justify the pronounced verdict of the people of Georgia." "A Declaration of the Immediate Causes which Induce and Justify the Secession of the State of Mississippi from the Federal Union .... Our position is thoroughly identified with the institution of slavery—the greatest material interest of the world." "An increasing hostility on the part of the non-slaveholding States to the institution of slavery, has led to a disregard of their obligations, and the laws of the General Government have ceased to effect the objects of the Constitution .... Thus the constituted compact has been deliberately broken and disregarded by the non-slaveholding States, and the consequence follows that South Carolina is released from her obligation." "In all the non-slave-holding States ... based upon an unnatural feeling of hostility to these Southern States and their beneficent and patriarchal system of African slavery, proclaiming the debasing doctrine of equality of all men, irrespective of race or color—a doctrine at war with nature, in opposition to the experience of mankind, and in violation of the plainest revelations of Divine Law .... By the secession of six of the slave-holding States, and the certainty that others will speedily do likewise, Texas has no alternative but to remain in an isolated connection with the North, or unite her destinies with the South." "The Federal Government, having perverted said powers, not only to the injury of the people of Virginia, but to the oppression of the Southern Slaveholding States... the people of Virginia, do declare and ordain that the ordinance adopted by the people of this State [in which] the Constitution of the United States of America was ratified [is] hereby repealed and abrogated."

When Lincoln assumed office on March 4, 1861, he was faced with what has been famously called a "slave-holder's rebellion". Since the time of the campaign, Lincoln had portrayed the conflict as a struggle to maintain the National Union and democracy: "We must settle this question now," he remarked, "whether in a free government the minority have the right to break up the government whenever they choose. If we fail, it will go far to prove the inability of the people to govern themselves." Although Lincoln was personally opposed to the institution of slavery, he did not openly adopt the abolitionist position of outlawing it—partly because of the political ramifications which that would have produced in the "border states" who, though opposed to secession, were ambivalent about the issue of ending slavery.

But, ideology and politics aside, now Lincoln faced the practical problem of dealing with the rebellion—and the focus of this attention fell upon Fort Sumter in South Carolina. When that state seceded, the US Army held two forts at the mouth of Charleston Harbor. Fort Moultrie had been built during the Revolutionary War and rebuilt since then: Fort Sumter, which lay directly across the channel, was larger and newer. Both forts were under the command of Major Robert Anderson, who had been there only a month. Although his personal views were pro-slavery, he was opposed to secession and remained loyal to the Union. When South Carolina seceded, Anderson decided that he didn't have enough troops or supplies to hold both forts: he therefore withdrew from Fort Moultrie and concentrated all his forces at Fort Sumter.

The political situation surrounding the Fort was delicate. South Carolina and the new Confederate States of America viewed the Federal troops there as foreign occupiers and demanded possession of the Fort; Anderson, a staunch Union supporter, refused to leave. Lincoln did not want to abandon Anderson and the Fort, and was determined to protect what he viewed as US Government property, but he also did not want to undertake any aggressive actions that might antagonize states like Virginia, North Carolina, Maryland and Kentucky, which had not yet voted to secede and which he hoped might all still be persuaded to remain in the Union. And Lincoln had a time limit: the Fort had enough provisions for about a month: if it was not relieved and resupplied by the middle of April, Anderson would be forced to surrender. (President James Buchanan, as one of his last acts in office, had tried to resupply Fort Sumter that February, but the unarmed merchant ship he sent had quickly retreated when the Confederate batteries in the harbor fired warning shots at it.)

Fort Sumter, in Charleston Harbor, viewed from one of the Confederate gun positions

Lincoln decided that he would send a convoy to Fort Sumter with supplies of food and water, but he would not reinforce it with new troops and weapons. Now, the political pressure was on Confederate President Jefferson Davis. He had already demanded the surrender of the Fort and had been refused: it was now up to him whether to use force to prevent the Federals from being resupplied. In the end, Davis made his choice: he ordered the local Confederate military commander, General Pierre Beauregard, to once more demand the Fort's surrender, and to take it if refused. At 4:30am on April 12, 1861, Beauregard's cannon batteries opened up. The Civil War had begun.

Bombardment of Fort Sumter, a contemporary illustration

Over the next day and a half, the Confederates poured over 3,000 shells into Fort Sumter. Finally, Major Anderson, low on supplies and with no hope of rescue or reinforcement, surrendered at 2:30pm on April 14. He and his men were carried back to New York on the convoy ships that had been unsuccessfully sent to supply them. Despite all the firing from both sides, nobody had been killed in the siege (except for one soldier who died in an accidental powder explosion).

Three days later, Virginia voted to secede, followed shortly afterwards by Arkansas, North Carolina, and Tennessee.

After the Civil War, the abandoned ruins of Fort Sumter were rebuilt, with lower walls and newer guns. It was abandoned again in 1876 and used as a lighthouse, but when the Spanish-American War broke out in 1898 Sumter was once again restored and new gun batteries were added. In 1948 the site became a National Monument, and in 1966 the Fort was added to the Register of Historic Places.

Today, the Fort is part of the Fort Sumter National Monument in Charleston Harbor, which also contains the Revolutionary War site of Fort Moultrie. The Visitors Center contains exhibits and artifacts, and is the departure point for the ferry that takes visitors to the Fort.

Just a few blocks from the Fort Sumter Visitor Center is the Charleston Museum, where the original desk at which the Declaration of Secession was signed is now on display.

Tredegar Iron Works
1861
Virginia

When the Confederate States of America was formed in 1861, it was the fourth-wealthiest country in the world at that time. But its agrarian-based economy was not suited for the new type of war which it faced, and that would ultimately prove to be its undoing.

Despite its geographic size, the Confederacy was only sparsely populated. Compared to the North's 23 million inhabitants the South had only 9 million—about 40% of which were enslaved. In military-age males, the North had 3.5 million; the Confederacy had only 1 million (of which over a third were slaves). The largest city in the South was New Orleans, with 160,000 people, but this was only the sixth-largest city in the US. The next-largest Confederate city was Charleston SC, with only 40,000 citizens (the 22nd-largest city in the US).

The American Civil War was in many ways the first "modern" war, in which large bodies of troops (both volunteer and conscripted) faced each other with a variety of new and deadly weapons that were churned out in vast quantities, making the "national economy" an important weapon of war. But in terms of the manufacturing industries which would play such a crucial role in the coming conflict, the Confederacy was far behind. The South had only 20,600 manufacturing plants, with around 200,000 factory workers (about 95% of which were slaves). The North, by contrast, had 100,500 factories which employed over 1.1 million workers. In total, the South was producing about $150 million worth of manufactured goods before the war: the North was turning out over $1.5 billion.

The new Confederate Government, recognizing the weakness of its industrial sector, convinced itself that it could remain financially viable through its strong export market. The Southern economy was almost entirely dependent on exports of tobacco, sugar, and, above all, cotton. The pre-war South accounted for 70% of the United States total exports, and cotton made up three-fourths of that. Because European nations like England and France were completely dependent upon Southern cotton to feed their vast textile industry, the Confederate Government at first declared an embargo on the sale of cotton, hoping that this financial blackmail would force the European powers into intervening on the side of the secessionists.

In the end, things did not turn out that way. When Europe refused to be coerced, Richmond frantically tried to resume the flow of cotton, but by this time the Federal blockades of Confederate ports had cut off their exports by 90%, ending the Confederacy's foreign exchange and crippling the entire economy. Southern states were forced to quickly improvise their own manufacturing capacity, but they lacked the raw materials necessary for this.

The Confederacy did begin the war with a fairly good transportation network of railroads and rivers, but quickly lost both, as the Union Navy closed off the river ports and the railroads deteriorated from the South's inability to manufacture new rails and replace damaged sections. Before the war ended, the destruction of the Southern transportation network meant that even food and agricultural products could not be delivered to cities where they were needed, and a wave of bread riots broke out across the Confederacy. The Confederate Government, wracked by inflation, was forced to pay for supplies with bonds redeemable at the end of the war—which were of course worthless. Much of the South was forced into a rudimentary bartering economy.

One of the most important economic assets that the Confederacy had was the Tredegar Iron Works, in Richmond. Founded on the banks of the James River Canal in 1836, Tredegar produced locomotive engines and railroad tracks, and by 1860 the plant covered five acres and employed 800 workers, both free and enslaved.

Tredegar Iron Works museum

When the Civil War broke out, Tredegar was the largest foundry in the South, and the only one capable of large-scale production of weapons. When the newly-declared Confederate States of America moved its capitol from Montgomery AL to Richmond in May 1861, it did so partially to concentrate its military forces to protect the vital industrial plants there. Under the direction of the Confederate Government, the foundry at Tredegar began manufacturing cannons, rifled muskets, and ammunition. The plant manager, Joseph Anderson, became a Brigadier General in the Confederate Army, was wounded at the Battle of Glendale, and was placed in charge of the army's Ordnance Department. For the rest of the war, the Tredegar works produced naval cannons, field guns, rifled muskets, carbines, artillery shells, boilers and iron armor for ships, and railroad rails.

Production did not stop until the day Richmond surrendered near the end of the war. However, as the war went on and materials became more and more scarce, the quality and quantity of the plant's output suffered. At one stretch, the foundry did not produce a single cannon for over a month. Towards the end of the war, when a copper shortage meant there was no more bronze, Tredegar began casting its cannons from iron instead. Anderson also opened a wool mill next to the iron foundry, which produced Confederate Army uniforms until it was destroyed by a fire in 1863.

When Richmond was evacuated near the end of the war, the Confederate Government ordered Tredegar burned along with the other remaining industrial plants in the city, to prevent their use by the Federals, but Anderson paid 50 armed guards to protect the foundry from destruction, leaving it as the only operational iron works in the South when the war ended. Anderson received a pardon shortly later and re-opened the plant, and Tredegar, now just a remnant of its former importance, produced railroad spikes for the next few decades. As 20th century steel manufacture began to replace iron products, Tredegar faded into obscurity.

In 1957, Anderson's heirs sold the site to the Ethyl Corporation, which undertook a restoration of some of the remaining buildings. For a short time in 1994 a museum was housed at the site, but it soon shut down. In 2000 the National Park Service and the American Civil War Center began joint management of the site as a satellite park, part of the Richmond National Battlefield. Today five of the original Tredegar buildings are preserved, containing exhibits of machinery and equipment as well as cannons, guns and other artifacts manufactured at the plant. They are listed as a National Historic Site.

Baltimore Riot
April 19, 1861
Maryland

After the bombardment and surrender of Fort Sumter, President Lincoln issued a call for an army of 75,000 volunteers to serve for 90 days to deal with the insurrection, and also ordered a number of troops to move in to protect Washington DC. Since all the railroads into DC passed through Baltimore, Federal soldiers began to concentrate in that city.

It was a tense situation. Southern sympathies were strong there: in the elections Lincoln had received less than 4% of the vote in Baltimore, and even before he had taken office there was an assassination plot to kill him as he traveled by train through the city—which was foiled by the famed Pinkerton Detective Agency. Even many Maryland citizens who did not support secession also did not want to see a war to prevent the Southern states from leaving. (Those anti-secessionists who were also against the war became known as "Copperheads".)

On April 17, a group of militia from Pennsylvania and several Army regiments that had been pulled from duty on the western frontier had stopped in Baltimore and were stoned by an angry mob. One of these units was the George Washington Artillery, and one of the regiment's members was Nicholas Biddle, an escaped slave who had joined as an officer's aide. Being an African-American in a Federal uniform, Biddle became the particular target of the Baltimore protesters, and was struck on the head and wounded by a rock. (Biddle went on to survive the war, and when he was buried years afterwards, his tombstone proudly proclaimed him to be "the first blood shed in the Civil War").

So when the 6th Massachusetts Infantry Regiment arrived in the city at noon on April 19, on their way to DC, everyone expected trouble. The soldiers had arrived at the Wilmington and Baltimore Line's President Street Station, but the only track that went on to Washington DC was the Baltimore and Ohio Line, at the Camden Station about ten blocks away. So the troop train had to be disconnected and dragged by horses, one car at a time, down the waterfront along Pratt Street. To prevent trouble, the troops were ordered to keep their window shades down so they would not be visible. But as the mob of citizens grew it became more and more unruly. When only two railroad cars remained at President Street Station, the crowd began piling up large stones, ship anchors, and wooden timbers to block the street at a bridge so they could not be moved.

The 240 remaining Massachusetts troopers were ordered out of the cars, loaded their weapons, and formed up in marching column before setting off down Pratt Street on foot, led by Captain Albert Follansbee. Things now became more violent, as groups of people began pulling up paving stones and hurling them at the troops. A small group of Confederate sympathizers marched in front of the Federals with a Palmetto Flag, the symbol of secession—soon one of the Union soldiers broke ranks, dashed ahead, and tore down the flag.

Shortly after that, rioters began appearing with pistols and muskets. Several shots were fired from the windows of buildings along the street and several troops went down. Finally Follansbee gave the order to fire: the soldiers leveled their muskets and shot directly into the crowd. Those rioters who had firearms shot back. In the ensuing melee, three Federal troops were shot dead, one was beaten to death, and a dozen members of the crowd were killed. Some 36 troopers and an unknown number of rioters were wounded in the fracas.

When Mayor George Brown arrived at the scene, having heard the shots, he picked up a fallen musket and placed himself at the head of the column in an attempt to end the violence. As more gunfire was exchanged (with Mayor Brown recorded as shooting one of the rioters himself), he was quickly joined by Police Marshall George Kane, who placed a line of officers between the troops and the crowd and declared to the rioters, "Keep back, or I shoot!"

With this police escort, the remaining Federal troops made it to their train and departed. The mob, meanwhile, moved on to the offices of the German-language newspaper *Baltimore Wecker*, which was openly anti-secession in its views. The printing presses were smashed, the building set afire, and the publisher and editor were run out of town.

The next day, Mayor Brown sent a message to President Lincoln urging him to stop sending troops through Baltimore, arguing that it would only lead to more conflicts. Lincoln, in turn, is said to have remarked that his troops simply had to cross Maryland to reach the Confederates—and they were not birds who could fly over it, nor were they moles who could burrow under it. In desperation, city officials sent local militia to burn several of the railroad bridges leading into the city, hoping to prevent any further troop trains from arriving.

During this time, another group of Federal troops, the 8th Massachusetts under General Benjamin Franklin Butler, was sent to Annapolis with orders to secure a safe passage from that city to Washington DC. When Maryland Governor Thomas Hicks refused him permission to land there, Butler replied that his troops hadn't eaten for several days and needed supplies: when Hicks declared that nobody in Maryland would sell anything to him, Butler pointedly noted that his men were armed and didn't necessarily need to *buy* their supplies. With this route to Washington now open, Federal troops began to arrive at the capitol in force.

It would be another three weeks before any Northern soldiers tried to enter Baltimore again, covered by a gunship in the harbor and with a heavy police escort.

When threats were then made in rebel newspapers to attack Fort McHenry, which was garrisoned by Union troops, the Governor ordered the state militia to help defend it: the Fort's commander in turn, knowing that there were Southern sympathizers in the militia, announced that any militiamen who approached within half a mile of the Fort would be fired upon.

All of these events caused a political crisis in Maryland. Governor Hicks called together a special session of the State Legislature to vote on whether to secede: they chose by 53-13 to remain in the Union, but also tried to defuse further conflict by asking Lincoln to withdraw Federal troops from the state.

Federal Hill, overlooking downtown Baltimore

Instead, realizing that he simply could not allow Maryland—which surrounded Washington DC itself—to be swayed to a pro-Southern stance, Lincoln dispatched General Butler to Baltimore with his troops. Butler declared martial law, suspended habeus corpus, replaced nearly all of the police force, and began arresting Confederate supporters and sympathizers— including the entire city government and, a few months later, most of the State Legislature. They were held without trial in Fort McHenry. (Ironically, one of these prisoners, arrested for criticizing the suspension of habeus corpus, was Frank Key Howard, grandson of Francis Scott Key who had written the National Anthem at Fort McHenry.)

To reinforce the point, Butler sent a detachment of New York Zouaves under Lt Col Abram Duryee to occupy a prominent hill next to the Inner Harbor that overlooked the Baltimore business district. On the night of May 13 the Zouaves constructed a series of bank and ditch earthenworks with cannons, and over the next few months this was strengthened with wooden palisades, 42 guns, and 1,000 troops. The fortress became known as Federal Hill. Its sole purpose was to control the residents of Baltimore.

The Confederate States of America, meanwhile, viewed Maryland as one of its member states which had become occupied by the Federals. But, while Baltimore remained a hotbed of resentment and Southern sympathies throughout the war, in the end Maryland was firmly on the Union side: she sent 55,000 troops to fight for the Federals, and only 22,000 to fight for the Confederates.

Today, Platt Street, where the riot took place, is one of the major thoroughfares of downtown Baltimore at the Inner Harbor. A series of historical plaques and interpretive signs marks the site of the Baltimore Riot, explaining its role as "The First Bloodshed in the Civil War". The nearby President Street Station (the oldest existing railroad station in the US) houses the Baltimore Civil War Museum. Federal Hill, across the Harbor, is now a city park, with monuments, cannon displays, and interpretive signs.

Elmer Ellsworth
May 24, 1861
Virginia

On May 23, 1861, voters in Virginia ratified by referendum a motion of secession that had been passed by the state legislature, and Richmond officially announced her withdrawal from the Union. It was now apparent that the war had all but begun. The next day, the United States would lose the first Federal officer to die in the Civil War. But this was no ordinary Union Army officer—Colonel Elmer Ellsworth was a personal friend of President Abraham Lincoln.

Born in New York in 1837, Ellsworth had served as a militia officer with units in Milwaukee, Madison and Chicago before taking up the study of law. In 1860 he went to work for Abraham Lincoln as a clerk in his law office. The two developed a close personal bond, with Lincoln treating the young Ellsworth almost as a younger brother. Ellsworth worked on Lincoln's presidential campaign and, after the election, accompanied him to Washington DC.

After the bombardment of Fort Sumter in April 1861, Lincoln issued a call for 75,000 volunteer troops to put down the "rebellion". He also tried to move his 24-year old friend Ellsworth into a staff job at the War

Department, but Secretary of War Edwin Stanton didn't have an open place for him. So Ellsworth went back to his native New York and recruited a unit of militia, the 11th New York Zouave Regiment, with himself as its commanding Colonel. Because most of its membership came from local fire departments, it became known as the Fire Zouaves.

The Regiment was quickly moved to DC to help defend the capitol, and its dashing young Colonel became a frequent guest at the White House. From Lincoln's office, they could look across the Potomac River to the city of Alexandria in Virginia. And through their spyglass telescope, they could see a large Confederate "Stars and Bars" flag fluttering from the roof of the Marshall House hotel. It was a reminder that Virginia was already moving towards secession, which would in effect put an "enemy country" within sight of the nation's capitol.

The day after Virginia formally seceded, Lincoln decided that he had to protect the capitol, and sent troops across the Potomac to occupy the city of Alexandria. The unit that was assigned the task was the 11th New York, commanded by Elmer Ellsworth.

Crossing by boat, Ellsworth found the city undefended. Dispatching a group of his Zouaves to occupy the railroad station, he brought another company with him to take control of the telegraph office.

On the way, they passed the Marshall House, where the huge Confederate flag still flew from the roof. Ellsworth at first passed by the hotel, intent on getting to the telegraph station. But then he seemed to have suddenly changed his mind and, turning about, he took four troopers with him and entered the hotel. Finding a half-dressed man there who had apparently just been sleeping, Ellsworth demanded to know "what the flag was doing up there". The man told them he was just a boarder, and Ellsworth and the soldiers left him and went up the stairs towards the roof.

But the man they had encountered was not a boarder—he was James Jackson, the owner of the hotel and an ardent secessionist. So when someone ran into the hotel and told him that the Federal troops were on the roof cutting down his flag, Jackson grabbed a double-barreled shotgun and started up the stairs.

There he ran into Ellsworth, who was on his way down, flag in hand. Jackson leveled his shotgun and fired once, hitting Ellsworth in the chest and killing him instantly. A moment later, one of the Zouaves, named Corporal Francis Brownell, killed Jackson in retaliation. (After the war Brownell would be awarded a Medal of Honor for his action.)

Death of Ellsworth, a contemporary illustration

A reporter for the *New York Tribune* had been accompanying the Zouaves, and now the word raced around the country. Although over 50 people had already been killed or wounded in Baltimore, the death of Col Ellsworth would cause an explosive reaction that could not have been predicted. Northern newspapers screamed that he had been "shot down like a dog"; Southern papers bragged that he was just the first of what would be many dead Yankees. Lincoln's request for 40,000 more troops was met by over 200,000 volunteers: their motivation was illustrated by the newly-formed 44th New York Volunteer Infantry

Regiment, which called itself the "Ellsworth Avengers". Ellsworth's image and depictions of his death appeared on mailing envelopes, lithographs, and drinking cups; "Col. Ellsworth's Funeral March" and "The Ellsworth Gallopade" became best-selling musical scores.

The secessionist South had also gained its first martyr. James Jackson, the man who had flown the Confederate flag and shot the Union officer, became a hero to the rebels. Within a year a biography appeared titled *Life of James W. Jackson, The Alexandria Hero.* Since the South lost the ensuing war, Jackson's name has fallen into obscurity. But the two deaths, and the war frenzy they whipped up at the time, insured that what had until now been largely a political conflict would turn into four long years of bloodshed.

Most affected was Abraham Lincoln. He had gotten the news of Ellsworth's death just as he was about to meet with two people from the Senate. Entering the White House library, they found Lincoln alone at the window. He was silent for a few moments, then turned and said, "Excuse me, I cannot talk," before breaking out in tears and burying his face in a handkerchief. "I will make no apology, gentlemen, for my weakness," he finally said, "but I knew poor Ellsworth well, and held him in great regard."

Ellsworth's body was, at President Lincoln's request, brought back to the White House, where it lay in state in the East Room before being carried back to New York, where it was displayed in City Hall and then taken to his hometown for burial. Thousands of mourners lined the streets as the carriage rolled by.

Today, the Marshall House hotel is long gone. A museum at Fort Ward in Alexandria, however, has a display which interprets Ellsworth's death and the effect it had on the war. Among the exhibits on view there is the Union Zouave uniform cap that Elmer Ellsworth was wearing when he was killed. A piece of the Confederate flag that he cut down is on display at the Smithsonian Museum of American History. Ellsworth's blood-stained uniform coat is on exhibit at the New York Military Museum in Saratoga Springs NY, and his gravesite is at nearby Mechanicville NY.

Philippi
June 3, 1861
West Virginia

Although blood had been spilled in Baltimore and Alexandria, the first intentional military battle of the Civil War happened in what is now West Virginia. It was part of an odd secession from the secession.

When the state of Virginia called a special convention in April 1861 to consider leaving the union, the delegates decided to hold off voting until after the situation at Fort Sumter was resolved. The state itself was divided: the eastern two-thirds was strongly Southern in sympathies, but the western portion was heavily pro-Union and largely anti-slavery. When the state delegates voted on April 17 to approve a resolution of secession and send it out for referendum, the westernmost counties staged a rebellion of their own: they walked out and set up their own rival convention in Wheeling, gathering there on May 13. Here they passed a resolution repudiating the act of secession and announced their intention to break away from Virginia and form a new state of their own, the pro-Union West Virginia, with Wheeling as its capitol. The Confederates in Virginia, meanwhile, continued to regard them as under Richmond's sovereignty.

The political conflict soon gave way to military maneuvering. A series of roads passed through the little town of Philippi, not far from Wheeling, where they ran both north and south over a large covered bridge. Also nearby were several railroad lines. It was a strategic area, and when the war broke out, both sides wanted military control of it (and of course both sides also wanted to establish undisputed political control as well).

The Union and Confederate forces had already sparred with each other in Virginia. On the day that the state seceded, secessionist troops seized a stretch of the Baltimore and Ohio Railroad and confiscated 56 locomotives and several hundred rail cars. The Federals, in turn, entered Virginia on May 24 and captured the city of Alexandria, just across the Potomac River from Washington DC.

To secure the pro-Union western region, the Confederate government sent a detachment of 1,000 Virginia troops under Colonel George Porterfield, while General George McClellan in Ohio sent troops of his own under General Thomas Morris. Porterfield established a base at Philippi, while Morris set up his camp at nearby Grafton.

The Federals did not know that they greatly outnumbered Porterfield's forces, and proceeded cautiously. A column of 3,000 Union troops (recruited in Virginia as well as Indiana and Ohio) was sent to Philippi under Colonel Benjamin Franklin Kelley and, in an elaborate ruse to keep the Southerners guessing at the target, split into two, with one group marching towards one end of town and the other group taking a train some distance away before doubling back to approach the other end.

When the Union forces arrived, it was raining. Porterfield expected that they would take at least another day to reach him, and planned to move to higher ground in the morning. Instead, the Federals marched all night in the rain. The two columns had planned to surround Philippi and attack from opposite ends at dawn with the pre-arranged signal of a pistol shot, but one of the groups had taken a wrong turn and was not in position.

The bridge at Philippi

At that moment, a woman from town happened to discover the Federals, who promptly captured her young son (to prevent him from running ahead and alerting the Confederates). Grabbing a pistol, she angrily took a potshot at them, inadvertently launching a premature attack by the Federal forces. Nevertheless, the Confederates had not put out any pickets or sentries, and were completely surprised when a wall of Union troops rushed over the covered bridge towards them. Inexperienced and untested, they panicked and ran. (Northern newspapers referred to the rout as the "Philippi Races".) The fighting lasted just twenty minutes. There were no deaths: the Confederates lost around 25 wounded and the Federals only a handful (including Colonel Kelley).

One of the wounded Confederates was Private James Hanger, whose leg, mangled by a cannonball, was amputated. During his recovery he made himself a hinged wooden leg that worked so well that the

Confederate Army contracted with him to make artificial limbs for other wounded soldiers. Today, the company that Hanger founded is still a major manufacturer of prosthetic limbs.

In the light of the Civil War battles that were to follow, the combat at Philippi was a mere scuffle. But it had lasting effects both political and military. The Federal forces won a subsequent series of small skirmishes and were able to secure the pro-Union areas of Virginia from Confederate attack, and shortly after this the provisional government in Wheeling applied for admission to the Union as the State of West Virginia. In Washington DC, General McClellan, who commanded the Army of Ohio, was lauded as a hero for the triumph at Philippi (though he was not actually there), and just a few weeks later, after General Irvin McDowell failed to win a victory at the First Battle of Manassas, McClellan was tapped to become the new Commander of the Union Army of the Potomac.

The commander of the Confederate Virginia militia, meanwhile, was General Robert E Lee. Although he was not at Philippi either, he was blamed by the Southern press for the loss of West Virginia, and was dubbed "Granny Lee". He was subsequently re-assigned to constructing coastal defenses and harbor forts in the Carolinas, and was later sent to Richmond to serve on Confederate President Jefferson Davis's staff.

Today, Philippi Covered Bridge is listed on the National Register of Historic Places and is part of the Philippi Historic District. It has been rebuilt several times after being destroyed by fire and floods. A small museum is housed in the railroad station next to the bridge, and each year the battle is re-enacted at nearby Blue and Gray Park.

Manassas
July 21, 1861
Virginia

Within two months of the outbreak of the Civil War, the Federals had an army of over 186,000 men. But in many ways it was just a paper army: it was ill-trained and ill-equipped. Everyone was expecting that the war would be over quickly. Most of the volunteers were "hundred-day men" who had enlisted for just three months, and they would soon be released from duty. Meanwhile, Lincoln was under tremendous political and public pressure to end the war with a quick single decisive drive to Richmond.

The commander of the Army of the Potomac, General Irvin McDowell, accordingly was ordered to make plans to attack the bulk of the Confederate Army, 20,000 men under the command of General Pierre Beauregard who were encamped along Bull Run creek near the Virginia town of Manassas Junction, an important railway station just 25 miles away from Washington DC. When McDowell objected that his men were untrained and not ready for battle, Lincoln reminded him, "You are green, it is true, but they are green also; you are all green alike."

On July 16, McDowell led his "Grand Army" of 35,000 troops—the largest American force that had ever taken the field up to that time—out of Washington DC and into Virginia. He didn't reach Bull Run until the 20th, where he now faced Beauregard's 32,000 men: unknown to McDowell, Beauregard had been reinforced that day by additional troops under General Joseph Johnston, arriving by railroad. (Though in the actual fighting both sides were only able to get around 18,000 men to the frontlines.)

As the armies gathered for the impending fight, it became a sort of spectacle. On the surrounding hills, society women from Washington DC and Richmond gathered for picnic lunches to watch the battle—each assuming that their side would make quick work of the other. One of the spectators was Confederate President Jefferson Davis, who arrived by train.

Matthews Hill and the Stone House

The battle began late. McDowell had planned to attack at dawn on the 21st, but a series of miscommunications meant that the Union forces were not in position until 10am. The Confederates had also planned an early attack, but they too were delayed, and the Union troops launched first. The early fighting centered around Matthews Hill, where the Confederates had a battery of artillery. This was soon overrun, forcing them to fall back to Henry Hill.

Focusing on a stone bridge at the left side of the Confederate line, the Union troops drove towards the farmhouse on Henry Hill and began pushing the Southerners back. A rout seemed imminent. Then Confederate General Barnard Bee spotted General Thomas Jackson's regiment atop a nearby ridge, calmly awaiting the Federal onslaught. "There is Jackson," Bee cried to his troops, "standing like a stone wall." The Confederates were able to rally, regroup, and stop the Federal advance, and "Stonewall Jackson" earned the nickname that would make him famous.

Confederate line at Henry Hill

At about two in the afternoon, Beauregard sent a counterattack towards the Federal lines. The Union troops fell back, then rallied and advanced. By 5pm it seemed as if the battle were over and the Federals held the field.

But then both sides saw another group of troops approaching—and nobody knew who it was. At this point in the war, neither side had yet adopted its familiar blue or gray uniforms: instead, each regiment adopted whatever uniform it liked and both sides were a riot of different colors. (During the battle several friendly regiments on both sides had mistakenly fired at each other, unable to tell friend from foe.) To add to the confusion, both sides had similar flags: the Federals flew the well-known Stars and Stripes, but the red, white and blue Confederate Stars and Bars looked similar at a distance, particularly when hanging limp. (Later, to avoid this uncertainty, the Confederates adopted their famous red and blue battle flag.)

The newly-arrived troops turned out to be Johnston's Confederates, and now they charged the Union position. The exhausted Federals broke and ran, some of them retreating all the way across the Potomac River into Washington DC. They had lost about 3,000 casualties. The Confederates, equally disorganized by the bloody fighting and having lost 1,800 casualties, did not pursue them.

At the White House, Lincoln received the news by telegraph: "The day is lost." Fearing that the victorious Confederates would march on Washington, he remained awake all night.

In the aftermath of the defeat at Manassas, Lincoln fired General McDowell and replaced him with General George McClellan, a masterful organizer who immediately set about reorganizing, equipping and training the army. It would be over a year before the Army of the Potomac would be ready to fight another major battle.

Today, the Manassas battleground is a National Battlefield Park, established in 1940 and run by the National Park Service. In 2013, a nonprofit group called the Manassas Battlefield Trust was formed to partner with the NPS and to raise money for preservation and expansion.

The Visitors Center at Henry Hill has a display of artifacts, and the Stone House is open for tours on weekends. There are hiking trails which cover most of the key sites, and a driving tour that goes to Matthews Hill. The battle is reenacted at Henry Hill each year.

Fort Ward

Summer 1861
Virginia

As the defeated Union Army retreated from Manassas, everyone knew there would now be no quick victory, and this would be a long and costly war. President Lincoln ended the 100-day enlistments and asked Congress to set the term for the next 500,000 volunteers at three years instead, and to authorize $250 million in loans and bonds for the war.

Meanwhile, the War Department realized that Washington DC itself was vulnerable. The White House was only a few days' march away from the Confederate capitol at Richmond, and the only defensive position that stood in the way was the old brick fortress at Fort Washington, which had served in the War of 1812 and had failed to stop the British when they burned the city in 1814. Although the Confederacy did not have either the desire or the means to actually march on the North and conquer it, nobody wanted a repeat of that debacle. A Confederate capture of Washington DC, even temporarily, would make it politically impossible for the North to continue the war, and would very likely lead to a negotiated peace which granted independence to the South. So, for Lincoln, defending the capitol city was absolutely vital.

During the summer of 1861, therefore, a large labor force consisting of both military engineers and civilians, under the direction of General John Barnard, was set to work constructing a series of forts that would completely surround Washington DC and parts of Union-occupied Alexandria. They became known as the "Ring of Forts". These were simple earthen-walled enclosures that could be thrown up quickly, with bank-and-ditch barricades, timber palisade fences, and a line of rifle pits. The initial strongholds were placed on commanding high ground at crossroads, rivers, and other potential invasion pathways, and a continuous line of trenches then interconnected them all. Within a year, a total of 48 forts had been built, garrisoned by 20,000 Federal troops.

Fort Ward

Over the next year, however, as the fighting in Virginia became more and more fierce, the Union Army found itself in need of trained manpower, particularly artillerists, and troops were gradually transferred from the Washington garrison and sent to join the Army of the Potomac. They were replaced in the forts by those soldiers who were considered too old or unfit for frontline duty or who had been wounded in action and invalided out of their units.

Then, in late 1862, General Robert E Lee made a thrust towards the North. Although stopped at Antietam, the move scared both Lincoln and Congress, and frantic efforts were made to further strengthen Washington DC's defenses. The effort was expanded again when the Confederates passed nearby on their way to Gettysburg PA, and by the end of 1863 there were 68 forts, 93 cannon batteries (most of these were empty, it being planned that the guns would be rushed into position from elsewhere if they were needed) and 25,000 troops in the ring of forts. Washington DC had become one of the most heavily-protected cities in the world.

In the end, only one of the forts around DC ever saw enemy action. In 1863, after the battle at Monocacy, a Confederate force under General Jubal Early briefly engaged the Union garrison at Fort Stevens before withdrawing back to Virginia.

At the end of the war, all of the ring forts were abandoned, and those which had been built on confiscated private land were returned to their former owners. The rest were left to erode and crumble away. In 1925, the municipal government of Washington DC decided to appropriate money in order to purchase the abandoned forts and turn them into a series of city parks, but this effort lagged until after the Second World War, when the National Park Service took over. Today, most of the former forts are gone, and only about 20 remain in various states of preservation. The National Park Service runs most of these sites as part of the "Defenses of Washington" National Park, and the remaining few are owned by Arlington County or the City of Alexandria.

The best-preserved of the still-intact sites is Fort Ward, in Alexandria VA. Finished in September 1861 after Federal troops occupied the Confederate city, it was one of the first to be built. Originally, the fort measured 540 yards around and contained 24 guns; in the aftermath of Antietam and Gettysburg it was expanded to 818 yards and 36 guns.

Today Fort Ward is the only remaining site that has an interpretive Visitors Center and a Museum, and nearly all of the original earthen walls are still present, though badly eroded in places. In 1961, the area was archaeologically excavated, and the Northwest Bastion was then restored to its 1864 appearance using period materials. The Fort is also surrounded by a city park, in which traces of rifle pits can still be seen. One of the Officer's Cabins has been reconstructed as well as the Entrance Gate. A walkway allows visitors to see the original earthen walls, the berms where the two bombproof shelters were located, and the reconstructed bastion and outside ditches. The Museum exhibits a collection of Civil War objects as well as artifacts from the archaeological excavation.

Hampton Roads
March 8, 1862
Virginia

When the American Civil War broke out, neither side was prepared for it. While huge numbers of enthusiastic volunteers rushed to enlist, neither the Federals nor the Confederates had enough weapons, uniforms, food or gunpowder to equip and sustain them.

But the Northerners quickly realized that they had the superior logistics advantage: most of the country's industrial capacity was concentrated in the North, as well as most of its transportation network and financial assets. The Federal forces could expect that soon their larger economic resources would come into play, while the Confederates would be forced to rely mostly on importing weapons and supplies from outside sources.

Under those conditions, it became a matter of crucial military importance for the Union to cut off any potential sources of foreign aid to the South. And so the Union Army commander at the beginning of the war, the aging Mexican War veteran General Winfield Scott, proposed a plan that came to be called "The Anaconda". It was basically an economic blockade: using its more powerful Navy, the North would bottle up all the

Confederate ports from South Carolina all the way to Texas and up along the Mississippi River, cutting them off from all foreign trade. Sooner or later, the snake would squeeze the life out of the Southern economy and strangle it into submission.

Although General Scott would shortly be retired and replaced by General George McClellan as Commander, his "Anaconda Plan" became the guiding principle for the overall Federal war strategy. On April 19, 1861, Lincoln declared a full blockade for every major port in the seceded states, later expanding this to include Virginia and North Carolina after they seceded too.

Over the next two years, the blockade was tightened ever further. Federal Navy squadrons were dispatched up and down the coast to bottle up Southern ports— where possible by landing US Marines to either capture existing gun forts or to build new ones—thereby allowing Union forces to control access to Southern harbors. The final piece fell into place with the capture of Vicksburg, which placed the entire Mississippi River under Federal control.

The Confederates, meanwhile, realizing the deadly threat that the blockades imposed and lacking sufficient naval strength to fight their way into the open sea, resorted to desperate measures. An entire fleet of small fast "blockade runners" was hurriedly put into action— they would slip away at night to attempt to sneak past the blockading Union ships and then furtively try to smuggle their badly-needed supplies back in. Although smuggling and blockade-running continued through the entire war, they were never able to bring in sufficient supplies for the Confederacy.

Other Confederate efforts sought out a technological breakthrough that would give the South an advantage and allow her to break the blockade. And the earliest of these attempts would indeed change the course of naval warfare around the world.

The last major naval war fought by the US had been the War of 1812, in which the frigate—a wooden ship powered by canvas sails—was the supreme weapon. In the years since, however, naval technology had begun to change. The first leap was the development of the steam engine and screw propeller. Fueled with wood and later with coal, the steam engine freed vessels from dependence upon the wind (although early steam technology did not have the best reliability, and most ships still carried a full complement of sails as a supplement, a configuration known as a "steam frigate"). By the time of the Civil War, nearly all of the navies of the world, including the US, were using steam-driven engines on their warships.

The next important innovation appeared in 1858. As cannons got bigger and more powerful, wooden ship hulls had to get thicker and heavier to provide protection, but this additional weight also limited speed and mobility. The French therefore built an experimental "ironclad" ship named *La Gloire*, which had a thin wooden hull that was covered over with flat pieces of iron armor. It was lighter, more maneuverable, and could sail in shallower waters. The British followed with an advance of their own, a warship with a hull made completely from iron plates and covered at the waterline with additional armor, named HMS *Warrior*. The United States had already experimented with iron hulls but had only deployed them on the Great Lakes, considering them not rugged enough for the open sea. But although all of these tentative designs had shown promise, the idea was not pursued.

In June 1861, however, with its fleet bottled up in port by the Federal Navy, the Confederates in desperation turned to this experimental technology, hoping it would give them enough of an advantage to break the blockade. Work began on a new "ironclad". As it turned out, the Confederacy had no iron foundry capable of building steam engines for the new ship, and so the engineers had to improvise. When the Union had abandoned the naval port at Norfolk VA after the secession, they had intentionally sunk a number of steam frigates to prevent them from being used by the South. One of these was the USS *Merrimack*, which had been set afire, burned to the waterline, and sunk. The Confederates now raised the wreck of the *Merrimack*, which, crucially, still contained her steam engines, and rebuilt her as an ironclad: her topside superstructure was reconstructed with sloping wooden ramparts that were sheathed with four inches of iron plate, fitted with ten cannons (ranging from 6-inch to 9-inch), and a large triangular iron ram attached to her front end. She displaced 3500 tons. The rebuilt ship, which, the newspapers reported, looked like "a floating barn roof", was christened the CSS *Virginia*.

The Federals had already heard about the new Confederate weapon, and were by now working on a response: in August 1861 the Navy approved a design submitted by Swedish engineer John Ericsson for a Union ironclad and began construction at the shipyard in Brooklyn NY. Christened USS *Monitor*, it was a revolutionary design that was far more advanced than the Confederate version. The iron-plate hull, containing the steam engines, projected just 18 inches above the water. A system of fans pulled air into the hull and circulated it for ventilation. On the flat deck was a small pilothouse from which the Captain could steer the ship.

Also on deck was the most striking feature of the design: a cylindrical turret, twenty feet wide and nine feet tall, which contained the ship's two guns. The steam-operated turret, covered with eight inches of steel plate, could be turned in any direction, giving an all-around field of fire (with the exception of the area blocked by the pilothouse). The *Monitor* was originally intended to be armed with two massive 15-inch cannons, but when these were delayed they were replaced by 11-inch rifled guns. So although the *Monitor* was relatively small (less than 800 tons), she packed lethal firepower. Contemporary newspapers would dub the strange-looking ship "the cheesebox on a raft".

Both ships happened to be finished and placed in service within days of each other in March 1862. As the *Monitor* was being towed down the coast from Brooklyn towards Norfolk, the *Virginia* (still known to the Federals under her old name *Merrimack*) went into action.

On March 8, 1862, the blockade at Hampton Roads Harbor, just outside Norfolk, was being maintained by three old Federal steamships: the sloop *Cumberland* and the frigates *Congress* and *Minnesota*. At around noon, the *Virginia* approached. Immediately the Union fleet and shore batteries opened fire—and were shocked to see their cannonballs bouncing harmlessly off the ironclad's armored hull. Steaming straight at the *Cumberland*, the *Virginia* rammed her: the wooden sloop sank in minutes. After briefly becoming entangled with the sinking *Cumberland*, the *Virginia* was freed when her iron ram twisted and broke off. Turning to the *Congress*, the Confederate ship opened fire with her cannons: the frigate was set ablaze and burned all night before sinking. The *Minnesota*, meanwhile, was desperately trying to maneuver into position to attack when she ran aground. With the tide out, the *Virginia* could not get into gun range of the stranded Federal frigate, and so turned for home. Flush with victory, her crew intended to return the next morning to finish off the *Minnesota*, destroy the rest of the Federal ships, and lift the blockade.

The Virginia *and the* Monitor, *a contemporary illustration*

But unknown to the Confederates, the *Monitor* had reached the Union fort at the harbor mouth that night, and by the morning of March 9th was sitting alongside the stranded *Minnesota*. When the *Virginia* steamed into sight, her captain did not know what the strange-looking object was—he at first thought it was a boiler being removed from the *Minnesota*. Then the object shot at him.

For the next four hours, the two ironclads blasted away at each other, sometimes from just yards apart. Neither was able to penetrate the armor of the other. Finally, both scored lucky hits: the *Virginia's* engine was damaged, and the *Monitor's* captain was temporarily blinded by shell fragments that entered through his viewing slit. Both ships withdrew.

Although the battle had been a draw, it changed the face of naval warfare. Around the world, navies from England to Russia hurried to begin constructing turreted ironclad "monitors" of their own. (These were intended as coastal and river vessels, since the low decks made them unsuited for the open ocean.) The US Navy, with its superior industrial ability, would churn out new and improved monitors for the rest of the war, over 60 in total, overwhelming the Confederates.

Neither the USS *Monitor* nor the CSS *Virginia* would survive long after their encounter, though. In May 1862 the Confederates withdrew from Norfolk, and set the *Virginia* afire so she would not be captured. Seven months later, the *Monitor* was being towed offshore when she ran into a gale off the coast of North Carolina south of Norfolk and sank.

In 1973, the wreck of the *Monitor* was discovered lying upside down in some 200 feet of water. To protect the site, Congress established a National Marine Sanctuary around the ship and it was declared an underwater archaeological site.

After years of study, it was decided that the ship was too deteriorated to be raised intact, and attention instead focused on obtaining and preserving the most significant parts of the wreckage, especially her revolutionary gun turret. Most of the work was done by Navy divers in cooperation with NOAA, as a way to train them and to test new equipment. The *Monitor's* propeller was raised in 1998, the engine in 2001.

The turret was raised in 2002 and was submerged in a special tank to remove the salt and halt the deterioration of the metal. Today the original turret can be seen still in its restoration tank at the Mariner's Museum in Newport News VA, and an exact cast replica is on display. Also on exhibit are the *Monitor's* propeller, a sheet of iron armor plate, and a number of artifacts from the wreck, and a cannon and piece of armor from the CSS *Virginia*. The Hampton Roads Naval Museum in nearby Norfolk VA displays several artifacts from the *Cumberland* and a section of armor plate from the *Monitor*. Other artifacts from the *Monitor* are on display at other museums, including the Richmond Battlefield Park in Virginia and the Civil War Naval Museum in Georgia.

Pea Ridge
March 8, 1862
Arkansas

From the outbreak of the Civil War, both sides had attempted to assert control over the "border states". In Missouri, which had already been the scene of conflict between pro- and anti-slavery militias during the Bleeding Kansas period, there was a small skirmish near Wilson's Creek before Union General Samuel Curtis was able to lead his 12,000 troops toward Springfield in February 1862. The Confederate forces, 8,000 men under General Sterling Price, retreated to Arkansas. Missouri was firmly in Union hands.

In Arkansas, Price's Confederate army was joined together with General Benjamin McCulloch's 6,000 troops and both were placed under the command of General Earl Van Dorn. They were joined by two regiments of Cherokee Native Americans, the only Civil War campaign in which a significant number of Indians participated. On March 2, Van Dorn marched this army back towards Missouri to try to drive the Federals out.

Van Dorn's strategy centered around the political struggle within Missouri. As the southern states began to secede in 1861, the Governor of Missouri, Claiborne

Jackson, had summoned a Convention under the chairmanship of Price (who had previously served as Governor) and urged it to vote to leave the Union. Instead, the Convention refused to do so, with most of the delegates arguing that while they opposed a war against the Confederacy, they were not in favor of secession.

At the outbreak of war, Union Army Captain Nathaniel Lyon was sent to Missouri by President Lincoln with orders to secure the Federal Arsenal at St Louis. After doing this, Lyon arrested a number of pro-Confederate militia units, then marched his troops to the state capitol in Jefferson City, where the entire state government removed itself from office and a military governor was appointed to run new elections. This action split the state, with Lyon's troops supporting the Unionists and the state militia, now under the command of General Price, supporting the Confederacy. Price and his militia troops, accompanied by Governor Jackson, assembled their own "state convention", issued a declaration of secession, and fled to Arkansas.

Meanwhile, pro-Southern militias continued to operate in Missouri and neighboring Kansas, assassinating Federal officials and executing Union sympathizers—the most famous of these guerrillas were "Quantrill's Raiders" and "Bloody Bill" Anderson. It was a continuation of the pre-war "Bleeding Kansas" violence. Van Dorn's plan, in turn, was based largely on information he was receiving from these Confederate guerrillas in Missouri, who reported that secessionist sentiment was rife and that thousands of people would flock to the Confederate banner if they were given the opportunity.

To travel quickly, Van Dorn left his baggage train behind and ordered his troops to carry their own supply of ammunition and food. As they marched, they ran into a late-winter snowstorm. The Federals also knew they were coming, and blocked the road with felled trees as obstacles.

Curtis had established a defensive position along the Little Sugar Creek, just inside the Arkansas border. Van Dorn reached him on March 7. His 14,000 Confederates outnumbered the 10,000 Federals, but Curtis had some

50 cannons and Van Dorn did not want to risk a direct assault on the Union lines, so he sent McCulloch's division around Curtis's right to attack while he moved his own forces around to the Elkhorn tavern, behind the Union lines. It was a mistake: the hills of Pea Ridge now ran between McCulloch and Price, preventing them from supporting each other.

Although the Federals were pushed to Ruddick's Field by McCulloch's charge, they soon rallied and fought back. During the fighting, General McCulloch was killed, and not long after that his replacement, General James McIntosh, was killed too. The Confederates were forced to retreat and establish a defensive line at Foster's Farm.

Pea Ridge battlefield

Van Dorn planned to attack the Federals in the morning, but during the night the Federals received reinforcements and on the morning of the 8th it was Curtis who took the offensive. A cannon bombardment tore into the Confederate lines at the Elkhorn Tavern, followed by a frontal attack. The Confederate General Price was wounded in the fighting. By this time the

Confederates were running short of ammunition and supplies, and Van Dorn withdrew from the field.

The Confederates had lost about 2,000 casualties at Pea Ridge, compared to about 1,300 for the Union. Price withdrew his troops to southern Arkansas: Van Dorn went across the Mississippi River and joined up with the Confederates in Tennessee. The battle left the Federals in complete control of Missouri and northern Arkansas.

In 1887, local Confederate veterans raised money to put up a stone obelisk memorial at the site, and two years later a reunion was organized for both Confederate and Federal veterans of the battle. They raised another memorial stone to "the united soldiery", and this led in 1914 to calls for establishing the site as a national memorial and the Pea Ridge National Military Park was established in 1956. There is a Visitors Center and trails, and a reconstruction of the Elkhorn Tavern (the original was burned by Confederate guerrillas while it was being used as a Federal telegraph station). A 7-mile loop takes visitors to all the important parts of the battlefield. Because the park is located in a rural area, it is much more intact and better preserved than most Civil War battlegrounds.

Shiloh
April 6, 1862
Tennessee

After the bloody combat at Manassas, General George McClellan withdrew and took several months to train and equip his army. Although Lincoln constantly urged him to attack the Confederates, McClellan felt that his troops were not ready yet, and also believed himself to be outnumbered.

In Kentucky, however, the Union General Ulysses S Grant went on the offensive. Grant's career had earlier fallen under a cloud because of his drinking habits, but when the Civil War broke out he was placed in command of the Federal forces in Kentucky.

Two Confederate forts stood in front of him, Fort Henry and Fort Donelson, which protected Tennessee and Nashville. Concluding that they were vulnerable, Grant attacked, capturing Fort Henry in February 1862 and laying siege to Fort Donelson. When the Confederate commander asked for capitulation terms, Grant famously replied, "No terms except unconditional and immediate surrender can be accepted." Fort Donelson surrendered with 15,000 prisoners, and US Grant earned the nickname "Unconditional Surrender".

He was given command of all the troops in Kentucky and Tennessee.

With the fall of these two forts, Nashville was open for occupation, and the remaining Confederate forces in the area, under General Albert Sydney Johnston, withdrew to Corinth MS. By April 1862, Grant had gathered his 38,000 troops at Pittsburg Landing, on Shiloh Creek in Tennessee, and was making plans to attack Johnston at Corinth.

Shiloh Church

Johnston, knowing that Grant's forces were about to be reinforced by 35,000 more troops under General Don Carlos Buell, decided that his only chance lay in attacking Grant before those reinforcements arrived. So on April 3, he marched out of Corinth with 40,000 troops. His plan depended on speed and surprise, but a series of weather difficulties delayed his arrival until April 5, where his advance cavalry skirmished with the Union picket line. Confederate General Pierre Beauregard, fearing that the Federals had not only been reinforced and now outnumbered them, but had also been alerted to the impending attack, now wanted to call it off and retreat back to Corinth, but Johnston was adamant, telling him, "I would fight them if they were a million."

Johnston launched his attack just after 5am on April 6. The Union Army had not expected that the Confederates would move away from their supply base, and the sudden sight of Southern troops rushing at them was a complete surprise. Heavy fighting followed. By noon the Federals had been pushed back several miles, until units led by General William T Sherman were able to stand firm and stop the tide: this section of the battlefield, near Shiloh Church, had so many bullets flying that it sounded like bees, earning the nickname "The Hornet's Nest". (Sherman himself was wounded twice in the fighting.) The Confederates made at least eight separate charges at the Hornet's Nest, and assembled a group of 11 batteries with more than 50 cannons to fire on the Federals there. Several of the green units on both sides who had not been in combat before broke and ran, but it took seven hours for the Southerners to capture the Hornet's Nest.

Confederate Memorial at the Hornet's Nest

Johnston, meanwhile, was at the front of his own troops, and about 2:30 in the afternoon, as the Confederates were attacking a cotton field on the Union left, he received a severe bullet wound in the knee that cut an artery. He bled to death (the highest-ranking officer to die in combat on either side during the war), and General Beauregard assumed command. Much of the fighting now took place around Bell's Farm. The duck pond here was one of the only places where the wounded from both sides could obtain water, and, it was said, the water was so stained that they were drinking each other's blood. It became known as "Bloody Pond".

By nightfall the Confederate advance had stalled in front of Pittsburg Landing, and the Federals were formed into a curved three-mile line supported by two wooden gunboats (USS *Lexington* and USS *Tyler*) on the Tennessee River. The two ships shelled whatever Confederate positions they could see within range.

During the night, moreover, Buell's reinforcements began arriving by boat, traveling up the river and disembarking at Pittsburg Landing. Now outnumbering the Confederates two to one, Grant launched a counterattack of his own at dawn. By the afternoon of the 7th, the Federals had recaptured all of the positions they had lost the day before. Beauregard withdrew from the battlefield and retreated back to Corinth.

Casualties at the Battle of Shiloh were tremendous. The Federals lost 13,000; the Confederates almost 10,700. Believing that the Confederate forces outnumbered him, and with his own army battered from the fight, Grant did not pursue Beauregard as he retreated. This caused a political controversy in Washington DC, where critics in the Lincoln Administration asserted that Grant was a coward and had probably been drunk during the battle. In a meeting at the White House, several Cabinet members urged that the General be fired. Lincoln stood silent for a moment, then concluded simply, "I cannot spare this man—he fights."

Despite Lincoln's defense of him, Grant was demoted when his superior General Henry Halleck arrived and took command. Grant had planned to attack

Beauregard at Corinth and surround his army, but Halleck now led a slow plodding march which gave the Confederates plenty of time to abandon their base before the Federals arrived. Grant, upset at being sidelined, asked several times to be relieved of command but was refused. Halleck, meanwhile, was shortly later promoted to commander of all the Union armies, leaving Grant once again in command of the Army of Tennessee.

After the war ended, the Federal Government established a National Cemetery on the site: according to some stories, this was done at the request of local farmers who were continually plowing up skeletal remains from the battle. The 20-acre Cemetery contains around 3500 Federal dead, and an unknown number of Confederates buried in unmarked mass graves.

After the Cemetery was established, the War Department, under pressure from Civil War veterans, took steps to protect the Shiloh battlefield, purchasing 2000 acres by 1897 and establishing a National Park in 1933. By 1954, another 1700 acres had been added, and since then the private Civil War Trust has purchased another 1200 acres. There is a Visitor Center and a 13-mile driving tour around the battlefield.

Albuquerque
April 8, 1862
New Mexico

After the outbreak of the Civil War, the Confederacy tried to expand westward, in an attempt to reach the port cities in southern California and evade the Union's naval blockade. In the first months of 1862, Jefferson Davis established the "Confederate Territory of Arizona" which contained what is now southern Arizona and New Mexico. A small Confederate force was sent to Tucson to take control in the name of the Confederacy, but it was driven out by a Union force from California in a series of skirmishes. One of these, between two cavalry patrols at Picacho Pass, near present-day Tucson, was the westernmost fighting during the Civil War.

In response, Lincoln sent troops under Colonel Edward Canby to the New Mexico area. Canby was followed by Confederate forces from Texas under General Henry Sibley, and the two forces fought some skirmishes. Canby initially occupied Albuquerque, then abandoned it on March 2, allowing the Confederates to move in and establish supply depots.

A few weeks later, Sibley sent a detachment of 300 troops under Major Charles Pyron to occupy Glorieta

Pass, a strategic route through the desert mountains. Pyron was met there on March 26 by 400 Federals under Colonel John Slough. After a day's inconclusive fighting, both sides spent the next day positioning reinforcements, and when the battle resumed on the 28th, the Confederates outflanked the Union troops and forced them to withdraw.

But it had been a Pyhrric victory: the Confederates held the battlefield, but during the fighting a Federal unit had attacked the Confederate wagon train and destroyed nearly all of it. With most of their supplies and ammunition now gone, Pyron's men had to withdraw to Santa Fe and then back to Texas. The drive to California had failed.

Replica cannon at Albuquerque battle site

On April 8, Canby's forces approached Albuquerque, unsure of how many Confederates were still there, but knowing that he didn't have enough troops himself to take and occupy the town in the face of resistance. Instead, he was hoping to drive the Confederates off and spook them into retreating with the rest of Sibley's army.

At first, Canby shelled the town from long range, until he was informed that there were a large number of civilians there. The next day, Canby sent a detachment of troops into the city to probe the Confederate defenses. After some skirmishing in the city plaza, the Federals withdrew back to their lines. Two days later, the Confederates, having exhausted their supplies and ammunition, destroyed their remaining depots, buried a pair of cannons in the plaza, and slipped out of the city, retreating all the way to Texas. The Southwest would remain firmly in Union hands for the rest of the war.

Today there is a commemorative plaque in Albuquerque's "Old Town" plaza marking the site of the skirmish, and replicas of the buried Confederate cannons are displayed here. The original cannons are part of an exhibit at the Albuquerque history museum commemorating the battle. The Museum is just a short distance away.

The National Park Service holds about one-fifth of the Glorieta Pass Battlefield. The rest is in private hands.

Fort Pulaski
April 10, 1862
Georgia

In 1862, the Confederate fortress at the mouth of the Savannah River was captured by Federal troops in a nearly bloodless battle, made possible by a technological advance that would change the way warfare was done.

After the War of 1812, the US decided to construct a large number of defensive forts to protect its harbors along the east coast. While the ground war had been a disaster for the young country (British troops had ransacked Washington DC and burned the White House) the naval war had been a bright spot. In particular, thick-walled masonry cannon positions such as Fort McHenry had proven their ability to withstand heavy bombardments from naval ships. Since all of the US's potential enemies at the time (England, Spain and France) were European naval powers, a wall of forts, some 200 in all, were planned to defend the entire coastline, from Florida to Maine, from naval attack. It became known as the "Third System".

In the end, only about 30 Third System forts were actually built. One of these was Fort Pulaski, just outside Savannah GA on Cockspur Island, overlooking the Savannah River. Begun in 1829, the Fort was planned as a three-story masonry structure, pentagonal in shape, but the swampy soil proved to be too soft to support that much weight, so it was reduced to two stories, and the extra bricks were carried by cart to strengthen the older Fort Jackson, a few miles away. Fort Pulaski was nevertheless one of the largest and strongest brick fortresses in existence at the time, and with its 7.5-foot thick walls it was considered virtually impregnable. (One of the Army officers who worked on designing the fort was a young artillery engineer named Robert E Lee).

But by 1846 American military needs were changing. The European powers had become less of a threat, and instead the US was entangled in conflict with Mexico and was beginning the long series of armed conquests in the West that would be known as "The Indian Wars". Naval forts were no longer a priority.

By January 1861, Fort Pulaski had still not been completely finished, and no Army troops had yet been based there. Meanwhile, the country was careening towards Civil War. The Federal Government had already sent a contingent of troops to reinforce Fort Sumter in Charleston SC, and the Governor of Georgia, Joseph Brown, assumed that Fort Pulaski would be next. On January 3 Governor Brown decided to pre-empt the Federals by ordering local militia to occupy the Fort. So 134 men from the Savannah Volunteers, the Ogelthorpe Light Infantry, and the Chatham Artillery moved in, arrested the two Union officers in the Fort, and began setting up cannons and clearing the defenses.

After Georgia formally seceded on January 19, the militia units became the 1st Georgia Regiment of the Confederate Army, under the command of Colonel Charles Olmstead. Fort Pulaski became a key defensive point; Savannah was a major shipping port and railway station, and everyone knew that the Union forces would try to take it. And indeed in November 1861, after the war began, a Union force of 12,000 troops, under the command of General Thomas Sherman, landed and occupied the lightly-defended Tybee Island, opposite Fort Pulaski on the other side of the Savannah River. An assault on the Fort would now surely follow. If the Fort fell, the port in Savannah would be choked off.

The Confederate General Robert E Lee, who had earlier helped to design the fort and was now in charge of the South's defensive works, briefly arrived to examine the situation. Both he and Olmstead thought the position was secure—the nearest land area from which the Federals could bombard the fort from Tybee Island was about a mile away, and the smoothbore cannon of the day did not have the range or accuracy to do any real damage. "They will make things hot for you," Lee told Olmstead, "but at that distance they will not breach your walls." Olmstead had 385 men and 48 cannon to defend the Fort.

On Tybee Island, the Union General Sherman knew that storming Fort Pulaski would be a costly and bloody fight, and he was not looking forward to it. But then his artillery commander, Captain Quincy Gillmore, offered an alternative. His Union batteries had just been equipped with a new weapon—the rifled cannon known as a "Parrott Gun". Firing a cone-shaped exploding projectile instead of a solid spherical cannonball, the rifled cannon had much better accuracy and range than the old smoothbores. If his guns could break down Fort Pulaski's walls with a sustained artillery barrage, Gillmore noted, the Confederates would be forced to give up without the need for any infantry assault. General Sherman agreed to let him try.

By April 10, 1862, Union artillery forces, working under cover of darkness, had placed 36 cannons and siege mortars, including 10 rifled cannon, along the edge of Tybee Island. The smoothbores and mortars were essentially useless, but the rifled cannon were all aimed at one corner of the Fort. Early that morning, Captain Gillmore and some soldiers rowed across the Savannah River under a white flag of truce, and presented a message to Colonel Olmstead demanding his surrender. Olmstead, in response, sent back a message declaring, "I am here to defend the fort, not to surrender it."

Gillmore's guns opened fire at 8:10 am that morning, firing some 3,000 shells throughout the day. Olmstead did not know that the Federals had rifled guns: he expected that the barrage would be inaccurate and ineffective. Instead, to his shock, the Union shells quickly zeroed in on the closest corner of his fort, and systematically pounded it to bits. When darkness fell and the barrage temporarily ended, Olmstead went outside the fort to inspect the damage, and was dismayed to see huge craters in his outer wall. Today, visitors can walk around the moated walls and see the gaping holes, along with the bricked-in repairs where the corner had been completely wrecked.

Battered walls at Fort Pulaski

The next morning the pounding resumed, and within a short time gaps had been blasted all the way through. At about 2pm a Federal shell went through one of these holes, traveled all the way across the inside of the fort, and exploded at the far corner, in front of the powder magazine. Olmstead now knew he was doomed: if a Union shell managed to hit the magazine with its 20 tons of gunpowder, the resulting explosion would level the entire fort and kill everyone in it. At 2:30pm, Olmstead ordered a white flag to be flown over the walls. Upon surrendering to General Sherman, Olmstead wistfully remarked, "I give up my sword, but not, I trust, my honor." The entire battle had resulted in only one Union soldier killed and two Confederates wounded.

The capture of Fort Pulaski changed the face of warfare. In just 36 hours, one of the strongest citadels in the US had fallen: the massive stone and brick fortress had become obsolete literally overnight. After this, gun fortresses would be transformed into low-walled positions with massive earthen banks to absorb artillery impacts—and when the modern recoil-absorbing field gun appeared a few decades later, that too was rendered useless.

Union troops occupied Fort Pulaski for the rest of the war, using it to control all of the shipping in and out of Savannah. When the city itself was captured by General William T Sherman's "March to the Sea", the fort was used a prison for captured Confederates.

Afterwards, just before the Spanish-American War, the Fort was strengthened by adding a series of earthen berms in front of the entrance gate, and some 3-inch gun positions nearby. But the position was already pointless. The guns were never emplaced, and the Fort was left empty.

For a time, the Fort was used as housing by the keepers of the nearby Cockspur Island Lighthouse, but was then abandoned. It became a National Historical Monument in 1924 and was restored during the 1930's. Today the Fort Pulaski National Monument is run by the National Park Service.

The Great Locomotive Chase
April 12, 1862
Georgia

During the 1850's, the US was still a nation of small farmers with barely any manufacturing. That situation changed, however, with the Civil War in 1861. The huge armies involved in the war required a massive amount of weapons, clothing, supplies and other manufactured goods, and spurred a rapid growth in American industrial capacity. And one industry that grew spectacularly and played a major part in the war was the railroads.

The Union had a huge advantage in this area: the industrial North had four-fifths of all manufacturing capacity in the United States and two-thirds of its railroad miles, while the agricultural South only had one factory capable of making or repairing railroad tracks. Despite this material disadvantage, it was the Confederates who first realized the utility of railroads in rapidly moving large armies. When a Union Army under General Irvin McDowell advanced towards the town of Manassas, the Confederates used trains to move their troops quickly into the railroad station there and defeated the Federals.

One of the primary arteries in the South was the Western and Atlantic Railroad line, which led from the storehouses and mills of Atlanta to the logistics center at Chattanooga. It was a major route for men and supplies heading from the Confederate heartland to the battlefields.

By the spring of 1862, the Union General Ormsby Mitchel was camped in central Tennessee, and was looking for a way to attack the Confederates at Chattanooga. In the first week of April he was approached by James Andrews, a civilian agent of the Federal intelligence service who was serving as a spy and scout, with a plan to cripple the railroad line.

The proposal presented by Andrews was audacious. First, he and his raiding party, dressed as civilians, would infiltrate into Marietta GA (near Atlanta) and all board a particular train there, the express locomotive known as "The General", and ride it as far as the station in Big Shanty (today known as Kennesaw). There, they would seize control of the train and drive it north, stopping along the way to pry up tracks, cut telegraph lines, and burn railroad bridges. By the time they reached Chattanooga, if all went well, the entire length would be unusable for weeks. This, Ormsby hoped, might give his own army enough time to move on Chattanooga and take it before the Confederates were able to repair the track and rush up reinforcements. And if nothing else, it would cripple the South's logistics network for a time.

Ormsby approved the plan, and Andrews selected almost two dozen volunteers from the Ohio regiments to go with him, including three who had worked as railroad engineers. Disguised as civilians, they all made their way in ones and twos to Marietta, arriving by the evening of April 11. Two of the volunteers didn't make the rendezvous, and two more overslept that night and didn't show up on the train the next morning as planned. So on the morning of April 12, Andrews and 18 men boarded "The General" at the Marietta station.

A short while later, the train pulled in to the platform at Big Shanty and made its regularly-scheduled half-hour stop to allow the passengers to go get breakfast and the engineers to resupply the locomotive's steam engine with wood and water. As soon as the train was empty, the Federal raiders went into action: they swiftly disconnected the passenger cars to leave them behind, then started up "The General" and pulled out. At the platform, conductor William Fuller stared in bewilderment as his locomotive left the station without him. "Someone is stealing our train," he was heard to say.

"The General", on display at Chattanooga in 1907

It now became apparent why Andrews had chosen this particular station to make his move: Big Shanty had no telegraph office, and there was no way for anybody to send word ahead that someone (at this time most of the officials at the station assumed it was Confederate deserters trying to get away from nearby Camp McDonald) had stolen a train. But Fuller now went into immediate action and took charge. First, he sent someone to make the eight-mile horse ride into Marietta to alert the telegraph station there to send out the alarm. Then, grabbing two nearby rail workers to take along with him, Fuller climbed aboard a hand-operated pump-car and began to follow after the train.

Andrews, meanwhile, had stopped "The General" a few miles away to cut the telegraph lines, then continued north. To avoid suspicion, he kept to the train's regularly scheduled timetable, informing each station as he arrived that he was on a special mission to deliver ammunition to Chattanooga—without any information from the telegraph, the station masters had no reason to suspect otherwise.

Andrews' intention had been to sabotage the tracks as much as possible. But now he began to encounter unexpected problems. At the Etowah Station, the Federals came upon another locomotive stopped on a side track and discussed whether they should halt long enough to capture that train and burn it. After a short debate, Andrews decided that there were too many railroad workers around and, even though the raiders were armed, it would take too long to overpower them and destroy the train. They passed it by.

When they did stop to try and burn one of the railroad bridges, however, they found that the previous night's rain had soaked all the wooden timbers and they were unable to set fire to them. Further, the crowbars they had were not large enough to allow them to easily pry up the rails and disable the track, and although at various places they were able to remove a rail or two and some ties (and cut the telegraph line), it was taking too long. Their sabotage mission was already a failure.

Fuller, meanwhile, had by now made his way by handcar to Etowah Station, where a mail train was sitting there. Commandeering it, he set off in pursuit of the hijacked "General". It would become known to the newspapers as "The Great Locomotive Chase". Twice over the next seven hours, as he ran into the sections of missing rails that had been pried up by the Federals, Fuller would run ahead on foot and requisition another locomotive to continue his hunt, ending up in an engine named "Texas"—which he was driving backwards because it happened to be sitting on the track facing the wrong way.

At the Kingston station, the Federals, still unsuspected, were delayed for an hour by traffic ahead of them. When they finally left, Fuller pulled in just a short time behind them in the "Texas". Andrews heard the whistle behind him and, aware that there were no scheduled trains from that direction, he now knew that he was being followed.

In desperation, as the "Texas" caught up to him, Andrews first tried to block his pursuers by setting one of his own boxcars on fire and disconnecting it on a bridge, then pushed a pile of timber railroad ties out onto the track. But at Ringgold Depot, 87 miles from where they had stolen "The General", the Union raiders ran out of luck—and out of water for the steam engine. With their locomotive now immobile, they all ran off into the woods and scattered. Within two weeks nearly all of them had been captured.

Since Andrews was a civilian and all of the Ohio troopers were dressed in civilian clothing, none of them had any rights as POWs, and all were tried as spies. Andrews and six others were hanged. Eight more were sentenced to death but were then released in a prisoner exchange. The rest of the condemned troopers escaped their captors and made their way back to Federal lines.

Although the Great Locomotive Chase was a military failure, the raiders were recognized for their courage and determination, and many of them became the first recipients of the newly-created Medal of Honor—except for Andrews, who, as a civilian, was not eligible.

Today, the original "General" locomotive is on display at the Museum of Civil War and Locomotive History in Kennesaw GA, where exhibits and interpretive signs tell the story of the raid. A historical marker in downtown Atlanta commemorates the spot where Andrews was hanged.

Williamsburg
May 5, 1862
Virginia

By April 1862, General George McClellan finally decided that his Army of the Potomac was once again ready for combat, and laid out a plan to advance towards Richmond, hoping to end the war. The Federal strategy was pretty simple: the Union still held Fort Monroe in Virginia, at the tip of the James Peninsula between the James and York Rivers. McClellan would transport his troops to the Fort by ship, then advance up the Peninsula, past the Revolutionary War battlefield at Yorktown and the old colonial state capitol at Williamsburg, and move on towards Richmond. With luck, the war would be over in a matter of weeks.

But the "Peninsula Campaign" did not go as planned. By the time McClellan's 100,000 troops had gathered at Fort Monroe, the Confederates under General John Magruder had expanded from 12,000 to almost 60,000 and had built two lines of defenses from river to river, consisting of breastworks, rifle pits, cannon redoubts and, in some places, earthen dams with flooded ditches. The Federals would have to get through them to make it to Richmond.

McClellan reached the first Confederate line on April 4. This stretched twelve miles, from the ruins of the old Jamestown settlement on the James River (where it was anchored by a group of cannon positions known as "Fort Pocahontas") across to the Warwick River, and then over to the old battlefield at Yorktown (in some areas reinforcing and utilizing some of the siege trenches built in 1781 by the British). As McClellan approached and the southerners realized how outnumbered they were, Magruder was ordered by Confederate commander Joseph Johnston to conserve his forces at Yorktown, but to delay the Federals, then withdraw to the better-prepared line at Williamsburg.

Union engineers, meanwhile, began laying siege to Yorktown, gradually moving over 100 cannons and mortars into position. It would have been the most heavily-concentrated artillery fire ever seen up to that time. After four weeks, however, as Union gunboats moved into position for a bombardment, Johnston, who had now taken field command from Magruder, decided it was time to withdraw. On the night of May 3, he pulled his troops back to Williamsburg. As a parting gift, he sowed the ground around his positions with buried "torpedoes", artillery shells with pressure fuses which acted like land mines. The next morning, the Federals found the Confederate breastworks silent, empty, and full of surprise explosions.

The southerners now occupied a second belt of defenses stretching out from Williamsburg. The lynchpin of this line was a group of earthen breastworks and cannon redoubts dubbed "Fort Magruder" which sat at the intersection of two roads. McClellan's advance force, General Joseph Hooker's division, reached it early on the afternoon of May 5 and immediately attacked, but was unable to break the walls. A counterattack by Confederate General James Longstreet pushed Hooker's men back.

There were attacks and counterattacks for the rest of the day. At one point, troops under Union General Winfield Hancock managed to occupy two Confederate redoubts and direct fire onto the southern lines, then fight off a charge by General Jubal Early's infantry.

Bank and ditch from Confederate cannon redoubt at Williamsburg

Johnston, however, concluding that his position was too weak, once again withdrew during the night, pulling back towards the much stronger defensive works surrounding Richmond. His actions on the Peninsula had delayed the Federals by over a month; the Federals had lost around 2300 casualties and the Confederates 1600.

Today, while a large portion of the Revolutionary War siege line of Yorktown is preserved as a National Battlefield, nearly all of the Civil War era earthworks are gone. The badly-eroded remains of a portion of "Fort Pocahontas" are visible in the Jamestown National Historic Site, while the fairly intact remains of two Confederate cannon batteries from Fort Magruder can be seen at Redoubt Park in Williamsburg.

Seven Pines
May 31, 1862
Virginia

As he continued his advance up the James Peninsula towards the Confederate capitol at Richmond, Union General George McClellan still outnumbered the Confederates under General Joseph Johnston some three to one, but, overly cautious as always, McClellan was slow and methodical. After spending over a month on the battles at Yorktown and Williamsburg, the Federals reached the Chickahominy River on May 21, just 12 miles from Richmond. And here they sat. Unwilling to repeat the carnage that had resulted at Manassas and Shiloh, the Union commander now planned to surround the Confederates and force them to surrender with a siege.

Johnston quickly moved to take advantage of McClellan's inaction. The Federals were busily building bridges across the Chickahominy, hoping to bring up their guns within range of Richmond. Two of the Federal corps had established camp across the river at a crossroads known as Seven Pines, where they were isolated from the other three corps, and Johnston saw his chance to inflict some damage. On May 31 he launched 51,000 of his troops against the 33,000 Union soldiers on his side of the river, hoping to trap and destroy them. The assault was aimed at the Federal corps commanded by General Erasmus Keyes, the least experienced of McClellan's units.

Seven Pines National Cemetery, on the battlefield site

But a series of miscommunications doomed the attack. Some Confederate units were five hours late in launching their charges. A series of hills masked the sounds of the fighting, and several commanders on both sides did not even know for hours that a battle was raging nearby.

After the fighting ended that night, both sides moved fresh units in. But when combat resumed in the morning it proved to be just as indecisive. By noon it was clear that the Union lines were holding their ground, and the Confederates withdrew back to Richmond. The heavy fighting had produced 5000 Union casualties and 6000 Confederate.

However, one of these casualties proved to be immensely significant: Confederate General Johnston had been hit in the shoulder and carried off the field.

While command of the Army of Virginia temporarily passed to General GW Smith, he was quickly replaced by General Robert E Lee, who till then had been serving as a military advisor to President Jefferson Davis. Lee immediately began a campaign to drive the Federals back from Richmond.

Today, nearly all of the Seven Pines battleground is gone, covered by the little town of Sandston. The National Cemetery, established in 1866, contains the remains of 1300 Federal troops from the battle (of which only 150 or so are identified) and covers about two acres. Interpretive signs scattered throughout the town describe the fighting which took place nearby.

Blockade Runner *Modern Greece*
June 27, 1862
North Carolina

As the Federal naval blockade tightened around the South and the US Navy began turning out large numbers of new *Monitor*-type ironclads, the Confederacy, in desperation, turned its efforts towards "blockade runners"—cargo steamships that could, it was hoped, evade the blockade and deliver weapons and supplies from Europe to ports in the Carolinas and Georgia. And one of the most famous of these is the *Modern Greece*.

Before the war, virtually all of America's ship-building capacity was located in New England. And so, while the Confederacy desperately needed cargo ships, it had no ability to make them. Out of necessity, they turned to Britain. Using a series of intermediaries to hide their intent from the Federals, Southerners began purchasing steamships in English ports. To further hide their real purpose, most of these continued to sail under a British flag.

One of these was a 210-foot steam frigate launched in 1859, named *Modern Greece*. Until 1862, this British ship sailed back and forth uneventfully between

England and Russia, mostly carrying timber from the Baltic coast. But in the spring of 1862, she was bought by the ZC Pearson Company and moved to the English city of Hull for refitting. Although the ship was legally owned by Zacharia Pearson (a former Mayor of Hull), the *Modern Greece* was financed by the Confederate Government through an intermediary in Bermuda, and she had only one purpose: to smuggle much-needed cargo past the Federal blockade into the port of Wilmington NC. While the harbor there was dominated by the long-range cannons of Fort Fisher, which prevented any Union ships from entering, the Federals were still able to maintain a line of blockading ships just outside the harbor entrance. The blockade runners were intended to slip past them and into the safety of the docks.

The *Greece* was, however, not well-suited for the role of blockade runner. Instead of being fast and capable of speeding through shallow water to evade pursuit, like later purpose-built smugglers, she was big, heavy, slow, and sat deep in the water. But the Confederates were desperate to obtain ships quickly. Her protection, the Confederates hoped, would come from the fact that she was British-registered and flew the Union Jack flag.

The *Modern Greece* left port on April 28, ostensibly with a load of timber for Tampico, Mexico. In reality, she was carrying food, cloth, whiskey, household goods, Enfield percussion muskets, gunpowder, and new Whitworth rifled cannons to North Carolina.

But when the *Greece* reached the mouth of Wilmington harbor at 4am on June 27, the Federals were not fooled. The Union ship USS *Cambridge* opened fire, and the *Greece* had no choice but to charge in at full speed, hoping to get far enough inside the harbor to be protected by the fearsome guns of Fort Fisher.

She didn't make it. Heavily-laden, the *Modern Greece* wasn't able to clear the shallow sandbar at New Inlet, and ran aground. Another blockader, the USS *Stars And Stripes*, joined the *Cambridge* and they both moved in to attack the stranded Confederate smuggler. A few shots from Fort Fisher, however, drove off the Union ships, and the Confederate shore batteries then turned onto the *Modern Greece* herself, to prevent the Federals from capturing her supplies. Over the next few days, teams of Confederate salvagers went through the wreck and took away whatever cargo they could, including four long-range naval cannons which they added to the arsenal at Fort Fisher. The ship was then bombarded again to destroy it. The top of the ship was blown apart: the bottom portion of the hull sank into the sand. The *Modern Greece* lay forgotten on the shallow ocean floor for the next 100 years.

The wrecked Modern Greece, *a contemporary illustration*

In all, over 100 Confederate blockade runners were purchased or built in British shipyards. Many of them operated from Bermuda or the Bahamas, where they would take on cargo brought over from England and then make the dangerous dash through the Union blockade and into the Southern ports. Over time, the design was standardized and became better suited to the needs of smuggling. The hulls became slim and low, with a shallow draft. The steam engines became more powerful, and side-wheel paddles became favored for speed. By the end of the war, blockade runners were being made from steel, which was stronger and lighter than iron.

In 1962, a fierce storm happened to uncover a small portion of the *Modern Greece* on the sandbar, in 25 feet of water just 300 yards from shore. The State of North Carolina, working with the US Navy, decided to attempt to recover as much of the wreckage as possible. Divers determined that the lower portion of the hull was fairly intact, and a large amount of cargo still rested within it. In March 1962 efforts began to recover artifacts. Over the years, some 11,000 objects, from china dishes to cannons, were recovered and conserved.

Today, a number of artifacts from the *Modern Greece* are on exhibit at the Fort Fisher State Historic Site in Wilmington and in the Transportation and History Museum in Fayetteville. The hull is too deteriorated to be raised, however, and it still lies on the sand in the harbor shallows, where it is legally protected as a marine archaeological site.

US Balloon Corps
June 1862
Virginia

By the time of the Civil War, manned balloons had already been flying for almost 70 years, beginning with the Montgolfier brothers in France. In the 1850s, American adventurer Thaddeus Lowe had been making balloon flights in the US and Europe, and at the outbreak of war, he decided to offer his services as a balloonist to the Union Army. On April 19, 1861, after the bombardment of Fort Sumter, Lowe took off from Cincinnati for a flight, intending to land in Washington DC as a way to demonstrate the capabilities of his balloon. Instead, he was blown off-course by a storm and landed in South Carolina, where he was briefly arrested by the Confederates on suspicion of being a spy.

Upon his return to Ohio, Lowe was contacted by the White House, where his flight had attracted the attention of government officials (including the Smithsonian Institution) who were now interested. On June 11, Lowe tethered his balloon *Enterprise* at the National Mall and ascended to 500 feet. From there, he used a telegraph wire running to the ground to send a message to President Lincoln at the White House: "This point of observation commands an extent of country nearly 50 miles in diameter. The city with its girdle of encampments, presents a superb scene. I have pleasure in sending you this first dispatch ever telegraphed from an aerial station, and in acknowledging indebtedness for your encouragement for the opportunity of demonstrating the availability of the science of aeronautics in the military service of the country."

Meanwhile, another balloonist named John Wise had also interested the Army in his balloon as a platform for reconnaissance and as a way of correcting the aim of artillery. The Army decided to place Wise in charge of the "US Balloon Corps" and to take Lowe and his balloon as one of the pilots.

When General Irvin McDowell took his troops to Manassas to face the Confederates, the Balloon Corps went with him. But when the general ordered a balloon sent aloft to make observations, Wise could not be found, and Lowe was ordered to launch his balloon instead. Wise then arrived at the scene, and an argument broke out over whose balloon should be used. When Wise finally got into the air, however, he was caught in the wind and entangled in a tree, destroying his balloon.

After this fiasco, Wise left, and President Lincoln appointed Lowe as the "Chief Aeronaut" for the Balloon Corps. With government funding, Lowe built a total of seven specially-reinforced balloons and twelve portable gas generators to produce hydrogen to fill them. In addition, he was given the use of an old river barge, the *George Washington Park Custis*, which Lowe converted into a sort of aircraft carrier by removing the boat's superstructure and fitting it with a flat deck from which he could launch his balloons. The whole apparatus was tested on the Potomac River, and by the end of 1861 there was a picket line of three or four balloons stationed along the shores of the Potomac to watch for any Confederate force that might approach Washington DC. In September 1861, Lowe's balloons successfully directed the fire of a Federal cannon battery onto a Confederate position.

Inflating one of Lowe's Civil War balloons; a contemporary photo

When General George McClellan advanced on Richmond in the Peninsula Campaign in 1862, he took Lowe and his balloons along. Although bad weather prevented any flights for the first few weeks, Lowe was able to launch tethered balloons from the deck of the *George Washington Park Custis* during the siege at Yorktown in April, then moved to the James River to keep a lookout for Confederate gunships.

At the end of May, as McClellan reached Richmond, Lowe's balloons were moved to Gaines Mill and Mechanicsville. From here, observers were able to direct cannon fire onto Confederate positions, and, with a view all the way into Richmond seven miles away, could also report the concentration of troops that would result in the Battle of Seven Pines.

By this time, the Confederates had a balloon of their own, hastily sewn together from local women's silk dresses. As the Battle of Seven Pines raged, the Union balloon *Intrepid* and the Confederate balloon *Gazelle* both watched from above.

Throughout the Seven Days' Battles, Lowe's balloons kept up a near-constant surveillance. During the Battle of Gaines Mill the Confederates advanced towards the Federal balloon station, and in his haste to abandon the position Lowe left behind a gas generator and other equipment that was captured by the Southerners and placed on display in Richmond. For the next few days, during the fighting at Savage Station and Malvern Hill, Lowe was retreating along with the Federal Army and was unable to make any flights. The Confederate balloon *Gazelle*, meanwhile, was making daily ascents from the deck of the tugboat *Teaser* on the nearby river, providing valuable information to General Robert E Lee until Union gunboats (including the USS *Monitor*) captured the boat and the balloon.

The Confederates were only able to build one subsequent balloon, which was quickly captured when it accidentally broke away and floated onto Union lines. Although the Federal balloons made over 3,000 ascents during the fighting in Virginia in 1862 and 1863, it was apparent that few in the Army fully appreciated their potential. McClellan valued the intelligence information that he got, and Union Generals John Sedgwick, Joseph Hooker, and then-Lieutenant George Custer (who had been trained to make topographic maps) would all make ascents in Union balloons, but Lowe and all his pilots were civilians and tended to be looked down upon by Union military officers as mere showmen and adventurers. The balloons were also often limited by weather and logistics, and were expensive to operate. (Lowe was not at Antietam because he was not provided with transportation to get there.)

During the retreat of the Federal Army back to Washington DC after the defeats at Fredericksburg and Chancellorsville, Lowe came down with malaria, then became involved in a dispute with the Army over his pay. He resigned in a huff and after a short time, in August 1863, the Balloon Corps was disbanded.

Today, the Tredegar Iron Works Museum, part of the Richmond National Battlefield Park, displays a valve from the equipment used to inflate the Federal observation balloons, and interprets their role in the fighting around Richmond.

Malvern Hill
July 1, 1862
Virginia

Upon assuming command of the Army of Virginia after the Battle of Seven Pines, General Robert E Lee knew that he was in trouble. The huge Union army under General George McClellan was only days away from besieging the Confederate capitol at Richmond, and was already preparing to move up their cannons to pound the city into submission. In the North, newspapers were jubilantly predicting that the war would be over in a matter of weeks.

But Lee knew that the Army of the Potomac also had a weakness—it was dependent upon the railroads that supplied it with food and ammunition. And Lee also knew his opponent: McClellan had, after the battle at Seven Pines, become even more unwilling to risk his troops in combat. Lee concluded that if he sent a major part of his army to attack the Federal supply routes, McClellan would be reluctant to take advantage of it by launching an assault on the city, and would instead withdraw to protect his logistics. Lee planned an attack for June 26.

Over the next seven days, Lee steadily pushed the Federals back in a series of flanking actions: there was fighting at the Chickahominy, at Gaines Mill, and at Glendale. Although the Confederate attacks were poorly coordinated and never had the tactical success that Lee hoped for, McClellan was unnerved by them and, abandoning his siege of Richmond, began cautiously retreating back down the James Peninsula. By July 1 the Federals were arrayed at Malvern Hill, a U-shaped ridge with an open wheatfield in front of it.

Union line at Malvern Hill Battlefield

It was a strong defensive position, but Lee boldly launched a direct assault into the teeth of the Union lines. The attack was a disaster: the Federals had a large number of cannons on the hill, and the Confederate barrage, which Lee hoped would open up a gap in the Union lines, failed to do so. In a withering 90-minute bombardment, the Federal batteries in turn knocked out most of the Confederate artillery. When Lee's charge came, it was ill-coordinated and launched piecemeal, with each wave being cut down by Union guns. At Evelington Heights, which overlooked the

Union positions, the Confederates only managed to emplace a single cannon before Federal infantry swarmed in and captured it. Lee's forces suffered over 5,000 casualties to the Union's 3,000. As one of Lee's subordinate generals described it, "It wasn't war: it was murder."

Despite the beating at Malvern Hill, the Seven Days Battles, as they became known, had saved the Confederacy. McClellan's lackluster performance led to his being placed subordinate to a new commander in chief of the Federal armies, General Henry Halleck. Lee, meanwhile, had lost some 20,000 casualties against just 16,000 for McClellan. But the Union army had been driven some 20 miles away from Richmond, and Lee was now poised to take the offensive.

Today, the Malvern Hill site is part of the Richmond National Battlefield Park, which commemorates most of the Seven Days battlegrounds. About 1300 acres of battleground have been preserved by the National Park Service and the nonprofit Civil War Trust.

Baton Rouge
August 5, 1862
Louisiana

When the state of Louisiana seceded in January 1961, it found itself in an important and strategic position. Once the Federal Government realized that the war would not be a quick and easy one, Union commanders formulated a grand strategy to choke off the South, cut its trade and supply lines, and starve it into submission. Called "The Anaconda Plan", it involved the blockade of every major Confederate seaport on the Atlantic and Caribbean coasts, and the capture of the Mississippi River ports—including Baton Rouge.

After secession, local militia troops in Baton Rouge seized the military Arsenal building with its weapons and ammunition, and also the Pentagon Barracks with its supply depot. At first, several thousand Confederate troops were stationed in the city. But as the war went on, most of these were transferred to other areas where they were vitally needed, and by the time New Orleans was captured by a Union fleet in May 1862, Baton Rouge, with its river port and its supply depot and arsenal, had barely any troops left. It was the next logical target.

On May 7, a week after New Orleans was captured, the Federal gunboat USS *Iroquois*, under Commander James S Palmer, sailed up the Mississippi and anchored at Baton Rouge. The state government had already fled to Shreveport, so Palmer sent a message to the city's Mayor demanding his surrender, and got a defiant reply announcing that while the town had no defenses and could not fight back, they would not voluntarily surrender, and the Federals could enter the city only "against the will of its peaceful inhabitants". Palmer landed a handful of troops who marched to the Arsenal and the Pentagon Barracks and raised the Union flag. Later that afternoon the Federal naval commander Admiral David Farragut arrived with 1500 Marines who made a show of force by marching through the city, then left for Vicksburg, further up the river.

Old Arsenal building

Vicksburg turned out to be too well-defended for Farragut's fleet (and indeed the city would not be taken without a long and extensive siege). But when Farragut's ships returned to Baton Rouge, Confederate snipers on shore fired upon them. In retaliation, Farragut shelled the capitol and surrounding buildings with two gunboats, then landed around 2,000 Federal troops under General Thomas Williams to occupy the city.

Now it was the Confederates' turn. General John Breckenridge marched from Vicksburg to Baton Rouge. He planned to attack the city on August 5 with a coordinated land and river assault: the new ironclad warship CSS *Arkansas*, which had already sunk several Union ships at Vicksburg, would attack the Federal gunships on the Mississippi River to prevent them from firing on the Confederates, while Breckenridge's 4,000 men would drive Williams' 5,000 troops out of the city. Though Breckenridge knew he was outnumbered, he assumed that his battle-tested troops would be able to defeat the newly-arrived Federals, most of whom had not yet seen combat.

It didn't work out that way. As the assault began, the *Arkansas's* engines failed and she floated helplessly adrift. To prevent her from falling into enemy hands, she was deliberately burned and sunk.

Breckenridge's troops fought furiously, reaching the center of the city. The Union General Williams was killed early in the attack, and his second-in-command, Colonel Thomas Cahill, took over. In a series of intentional retreats, Cahill led his troops back towards the riverbank—drawing the Confederates into range of the Federal gunboats. Without his ironclad to neutralize the Union fleet, Breckenridge realized that he could not hold the city. That night he withdrew his troops to nearby Port Hudson.

The Battle of Baton Rouge had cost the Federals 484 casualties and the Confederates 456. One of the Confederate troopers who died in the fighting was the half-brother of President Lincoln's wife Mary Todd.

To strengthen their position, the Federals burned most of the buildings along the Baton Rouge riverfront to give clear fields of fire for their gunships, and soon moved in another 8,000 troops. Baton Rouge was occupied for the rest of the war.

Today, virtually none of the original battlefield in Baton Rouge remains. The Old Arsenal is now a museum. The nearby Pentagon Barracks is being used as a state government office building, and while visitors cannot enter the building they can walk around the outside of the structure. Much of the fighting occurred at the site of the current Magnolia Cemetery and Baton Rouge National Cemetery, which contain the graves of some of the Union and Confederate troops killed in the battle, and also a memorial.

Second Manassas
August 28, 1862
Virginia

Not long after withdrawing from Richmond, Union General George McClellan was ordered to move his army north to Manassas and join the new Army of Virginia commanded by General John Pope. But viewing Pope as a rival and angered by his own subordination to General Henry Halleck, McClellan dragged his feet and took almost two weeks to begin moving his troops.

And in that, Confederate General Robert E Lee saw an opportunity. Moving quickly, Lee intended to attack Pope and defeat him before McClellan could arrive. On August 25, Lee sent half of his army, under General Stonewall Jackson, to circle around behind Pope's lines and attack the Federal supply depot at Manassas Junction (the same site as the first Battle of Bull Run). When Pope turned to deal with the threat, Lee planned to attack with the other half of his troops, under General James Longstreet. He hoped to surround and crush Pope's entire army.

The initial move began on August 25, when Jackson's 24,000 troops marched an incredible 50 miles in just 24 hours, placing them about 25 miles behind

Pope's force of 66,000 men. On the morning of August 26, 6000 Confederate cavalry swept into the poorly-protected Federal supply depot at Manassas Junction, burning it. Jackson then took up a defensive position on Stony Ridge, just west of the site of the 1861 battlefield.

As Lee expected, Pope turned his army to face the threat. On the afternoon of August 28, fighting broke out around Brawner Farm as the Federals reached Jackson's position. By the time night fell, Jackson had fought off the Union assaults and held his ground.

Brawner Farm House

The next morning, the Union attacks resumed, and again Jackson fended them off, until Longstreet's troops joined the fight and pushed the Federals back. The Confederates established a line along an unfinished railroad cut, which gave them a good defensive position.

As night fell again, Pope was now caught between two Confederate forces; seemingly unconcerned with the danger and thinking he had Jackson trapped, he telegraphed Lincoln to report that he had "pushed the enemy off the field" and expected to defeat him the next day. McClellan, meanwhile, was not far away with 25,000 men, but in the absence of a request from Pope for reinforcement he did not move to join the fight, preferring to keep his troops in a position to defend Washington DC if it became necessary.

On the afternoon of August 30, Pope launched a large assault at the Confederates, who held their ground with an intense artillery barrage and then counterattacked towards Chinn Ridge with 25,000 troops—one of the largest charges in the entire war. The Federals were driven back to Henry Hill, the scene of heavy fighting in the First Battle of Manassas, and then were pushed further to a stone bridge over Bull Run, where they held until nightfall and withdrew to Washington DC the next morning.

Chinn Ridge

Pope had lost about 15,000 men, roughly one-fifth of his army. He was relieved of command and sent to a minor post. McClellan was nearly fired too, but Lincoln decided to keep him, recognizing that despite his battlefield flaws his organizational skills were needed to rebuild the beaten Federal army.

Lee, meanwhile, had won the battle but failed in his strategic objective to destroy Pope's army. But he was already planning his next campaign.

Today, the battleground is contained within the Manassas National Battlefield Park, established in 1933. The Park preserves the sites of the First and Second Battles of Manassas, which were fought largely on the same ground. There is a driving tour that reaches the key sites of the Second Battle.

Harpers Ferry
September 12, 1862
West Virginia

After his victories in driving the Federals from Richmond and in defeating an army twice his size at Second Manassas, General Robert E Lee decided that it was time to take the war into the North, to relieve some of the strain on his army and also to threaten the Federal capitol at Washington, perhaps even provoking enough political pressure to entice Lincoln into seeking a negotiated solution to end the war. And so in September 1862, some 40,000 Confederate troops entered Maryland and made camp at Frederick. From here, Lee hoped to go on to enter Pennsylvania, where he could seize agricultural supplies for his army and also take control of several important railroad routes.

Lee had assumed that when he entered Maryland the Federal garrison at Harper's Ferry would withdraw to the north ahead of his advancing army, which would allow him to capture the railroad lines there and use them as his logistical base. Instead, to his surprise, the Federals—14,000 troops under Colonel Dixon Miles—remained stubbornly in place, where they constituted a threat to Lee's supply lines. So Lee decided on a potentially dangerous move: even though the Union forces under General George McClellan outnumbered him, he would split his army and send General Stonewall Jackson with three groups of cavalry and artillery to capture the town. Lee knew his opponent, and counted on McClellan's risk-averse nature to prevent any attack on his outnumbered troops.

The terrain greatly favored Jackson's troops. Harper's Ferry was surrounded on three sides by hilly terrain: two of these were defended by Federal soldiers and cannons, and the third was left undefended (it was presumed to be too steep for guns to be brought there). Each of the three "heights" was to be attacked by one of Jackson's units.

The Heights overlooking Harpers Ferry

The assault began on the morning of September 12. Within two days the undefended part of the heights had been taken, and another fell after several hours of fighting. On the morning of the 14th, Confederate troops attacked the Federal position at Bolivar Heights, and fierce fighting raged in the vicinity of Murphy's Farmhouse. After a time, the Confederates were able to drag additional cannons up the heights, and the Federals were forced back into town. By the night of September 14, cannon shells were falling on Harpers Ferry from all sides. The next morning, Colonel Miles ordered a surrender, just before he was hit and killed by a Confederate cannonball. In all, some 12,700 Federals surrendered at Harper's Ferry—the largest number of Union prisoners taken in any Civil War battle.

Lee, meanwhile, had detached another portion of his army to capture a smaller Federal garrison at nearby South Mountain, but they had failed and been forced to retreat. Lee had seriously considered abandoning the Maryland operation and returning to Virginia, but when word came of the Federal surrender at Harper's Ferry, he decided to stay in place and confront the Union General McClellan, who was camped at Sharpsburg near Antietam Creek. General Hill's troops returned to Lee's camp, with captured Federal weapons and supplies, just in time for the impending battle.

Although Harper's Ferry is now a National Historic Site, it is far better known as the location of John Brown's Raid than for the Civil War battle. But there are walking trails and interpretive signs at key locations from the fighting, including Murphy's Farm. The farm itself was on private land and scheduled for demolition for the construction of a condo unit, when it was obtained by the National Park Service in 2002.

Antietam

September 17, 1862
Maryland

In laying out his plan for attacking Harper's Ferry and South Mountain, Robert E Lee had given detailed written instructions to his subordinate generals, known as Special Order 191. But unknown to Lee, a copy of that order had somehow fallen into the hands of the Federals, and Union General George McClellan, a man who was overly cautious by nature, now knew that Lee's forces were divided and vulnerable. As a result, McClellan decided to make a stand and fight it out with Lee at Sharpsburg. By September 16, the two armies faced each other along Antietam Creek. It would result in the single bloodiest day in American history.

At sunrise on September 17, McClellan launched his attack. His plan was relatively simple: he would assault the Confederate left flank, force Lee to move troops from his center to reinforce it, then the Union troops would drive into the weakened center. But things fell apart quickly. The initial attack passed through a large cornfield on the Miller Farm. In the head-high cornstalks, neither Federal nor Confederate troops could see each other, and the result was a fearful close-action fight that lasted nearly three hours. There were over 10,000 casualties in just the first two hours, and some units lost as much as 80% of their strength. "The Cornfield", as it became known, changed hands numerous times before the Federals sent forces around it, to the area near Dunker Church. Here they ran into Confederate artillery and were stalled for a time.

Miller Cornfield

After fighting their way past the Church and through the Mumma and Roulette farmhouses, the Federals approached the small farm road that ran through the area. Here, the Confederates were positioned in a stretch of pathway with high banks that formed a natural defensive trench, known as the "Sunken Road". Once again the fighting became intense, as some 2000 Confederates held off over 10,000 Federals for almost three hours, inflicting savage casualties. Then, around noon, a small force of Union infantry and artillery were able to flank one end of the Sunken Road and fire along its length. Now it was the Confederates who were slaughtered. The country wagon path became littered two and three deep with dead and dying soldiers. It became known as "Bloody Lane".

The final fighting of the day took place at the Lower Bridge, which crossed Antietam Creek. In an attempt to outflank the Confederates, General Ambrose Burnside launched his troops at the stone bridge. But the crossing was protected by several hundred Confederates atop a steep 100-foot bank that ran along the creek and overlooked the bridge. For three hours, the Confederates held firm, and Union casualties soared. Finally at around 1pm the Federals managed to cross the bridge in sufficient force to clear out the Southerners. Today the area is known as "Burnside Bridge".

Burnside Bridge

After taking a few hours to reorganize his men, Burnside moved forward to engage the extreme right end of the Confederate line. But there he was stopped by the Southern division commanded by General Ambrose P Hill, who had just arrived after marching all the way from Harper's Ferry.

As night fell, the guns became silent. The next morning, Lee pulled his troops together into a defensive line and awaited McClellan's attack. It never came.

Although McClellan had stopped Lee's advance, it came at a horrible price: the fighting produced almost 23,000 casualties out of the 100,000 troops engaged, making it the single largest military loss ever suffered by the United States. In 23 hours of combat, the Federal Army had lost 17% of its total force, while the Confederates had lost 27%.

Early in the afternoon of September 18, Lee withdrew his army across the Potomac River back into Virginia. McClellan did not pursue him—which angered President Lincoln. McClellan and Lincoln already had a checkered past with each other. McClellan's reluctance to engage the Confederates had led Lincoln to remark at one point that "If McClellan doesn't want to use his army, I would like to borrow it for a while". Two months after Antietam, Lincoln replaced McClellan with General Ambrose Burnside. In response, McClellan ran against Lincoln in the 1864 elections on a platform of negotiated peace with the Confederacy, and lost.

In the autumn of 1862, meanwhile, photographer Matthew Brady opened an exhibit in New York City titled simply, "The Dead of Antietam". In stark black and white imagery, Brady brought home the true horrors of war as the public had never seen it before.

But the battle also had a more concrete effect on the war. As early as late 1861 Lincoln had been considering a decree that would both free the slaves and adopt them into the Federal Army: his cabinet was opposed to the idea, however, and Lincoln also did not want to present it while the Union troops were doing badly on the battlefield as it might look like a sign of weakness and desperation.

As the war dragged on, however, Lincoln became more and more worried that France or England might give diplomatic recognition to the Confederate States of America, perhaps even leading to military aid or intervention. And so, in early 1862, Lincoln took the step of drafting an "Emancipation Proclamation" which declared that all the enslaved people in Confederate-held territory were now considered to be free. In the wake of

Antietam, Lincoln considered that battle enough of a "win" that he officially released the Proclamation: overnight, the aim of the war changed from merely holding together the Union to a crusade against slavery. Neither France nor Britain, which had both outlawed slavery in their own territories, could be seen diplomatically as supporting a slave-holding state, so the Proclamation ended virtually any chance of the European powers giving aid to the Confederacy.

After the War, Antietam became a National Cemetery, with about 5,000 graves. The battlefield then became one of the first Civil War sites to be incorporated as a National Monument, set up by the War Department in 1890 and transferred to the National Park Service in 1933.

The park today consists of around 2700 acres. An 8-mile driving tour leads to all the significant portions of the battlefield, including the Cornfield, Bloody Lane, and Burnside Bridge. There are also about 40 miles of walkways and paved paths. The Pry House, which served as McClellan's headquarters and a temporary hospital, features exhibits which interpret Civil War medical practices.

Corinth
October 3, 1862
Mississippi

After their loss at Shiloh, the Confederates under General Pierre Beauregard withdrew to Corinth. This Mississippi town was an important supply base for the South: both the Memphis & Charleston and the Mobile & Ohio Railroads ran through Corinth. These were the major supply arteries for the entire Confederacy.

That made the city an inviting target, and in May 1862 Union General Henry Halleck led 120,000 troops to besiege Corinth. Beauregard knew he could not withstand a siege, and on May 30 he abandoned the city. The Federals moved in, seized the vital railroads, and turned Corinth into a huge supply depot of their own, establishing storehouses for food and weapons, training camps for Federal troops, and a "Contraband Camp" for freed slaves. Many of these former enslaved people were armed and trained to form the 55th Infantry Regiment United States Colored Troops.

By the next autumn, however, the Confederates decided to recapture Corinth and its vital railroad network, and an army was dispatched under General Earl Van Dorn. The city was defended by 23,000 Federal troops under General William Rosecrans. On September 19, portions of both armies clashed at Iuka, about 20 miles away. Van Dorn suffered heavy casualties, and merged his remaining army with that of General Sterling Price before moving again, now with 22,000 men, towards Corinth.

On October 3, Van Dorn began his attack on the Federal strongholds that surrounded the city (most of which had originally been constructed by the Confederates themselves during Halleck's siege in May). After fierce fighting, the Union troops were driven back over two miles to a secondary line of cannon redoubts. When darkness fell, Van Dorn decided to halt the attack and resume in the morning. The Federals were already planning a counter-attack, but miscommunicated orders delayed it until it was too dark to carry out. Both sides waited for daylight.

Reconstruction of Battery Robinett

Rosecrans seized the opportunity to reorganize his troops and strengthen his defensive breastworks. The next morning, the Southerners attacked first, with a cannon barrage at 4:30am. An infantry charge, after several hours' delay, then captured the Union cannon redoubt at Battery Powell and managed to fight their way into the center of the city itself, with a small force reaching the railroad yards.

But the Confederate advance stalled at Battery Robinett, and a Union counter-attack then pushed the Confederates back. The Federals recaptured their positions, and Van Dorn withdrew. He had suffered 4200 casualties compared to Rosecrans's 2300. Corinth remained in Union hands.

In the aftermath of the battle, Rosecrans was sent to Ohio and given command of the Union forces there; Van Dorn was demoted and replaced by General John Pemberton. Meanwhile, with his supply base at Corinth now secure, Union General Ulysses S Grant made plans to advance towards the Confederate river port of Vicksburg.

When the focus of the Civil War shifted in January 1864, Corinth was too far away to serve as an effective supply center, and it was abandoned by the Federals. The Confederates then placed a small garrison in the town, but it never played any active role in the rest of the war.

After the war, the Corinth National Cemetery was established, which contains the gravesites of 6,000 Union soldiers and unmarked mass graves of several thousand Confederates. In 2004, the National Park Service obtained a portion of the Corinth battlefield and incorporated it as a satellite of the Shiloh National Military Park. An Interpretive Center stands where the bulk of the fighting took place at Battery Robinett, with a reproduction of the ramparts. Much of the battlefield is still covered by houses and streets, however.

There is a driving tour which visitors can make to significant areas around town, including the site of the Contraband Camp, the railroad depot, the Corinth Cemetery, and several houses which were involved in the fighting including General Leonidas Polk's headquarters.

Perryville
October 8, 1862
Kentucky

After the retreats from Shiloh and then Corinth in the spring of 1862, Confederate General Pierre Beauregard was relieved of command and replaced by General Braxton Bragg. At first, Bragg gave thought to an assault to re-take Corinth in June, but concluded that the Federals were too strong and delayed the Confederate attack there for several months.

In the meantime, he was presented with an alternate objective by Colonel John Hunt Morgan, the Confederate cavalryman who was conducting a guerrilla war against Federal units inside Kentucky. Morgan told Bragg that the people in Kentucky were weary of Federal occupation and would rise up and support the Confederacy if a sizable military campaign were to enter the state. (A group of politicians had set up a pro-Southern "state assembly" in Bowling Green and declared their secession, but although the Confederacy recognized them and considered Kentucky as a member state, they never had any actual governmental power.) As Bragg considered the idea, he received word that the Union General Don Carlos Buell was moving across northern Alabama towards Chattanooga, which was defended by Confederate General Edmund Kirby Smith. Kirby Smith frantically telegraphed for reinforcements.

Bragg drew up a plan that would both protect Chattanooga and bring Kentucky under Confederate control. He would take his army north to join with Kirby Smith at Chattanooga, defeat Buell's army there, then advance to Lexington and Louisville, install a pro-Confederate Governor in Frankfort—and perhaps be in a position to attack Nashville and recapture Tennessee.

Because the Federals controlled the transportation hubs in Nashville and Corinth as well as the Mississippi River ports, however, Bragg and his army had to take a long circuitous route: leaving Tupelo on July 23, he crossed over Mobile Bay by boat, then took various railroad lines through Atlanta to Chattanooga. In all, his troops traveled almost 800 miles in less than a week. It was a stunning logistical feat.

But Bragg's ambitious plan ended before it even started. Although Kirby Smith had agreed to the strategy, he now changed his mind. Even as Bragg's troops were still making their way to Chattanooga, Kirby Smith marched his own army north towards Kentucky. His motives remain a mystery: perhaps he wanted all the glory himself, or perhaps he had a personal grudge with Bragg. In any case, Kirby Smith's troops entered Kentucky on August 30 and defeated a Union garrison in the town of Richmond KY. Buell, in turn, first retreated all the way to Nashville, then set out towards Louisville to protect his supply lines. At the same time Bragg marched towards the Kentucky capitol of Frankfort to install a new Confederate state government. He optimistically hauled 15,000 rifled muskets along with him, intending to use these to arm the new recruits he expected to gain in Kentucky.

As it turned out, the weather took an unusual turn for the worst. An intense heat wave developed, leading to heat stress for the marching troops on both sides and, more importantly, producing a drought that dried up most of the water sources in the region.

On October 7, a part of Bragg's army, under the command of General Leonidas Polk, entered the little town of Perryville KY, through which passed most of the roads in the region—including the ones being used by Buell's Federal army. But more immediately, it had a supply of available water along a short stretch of the Chaplin River. Confederate and Union cavalry scouting parties had already skirmished nearby. Polk, thinking that he was confronting only a small part of the Federal forces, decided to make a stand, and set up a defensive line in Perryville.

Buell also knew there was water available in the river and that the Confederates were nearby, and dispatched a cavalry patrol to find both. They ran into a Confederate cavalry force at Doctors Hill. The battle grew as both sides rushed in reinforcements.

The Confederate Cemetery

When Bragg arrived at daylight to join his forces with Polk's, he found a poorly-organized defensive line with little protection at the flanks. Still believing that they only faced a small force, the Confederates filled the gaps in their lines with Bragg's troops and then attacked, pushing the Federals back to Starkweather's Ridge, where they were halted.

Darkness now brought an end to the fighting, but Bragg had finally realized that he was confronting only the advance force of Buell's entire army, some 80,000 men in all. Hopelessly outnumbered, the Confederates abandoned Perryville in the night and began the march back to Tennessee. The retreat was so hasty that they left behind all their dead and wounded: the wounded were treated by Federal surgeons and "paroled" (released upon the promise to not fight again), while the Confederate dead were buried in a mass grave located near the center of the battlefield, next to the modern Visitor's Center.

Although the Battle of Perryville was small in terms of number of troops, the cost to both sides was disproportionately high—of the 23,000 Federals engaged in the fighting, some 4,200 were casualties; the 15,000 Confederates had lost 3,400. But the primary effect of Perryville was political: despite Bragg's hopes, the population had not risen up in rebellion, and Kentucky remained firmly in Union hands for the rest of the war.

After the battle, Federal troops buried over 800 Confederates in a mass grave, which was marked by a memorial statue in 1902. Another 1000 Federal dead were also buried, but were relocated in 1867 to a new cemetery at Camp Nelson, some distance away.

Today, the site of the fighting is preserved as the 750-acre Perryville State Historic Park, incorporated in 1936. A number of walking trails cover the battlefield and the Confederate Cemetery, and the Visitors Center houses an interpretive film and displays of battlefield artifacts. In 1991, the local Perryville Battlefield Preservation Association was formed to raise money for land acquisition, and in 2017, an additional 70 acres of land were purchased by the Association and the Civil War Trust and, after some modern structures were removed, added to the park. Today the park totals a little over 1,000 acres.

Fredericksburg
December 11, 1862
Virginia

When Union General George McClellan failed to pursue the defeated Confederate forces after the Battle of Antietam, a frustrated President Lincoln fired him and appointed General Ambrose Burnside as commander of the Army of the Potomac. Burnside had already been offered command back when McClellan was floundering after the battle at Manassas and had turned it down, explaining that he didn't think he was suited for it. But now Lincoln ordered him to take the offensive and attack General Robert E Lee's forces in Virginia. Reluctantly, but giving in to pressure, in late November Burnside moved 120,000 troops across the Potomac into Virginia and lined them up along the Rappahannock River, protected by over 200 cannons.

Burnside's plan was a simple one: he would cross the Rappahannock and advance as fast as he could towards Richmond, hoping to reach it before Lee could intercept him. But immediately he ran into problems: the river was too deep to ford, so Burnside sent for engineers and pontoon bridges. They were delayed and didn't reach him until December 10. As they built the six bridges, the engineers came under deadly sniper fire.

Lee had originally planned to fall back to another defensive line closer to Richmond and make his stand there. But Burnside's difficulties allowed him to be joined by General James Longstreet and General Stonewall Jackson, and gave them sufficient time to strengthen the defenses at Fredericksburg, in particular the strong position at Marye's Heights held by Longstreet. Longstreet's cannons lined the ridge, and his men took advantage of a road and stone wall that ran along the bottom of the hill. In total, the Confederates now had 80,000 troops around Fredericksburg. This would be the largest battle of the Civil War.

The stone wall on Marye's Heights

Burnside in turn was forced to give up his planned rapid advance, and now, still under pressure from Lincoln to take the offensive, chose to attack Lee in his well-built stronghold. It would be a fatal mistake.

When the Federals crossed the river on December 11, Lee did not attack them, but waited patiently behind his breastworks. On December 12 there was a huge

Union artillery barrage on the town of Fredericksburg, followed by some skirmishing as Burnside's troops advanced through the streets towards the Confederate lines, pillaging as they went.

The Union attack finally came on the morning of December 13. It was a disaster. Lee's defenses were virtually impregnable, and confusing orders from Burnside meant that the attacks were made piecemeal instead of all at once. On the Confederate right, at Prospect Hill, General Stonewall Jackson held firm. The Union General George Meade's division made some headway but was not reinforced, and bogged down in an area that became known as "The Slaughter Pen". On the left, Longstreet's artillery on Marye's Heights cut down the waves of attacking Federals. Throughout the morning, Burnside's troops lost thousands of men in repeated futile assaults. It was, one Union officer later wrote, "butchery".

Prospect Hill

The Confederates launched a counter-attack that afternoon, but were halted by the arrival on the battlefield of Union General Daniel Sickles and his troops. By nightfall, the Confederates were still in their defensive positions, and the Federals had withdrawn back to their lines.

That night, at a council of war, General Burnside grandly announced that he himself would personally lead the army in another assault on Marye's Heights: his subordinates sensibly talked him out of it. Instead, the next day, both sides agreed to a temporary truce to remove the dead and wounded.

On December 15, Burnside retreated back across the Rappahannock. He had been soundly beaten: the Federal casualties were over 13,000: the Confederates had lost only 5,000. Morale in the Union Army plummeted; desertions began to increase. Less than a month later, Burnside was replaced as commander by General Joseph Hooker.

In July 1865, a National Cemetery was established at the battlefield and 15,000 Union soldiers were buried here. In 1927, four Civil War battlegrounds—Fredericksburg, Chancellorsville, the Wilderness and Spotsylvania, all located near each other—were incorporated into the Fredericksburg and Spotsylvania National Military Park, which was then transferred to the National Park Service in 1933.

Today, the Park consists of around 8,000 acres encompassing parts of all four battlefields. There are two Visitors Centers: one of these is at the Fredericksburg location on Marye's Heights. In May 2002, plans were announced to build a housing development on a privately-owned tract of land where some of the initial fighting in the battle had occurred. The Civil War Trust took up the fight to save the area, and successfully blocked a rezoning request. Working with the NPS and local citizens, the Trust then bought the land in question. The park also was expanded with additional purchases in 2004 and 2006, obtaining a tract that included The Slaughter Pen, which had also been under plans to be sold as a housing development.

USS *Cairo*
December 12, 1862
Mississippi

In May 1862, a group of US Navy ships under Admiral David Farragut had attempted to sail up the Mississippi River from Baton Rouge and capture the port at Vicksburg MS, and had been driven away by the powerful Confederate shore batteries there. But Vicksburg was still an important target for the Federals, and in December 1862 it was decided to make another attempt to take out some of the city's defensive guns, paving the way for another attack. This time, the focus would be on the batteries along the Yazoo River, just north of Vicksburg.

The ship selected for the task was the USS *Cairo*. In January 1862, the Navy made a deal with two shipbuilders in Illinois to construct seven nearly identical ironclad steam-driven gunboats, to be known as the "City Class". One of these was the *Cairo* (pronounced "kay-ro" and named after a town on the Mississippi River, not after the city in Egypt). The contract specified that all seven ships had to be finished within 90 days, so to speed up the work, the design was much simpler than the USS *Monitor*: the City Class had no moveable turret, but instead used a total of 13 fixed cannons at the sides, front and back. Since the boats were intended for river service against mostly shore targets, this was considered to be suitable. These were intended to be 8-inch Dahlgren naval guns, but in the rush to finish the ships, the builders simply installed whatever spare cannons were available, including obsolete 32-pound smoothbores and old 42-pounders that had rifling grooves machined into their barrels. To repel boarding parties, each ship also had a 12-pounder howitzer deck gun to be loaded with canister shot.

USS Cairo *on display*

The boats were steam-powered, with five steel-plate coal boilers that operated at 140 psi. Two pistons operated a pair of paddle wheels. The wheels were fitted into a recess at the back of the boat so they were protected from enemy fire. Top speed was around 7 knots.

The ship's topside was protected by a layer of iron plates, two and a half inches thick, which was backed by two feet of oak timber to absorb the shock of enemy cannonballs. In addition, the crew of the *Cairo* fitted an additional layer of armor to the front sides, made by bolting down pieces of railroad track. The finished ship weighed 500 tons, was 175 feet long, and carried a crew of 175.

On December 12, 1862, the *Cairo* and four wooden Union gunboats made their way down the Yazoo River. This area bristled with shore batteries, but the Confederates had also deployed a new type of weapon: a wooden barrel that had been packed with black powder explosive and an electric detonator. These were tethered in the river, with two wires running back to an operator who was concealed on shore. When an enemy ship got close, the operator closed a switch which set off the explosive. Back then they were called "torpedoes": today we would know them as naval mines. The *Cairo's* task was to sail down the river, clear out these Confederate torpedoes, and take out as many shore batteries as possible.

Suddenly two explosions lifted the *Cairo* out of the water as mines detonated under the left side of her bow. Water poured in, and the gunboat sank in just 12 minutes, settling onto the mud at a depth of 35 feet. Remarkably, her entire crew managed to get out of the sinking wreck, and nobody was killed. But the boat was gone: only the tops of her two steam chimneys protruded above the water. A few days later, US ships plowed over the smokestacks to knock them over and hide the wreck's position so the Confederates would not be able to salvage her guns.

The *Cairo* was forgotten. As the top portions of the wreck washed away, the bottom portion sank into the muck and was covered with river silt. The cold water and oxygen-poor mud preserved her almost intact.

Then, almost 100 years later, a historian at the Vicksburg National Military Park became interested in the *Cairo*, and using old Civil War maps he began to look for the wreck, using an ordinary magnetic compass to search for large metal objects in the river. In 1956, searchers found what they presumed was the wreck, but it wasn't until 1960 that a team of divers was able to bring up artifacts that allowed a positive identification.

After years of fundraising and planning, an attempt was made in October 1964 to lift the *Cairo* out of the river. But the hull had been weakened so much that the cables were causing too much damage. It was then decided to cut the hull into three pieces and lift them out separately. In December the hull sections were placed on barges and towed to a shipyard on the Mississippi coast, where they were treated, preserved and reassembled.

Since the crew had abandoned the stricken ship in such a hurry, they left all their equipment and personal articles behind, and the interior of the wreck was a perfectly-preserved time capsule from the Civil War era. Hundreds of artifacts were found and conserved, ranging from artillery shells for the cannons to personal shoes and pocketknives. The restoration was completed in 1980.

Today, the USS *Cairo* is on display as part of the Vicksburg Battlefield National Military Park. With the missing parts of the ship reconstructed, visitors are able to go onboard and examine the guns, the boilers, the pistons, the iron ribs for the paddlewheels, and the armor plate. The nearby museum displays many of the artifacts recovered inside the wreck.

Chancellorsville
April 30, 1863
Virginia

After the crushing defeat at Fredericksburg, the Union Army of the Potomac was in disarray, and the new commander, General "Fighting Joe" Hooker, needed several months to bring it back into combat readiness. By early 1863 he had an effective force of 130,000. But he was also under a time pressure; many of his troops had enlisted for two-year terms, and they were about to run out.

And so Hooker moved his troops across the Rappahannock into Virginia where Confederate General Robert E Lee was still encamped with 60,000 troops (General James Longstreet's corps had been dispatched elsewhere). By April 30, the Federals had 80,000 troops in the tiny crossroads of Chancellorsville, behind Lee's position, and another 40,000 in front of him across the river, and Hooker was confident that he had the Southerners trapped.

He was in for a shock. On May 1, Lee, although he was outnumbered over two to one, boldly decided to attack. Leaving a small portion of his forces at Fredericksburg to defend against a possible Union drive across the Rappahannock, he took the rest of his army and split it in two, sending half against each of the Union flanks. Taken by surprise, Hooker lost his nerve, and withdrew his troops back to a defensive line at Chancellorsville, at the intersection of two roads. Perhaps he hoped to goad Lee into launching his smaller force against a superior defensive position and destroying himself, just as Burnside had done at Fredericksburg.

Union position at Chancellorsville battlefield

But Lee, now with the initiative and a fixed target, did not make a frontal assault. Instead, in a brilliant tactical move, he now made another daring offensive: he sent General Stonewall Jackson and 22,000 men in a 12-mile circular sweep around the side of the Union lines, hitting them in their vulnerable flank at Wilderness Church just as Lee's troops attacked from in front. The effect of the two-pronged assault was devastating: many of the Federal troops were just sitting down to dinner when the Confederates hit them. They lost over 2500 casualties. Hooker, who had made his headquarters in the Chancellor family home, was temporarily dazed and put out of action when a cannonball shattered a porch pillar he was leaning against. Only darkness halted the Confederate advance.

General Jackson wanted to continue the attack even in the dark, hoping to destroy most of Hooker's army before he could regroup. At around midnight, Jackson and a few staff officers rode out to inspect the Union positions, wanting to see if it would be feasible to launch a night attack. As they rode back towards the Confederate lines, however, they were mistaken by Southern pickets for a Union cavalry patrol and were fired upon. Stonewall Jackson was hit three times: after having his arm amputated he contracted pneumonia and died a week later.

Stonewall Jackson Memorial

At daybreak on May 3, the Union division commanded by General Daniel Sickles, at Hazel Grove, found itself between the two Confederate armies, and withdrew. That hill was quickly occupied by Confederate artillery, which then supported an infantry charge against the heavily dug-in Federals. After several hours, the Union troops were driven back towards the

Rappahannock. Together, both sides had lost around 21,000 men, making this the second-bloodiest day of the war, behind only Antietam.

The final fighting of the battle took place on May 4 when the Union forces under General John Sedgwick crossed the Rappahannock and attacked the 11,000 troops that Lee had left behind in Fredericksburg. The Confederates were entrenched on Marye's Heights and fought off the attack. When Sedgwick withdrew back across the river, the Battle of Chancellorsville came to an end. Hooker retreated back to Maryland. He had lost 17,000 casualties. Lee had won a stunning tactical victory, but in the process he had lost 13,000 men— almost one-fourth of his total forces. He had also lost Stonewall Jackson, one of his most capable subordinates. It was a price that the Confederacy could not afford.

But Robert E Lee was now flush with victory: his army had delivered a crushing defeat to one that was twice its size. And, seizing upon what may have been an opportunity to win the war, he formed a bold plan: he would cross Maryland, invade Pennsylvania, threaten Washington and Philadelphia, and force the North to make peace on favorable terms. He set his sights on the transport hub at Gettysburg.

The back to back Federal losses at Fredericksburg and Chancellorsville also had international implications. Neither England nor France wanted to be seen as actively supporting a rebel nation that was fighting for its right to hold people as slaves, but the string of Northern military defeats now convinced them that the time had come for the two European powers, perhaps accompanied by Russia, to possibly intervene as mediators, offering to broker a peace agreement based upon the separation of North and South.

At the time of the battle, Chancellorsville consisted mostly of a farmhouse and inn at the intersection of two dirt roads. Owned by the Chancellor family, the building was burned down by cannon shot during the fighting. With their livelihood ruined, the Chancellors sold their land and left. Their original house was rebuilt, but this too was later destroyed by a fire, and today only the stone steps and foundation remains. In 1927, Congress authorized the Fredericksburg and Spotsylvania National Military Park, protecting four different Civil War battlefields, and obtained the land.

One of the two Visitors Centers is located at the Chancellorsville battle site. There is a short walking trail which leads to the place where Stonewall Jackson was shot. Not long after the war ended, the spot was marked by a large quartz boulder. Later, a stone monument was placed at the site.

A driving tour takes visitors around the battlefield, including the location of the Chancellor family home and Hazel Grove, where the heaviest fighting occurred. Another spot on the tour is the ruins of Catharine Furnace, an iron smelter that was the scene of brief fighting.

Gettysburg
July 1, 1863
Pennsylvania

The Battle of Gettysburg is certainly the most famous conflict of the Civil War and the most-visited battlefield in the US. And for good reason: it was the turning point that ended the Union's string of defeats and set the North on the path to victory.

After his clear wins at Fredericksburg and Chancellorsville, Confederate General Robert E Lee decided that he no longer needed to sit on the defensive, but could take the war to the Yankees. He had tried this before, in 1862, and had been stopped at Antietam, but now he would try again. Lee knew that disenchantment with the war was growing in the North, and another Confederate victory might be enough to provoke a political settlement to end the conflict. He began to move his troops into Maryland.

Union General Joseph Hooker followed, being careful to keep his army between Lee and Washington DC. But after the debacle of Chancellorsville, Hooker had lost the confidence of his officers and of President Lincoln, and on June 28, after an argument with General Henry Halleck, Hooker submitted his resignation: command of the Army of the Potomac was given to General George

Meade. By the end of the week Meade would fight the most important battle of his life.

Lee's plan was to assemble his 75,000 men at the small town of Gettysburg PA, which was a strategic transport hub with vital roads and railways radiating out from it. Using this as a staging area, he then expected to attack the Pennsylvania state capitol of Harrisburg.

But when Confederate General Richard Ewell reached Gettysburg with his advance force on July 1, he found two brigades of Union troops already there. In a day-long fight that began near McPherson Ridge, Ewell pushed the outnumbered Federals back through the streets of Gettysburg: they withdrew to a long hill known locally as Cemetery Ridge. Ewell decided that the Union defensive position here was too strong for him, so he formed a line of his own along Seminary Ridge, which paralleled the Federals. For the next 24 hours both sides would rush in reinforcements, until the Union had 90,000 troops and the Confederates had 70,000. Both Lee and Meade knew that this would be a decisive battle.

Cemetery Ridge

That night, Lee and his second-in-command, General James Longstreet, debated strategy. Longstreet concluded that the Federal position along Cemetery Ridge was too strong to attack directly, and advocated moving the Confederate Army away towards Philadelphia, which would force Meade to move out from his defenses and fight in the open. Lee, however, decided to assault the Federal lines. "The enemy is there," he concluded, "and I am going to attack him."

Lee's plan was to launch a two-pronged move at first light, against the two ends of the Federal line. But a series of delays meant that the first attack, by General Longstreet, did not begin until 4pm that afternoon. His target was a pair of hills called Round Top and Little Round Top: if these could be captured, they could dominate the entire Federal line with cannon fire and force Meade to withdraw. Little Round Top, moreover, had been mistakenly left undefended by the Federals: only a last-minute move by Union troops of the 20th Maine and 140th New York Regiments protected the hill and avoided a disaster. After several hours of bloody fighting at the Peach Orchard and the Wheatfield, the Confederates managed to capture a patch of large rocks known as the Devils Den (which became a sniper's lair), but were unable to break the Federal line.

Meanwhile, General Ewell's troops were attacking Culp's Hill, at the other end of the Union line. Despite fierce fighting, they were no more successful. As night fell, the Union troops were still secure on Cemetery Ridge. It had been a bloody day: both sides had lost over 9,000 casualties.

On the morning of July 3, Lee thought he was on the verge of victory. After sending another attack against Culp Hill, which he hoped would force Meade to move reinforcements, Lee ordered a 90-minute barrage from 150 Confederate cannons, intended to knock out the Union guns and weaken their lines. When the barrage lifted, he would send 15,000 of Longstreet's men, under General George Pickett, directly into the center of the Union lines. It would, he thought, be enough to break the Federals. Longstreet was horrified: his troops would have to march over a mile in open country into the teeth of Union cannons and long-range rifle fire. But Lee was adamant. "Pickett's Charge", as it became known to history, was launched at 3pm.

Devils Den

It was slaughter on a scale that had scarcely been seen before. The Federal cannons began with long-range solid shot, then canister shot as the Confederates got closer. At several hundred yards the Union troops poured rifle fire into them. While a tiny portion of the charge actually managed to briefly penetrate the Federal lines, the rest of the Confederate units were shattered. Many threw down their muskets and surrendered: a few thousand survivors made their way back to the Confederate line on Seminary Ridge. More than half of Pickett's troops lay on the field. To most historians, this was the point at which the Confederates lost the war.

Lee pulled the remnants of his shattered army together on Seminary Ridge and, throughout the day of July 4, in a heavy rain, waited for Meade's counter-attack. It never came. Meade's army, though victorious, was also severely crippled. When Lee withdrew to Maryland and ultimately back to Virginia, Meade made only a half-hearted attempt to follow him. The Federals had lost 28,000 men at Gettysburg. Lee had lost 24,000—around one-third of his entire army.

Meanwhile, even as the Battle of Gettysburg was raging, the Confederates were, a thousand miles away, suffering another defeat at Vicksburg which would prove to be equally as devastating.

A week after the battle, the State of Pennsylvania began plans to obtain a portion of the field as a cemetery. On November 19, 1864, the National Cemetery was dedicated, and President Lincoln was invited to speak "some appropriate words". His Gettysburg Address, only two minutes in length, is now one of the most famous speeches in history.

After the war, the Gettysburg Battle Memorial Association purchased some of the land and set up a wooden observation tower for visitors. For the next twenty years, Civil War veterans groups placed over a thousand statues, plaques and memorial stones on the battlefield.

In 1895, Congressman Daniel Sickles—a Union General who had fought at Gettysburg—introduced a resolution for Congress to obtain the battlefield and dedicate it as a National Military Park. The War Department purchased all the lots owned by the Memorial Association. For many years, the Army used the site as a campground for training troops.

In 1933, after the National Park Service came into existence, ownership of the Park was transferred from the War Department to the NPS. In 1962 a new Visitors Center was completed, featuring a 360-degree cyclorama painting of the battle. In 2002, after it was decided to restore the battlefield in a closer resemblance to its original condition, this building was demolished and a new Visitors Center constructed at the edge of the park.

Today, only about half of the actual battlefield is contained within the park's borders. Much of the fighting, particularly on the first day, occurred inside the town of Gettysburg itself, and several historic buildings have been designated there, some still showing battle damage.

In 2017 a seven-acre tract of land was preserved at the site of Powers Hill, where the Union forces had placed a cannon battery. The Civil War Trust considers several other historically-significant locations outside the protected boundaries to be in serious danger of development and loss.

Vicksburg
July 4, 1863
Mississippi

Although the siege of Vicksburg came to an end on the day after the Battle of Gettysburg, and provided another crippling blow to the Confederates, the actual fighting there had begun long before.

Vicksburg was an important port on the Mississippi River, and was targeted as part of the Anaconda Plan to cut off the flow of commerce up and down the Mississippi, thereby dividing the Confederacy in half. The first attempt to take the city had been in May 1862, when Admiral David Farragut, after capturing New Orleans and Baton Rouge, sailed up the Mississippi River with a fleet of gunships, but was driven back by the port's shore batteries.

In 1863, Union General Ulysses S Grant, at his base in northern Mississippi, made plans to move on Vicksburg and thereby remove the last remaining major Confederate port city on the river. In March his army arrived at Milliken's Bend, on the Louisiana side of the Mississippi River.

But now Grant had to get his troops to the other side of the River, and the Confederate defenses were too strong for a direct assault. His first landing attempt, at

Grand Gulf, was beaten back by Confederate fire. In desperation, the Union troops now tried to dig a canal that would allow Federal gunboats to bypass the Confederate shore batteries. This proved to be too difficult, however, and was abandoned.

Union trench at Vicksburg

Finally, a second landing on May 1, at Port Gibson, was successful, and Union troops marched through swamps and bayous towards Jackson, the state capitol, to force its surrender and to cut off the supply lines to Vicksburg. Two weeks later, the defenders at Jackson, under Confederate General John Pemberton, were forced out of the city and withdrew towards Vicksburg. Grant followed, and skirmishes took place at Champion Hill and the Big Black River before Pemberton's remaining forces reached Vicksburg.

When Grant reached the city on May 18, he desperately wanted to avoid a long drawn-out siege, and searched for some way to take the town quickly. So the next day he launched troops under General William T Sherman against Stockade Redan, one of the

Confederate strongholds. The attack was beaten back and Sherman's men suffered heavy casualties. Three days later, on May 22, Grant tried again, bombarding a three-mile section of Confederate defenses before sending in the infantry. Once again, the Confederates inflicted heavy losses.

Grant now realized that his only hope of taking the city was through an old-fashioned siege. As his number of troops swelled from 35,000 to 77,000, Grant began digging trenches around the city, gradually working his way closer and closer to the Confederates. Meanwhile, Union cannons and gunboats on the Mississippi River kept up a steady bombardment. Vicksburg was reduced to a tangle of shell craters. Most of the defending troops and remaining civilians lived in caves dug into the hills: the Federal soldiers referred to it as "Prairie Dog Town". Food quickly ran out, and dogs, cats and horses began to disappear from city streets.

On June 7, a contingent of Confederate soldiers from Louisiana made an attack on one of the Federal outposts at Milliken's Bend, hoping to cut off the Union supply lines and force Grant to withdraw at least part of his army. Milliken's Bend was defended by inexperienced African-American troops, but they held firm and repelled the Confederates. With the Federal supply lines now secure, Union troops surrounding the entire city, and ironclad gunboats shelling the whole area, the fate of Vicksburg was all but sealed. It was just a matter of time.

In late June, Grant tried out a new tactic when he assigned a group of soldiers who had been miners before the war to dig a tunnel under one of the Confederate strongholds and pack it full of black powder. On June 25 the mine was detonated, destroying the position. But when Federal troops rushed forward into the resulting crater, they were pinned down and suffered heavy losses before withdrawing.

By July, however, the siege was taking its toll on the city's defenders. On July 3, Pemberton asked Grant for surrender terms. Grant initially replied that he would only accept an unconditional surrender, then changed his mind and offered to parole and release all 29,000

prisoners. The surrender of Vicksburg came on July 4—
the day after the Battle of Gettysburg. According to local
legend, Pemberton had offered to surrender several days
previously, but Grant had rejected it because he wanted
to announce the surrender on the Fourth of July: the
city did not celebrate the holiday again for almost 100
years.

The twin defeats at Gettysburg and Vicksburg
marked the end of the South's dream of independence.
The Confederacy never again took the strategic offensive,
and in Europe the rebellion was now viewed as a lost
cause. Although the war would last another two years,
the outcome was no longer in doubt.

In 1866, Congress set up the Vicksburg National
Cemetery, and 18,000 graves were placed here. The War
Department obtained ownership and established a
military park in 1899, but most of the original
battleground had already been lost. In 1933 the site was
taken over by the National Park Service.

Today the Vicksburg National Military Park covers
about a third of the area where the Union and
Confederate positions snaked around the city. It
contains almost 2000 acres of original and
reconstructed trenches, defensive works, caves, and gun
positions. There is a driving tour and almost 15 miles of
walking trails. Located across the Mississippi River in
Louisiana are the preserved sites of Grant's Canal and
Milliken's Bend, which are also part of the Park.

Lowry War

1863
North Carolina

During the Civil War, a band of Lumbee Indians in North Carolina known as the Lowry Gang waged a "Robin Hood" war against the white aristocracy, and became a local legend.

The mid-19th century was a time of tragedy for Native Americans in the US. The policy of the United States was "removal", in which native tribes were forcibly relocated to the "Indian territory" in Oklahoma. In the most famous instance, the Cherokee Nation appealed their removal all the way to the Supreme Court, which ruled in their favor. The tribe was forcibly deported anyway, with President Jackson famously remarking, in reference to Chief Justice Marshall, "He's made his decision—now let him enforce it". The mass relocation became known as "The Trail of Tears".

By the time the Civil War broke out in 1861, only scattered groups of Native Americans remained in the east. One of these was the Lumbee tribe in North Carolina. Under the racial laws which enforced the Southern slavery system, Native Americans were classified as "free people of color"—a category which also included non-slave African-Americans. The slave-owning aristocracy considered them all to be a dangerous threat to the social order (especially in the wake of Nat Turner's unsuccessful slave revolt), and passed a series of laws to keep them powerless. "Free people of color" were banned from voting, from serving on juries, and from possessing firearms. As a result of this legal discrimination, the Lumbees lived mostly in poverty, on small farms on the worst land outside of town.

After the Union victories at Vicksburg and Gettysburg, the war began to turn against the Confederates. In the South, local militias appeared, known as the Home Guard, consisting of discharged soldiers and men who were not suitable for service at the front. A series of defensive forts and strongpoints were planned, and the Home Guards were sent to forcibly recruit all able-bodied males who could be pressed into service to build them. And "free people of color" were specifically targeted. To escape this impressment, many Lumbee Indians, free African-Americans, and escaped slaves, as well as Union sympathizers, left town and retreated into the nearby forests and mountains. Here, they were dependent upon local supporters for food and supplies, and many of them turned to thievery to survive.

One of these bands, in Robeson County NC, was led by the Lowry family. Before the war, the Lowrys had a farm of about 2,000 acres. Some documents list them as Lumbee, others as African-American: they may have been of mixed ancestry. During the war, local Home Guards began forcibly recruiting local men to work at constructing nearby Fort Fisher, and to avoid this, most of the Lowry sons fled into the swamps.

In December 1864, members of the family stole two pigs from the plantation owned by James Barnes. Barnes led a group of Home Guards to arrest the Lowrys, but a gunfight broke out and he was killed. The Lowrys, accompanied by local supporters, now waged an open guerrilla war against the local aristocracy. In a daring attack, they broke into the county courthouse and took guns and ammunition from the armory, then launched a series of nighttime raids against local plantations, stealing food and supplies and distributing them to other Lumbee bands hiding in the swamps. In

March 1865, Home Guards raided the farmhouse of Allen Lowry, the elderly patriarch of the family, and found guns hidden there. In retaliation, the militia convened a drumhead "trial" and summarily executed Allen and his son William.

Henry Lowry, in a contemporary photograph

The executions sparked a private war, led by Lowry's son Henry, that would last for the next seven years, long after the Civil War was over. The Lowry Gang, as it was known, specifically targeted the area's wealthy white plantation owners, and over the years carried out a number of raids, robberies, assassinations, and gunfights with lawmen. To the authorities, the Gang was just a bunch of thieves and "swamp outlaws"; to many of the local people—especially Lumbee Indians and African-Americans—the Lowrys were modern-day Robin Hoods who were fighting for social justice. This reputation was enhanced when the Lowrys ambushed and killed the head of the local Ku Klux Klan. Henry Lowry became the most famous outlaw in North Carolina, with a $12,000 reward on his head, and his exploits were reported by newspapers in faraway New York and Chicago. Southern newspapers, meanwhile, depicted the Lowry Gang as "the African Ku Klux", a terrorist group that targeted white citizens.

In February 1872 the band made its most famous robbery, attacking a depot in Lumberton and making off with a safe containing $20,000 in cash. After that, Henry Lowry disappeared, and it is still unknown what happened to him. Some have speculated that he died of a gunshot wound from a raid; others assert that he moved away to the Wild West to start a new life. Leadership of the Lowry Gang fell to his son Steve, but the raids were already slacking off. When Steve Lowry was shot by bounty hunters in 1874, the Lowry War came to an end.

A revolver that once belonged to gang member Tom Lowry is now on display at the North Carolina Museum of History in Raleigh, part of an interpretive exhibit on the Lowry War.

Corydon
July 9, 1863
Indiana

As General Robert E Lee and his Army of Virginia approached Pennsylvania in June 1863, he was receiving some help from another much smaller Confederate force, several hundred miles away. General John Hunt Morgan and 2500 Confederate cavalry troops were approaching the Ohio River, which separated Kentucky from Indiana. Morgan intended to launch a raid towards Indianapolis and Cincinnati that would force the Union to pull some of its forces from Pennsylvania, away from Lee's army. After wreaking whatever havoc he could in Indiana and Ohio, he planned to then move his troops to Pennsylvania to join up with what he presumed would be Lee's victorious Confederates.

On July 8, 1863, Morgan's raiders captured an Ohio River merchant steamboat, the *J.T McCombs*, when it landed on its regularly-scheduled trip to Brandenburg KY. Sailing her out into the middle of the river, the Confederates then set out a false distress flag which attracted another riverboat, the *Alice Dean*. When the *Dean* pulled up alongside the *McCombs*, she was captured too, and Morgan now planned to use both boats to ferry his men across the river. A small force of Indiana militiamen fired a cannon at them from the far bank, but they were inexperienced and inaccurate, and caused little damage before they were driven off by the Confederates' own cannons.

While this was going on, though, a Union gunboat, the USS *Springfield*, arrived at the scene. As the two captured Confederate ships retreated, the *Springfield* shelled the town until she ran out of ammunition, then withdrew. Morgan's little fleet set out once again, but now two more gunboats, the USS *Elk* and the armed merchant steamer *Grey Eagle*, appeared; both quickly sailed away, however, after coming under fire from the Confederate cannons on shore. Finally, Morgan was able to board his troops and cross.

Once on the Indiana side of the river, Morgan burned one of his boats and allowed the other to leave, then formed a marching column and set out along the Mauckport Road for Corydon, about ten miles away. During the night the town received word that the Confederates were approaching, and the next morning a force of about 450 Indiana militia hurriedly constructed a series of log breastworks across the top of a hill just south of town. None of them had ever been in a battle before, but they were hopeful that they could beat Morgan's raiders back, or at least delay them until help could arrive from New Albany.

Morgan and his 2500 cavalry arrived at about noon. His advance guard, seeing how few militia there were manning the hill, tried to launch an assault but were driven back. Sixteen captured Confederates were triumphantly marched to Corydon and secured in the town jail.

But as the rest of Morgan's men arrived, the tiny Federal force was outnumbered over 6 to 1. Sending the two flanks of his force to attack the Union hill on both sides, Morgan simultaneously opened up with his guns. To avoid being surrounded, the Federal militia fell back from their hilltop fortress and retreated into town, with the Confederate cavalry close behind. There, recognizing that their position was hopeless, the tiny Union garrison surrendered. The battle had lasted about an hour.

Morgan had lost around 50 casualties, and the Indiana militia about 20.

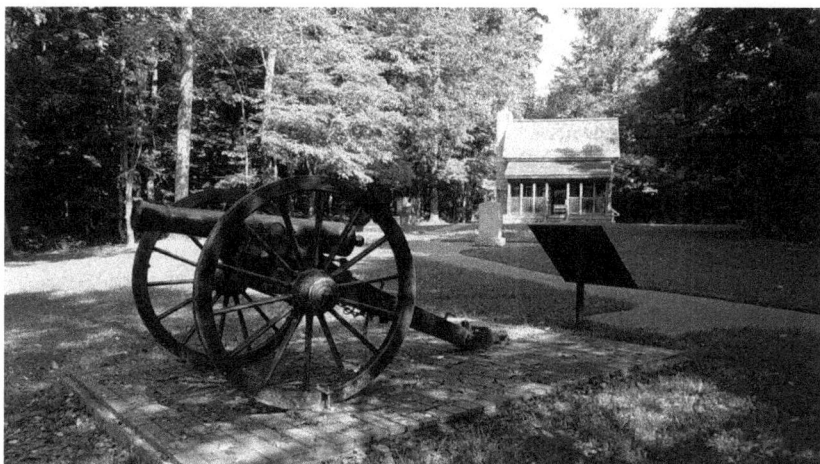

Corydon Battlefield Park

The Confederates now swarmed through the town looting anything valuable and stealing most of the horses. (They also freed their captured comrades in the town jail.) The raiders disarmed all the militia members, then agreed not to burn the town in exchange for a cash ransom payment. General Morgan triumphantly entered the Kintner House Inn, which became his headquarters.

But here Morgan received some bad news of which he had been unaware: reading a local newspaper, he learned that not only had the Confederate garrison at Vicksburg surrendered, but Lee's army had been defeated at Gettysburg and had withdrawn to Maryland.

Morgan now realized he was in a serious position: not only was he alone and isolated deep in Federal territory without any nearby Confederate forces to join up with, but without any riverboats he had no way of crossing the Ohio River back to safety. So he did the only thing he could: gathering up his troops, he began marching north along the river towards Ohio, raiding and foraging for supplies along the way and searching desperately for a way to cross. As he moved north, more and more local militia gathered to pursue him, accompanied by 6,000 Union cavalry.

Today, the hill around which the fighting at Corydon was centered is preserved as a county park, the Battle of Corydon Memorial Park, established in 1976. There are interpretive signs and stone markers and memorials. The wooden cabin that once stood at the flank of the Confederate line and served as a field hospital was disassembled in 2011 and rebuilt on the top of the hill.

Morgan's Raid
July 26, 1863
Ohio

After the Battle of Corydon, Confederate raider General John Hunt Morgan found himself isolated and pursued deep in enemy terrain, with no way to return to friendly territory. For over two weeks, Morgan and his remaining troops were forced to retreat further and further north, away from Confederate territory, in a desperate move to evade the Federals and find a way across the Ohio River. They passed through over a dozen towns. According to legend, in one village a few Confederate troopers looted a local Masonic Lodge, stealing some gold coins and jewels: Morgan, himself a Freemason, had them arrested and returned the pilfered booty.

At Buffington Island, about 250 of his cavalry troops managed to escape across the Ohio River into Kentucky, but another 1,000 were captured by the Federals, leaving Morgan with just 400 troops, and pursued by several thousand Union soldiers and militia commanded by General Edward Hobson.

Finally at about noon on July 26, 2600 Union cavalry under Major George Rue intercepted Morgan's force at Salineville and surrounded it. After less than an hour of fighting, Morgan realized that his position was hopeless. He retreated from the battlefield and made his way to the nearby town of West Point, where he decided to give up and offered his surrender to one of the people he had captured, a man named Burbridge who claimed to be an Ohio Militia Captain. Burbridge and Morgan reached an agreement in which parole was granted to the Confederates once they had laid down their arms (which would have removed them as combatants and allowed them to return safely to Confederate territory as civilians).

Memorial at Buffington Battlefield Park

But when Major Rue arrived, he discounted this informal agreement, insisted that Morgan formally surrender his forces to him, and then refused to grant parole. (Later, it was discovered that "Captain" Burbridge was actually just a civilian with no military office and no authority.) Most of Morgan's force was sent to the Union POW center at Camp Chase, near Columbus OH, and the officers, including Morgan himself, were kept in the Ohio Penitentiary.

Then, in November 1863, using kitchen utensils as tools, Morgan and six of his officers tunneled their way out of the jail yard and escaped: wearing civilian clothes, they boarded a train and made their way to Cincinnati, then crossed the Ohio River into Kentucky. But Morgan's freedom was short-lived; after rejoining the Confederate Army, he was killed during the fighting at Greeneville TN less than a year later.

Morgan's raid in Ohio is considered by most to be the deepest penetration by Confederate troops into Union territory.

After the war, a memorial stone obelisk was erected at the Buffington battle site. In 1929, the Ohio Historical Society obtained a 4-acre section of the battleground, and today, this small portion of the battlefield at Buffington Island is run by the Society as a historical park. The other 600 or so acres where the fighting occurred are in private hands, and much of the battle site has been lost to a quarrying operation. While some archaeological excavations have taken place near the site, the location of the mass graves where the Confederates were buried on the battlefield remains unknown.

Camp Chase
1863
Ohio

In May 1861, the Union established a training center at Camp Chase, just outside of Columbus OH, which also served as a railway transport center for dispatching Ohio troops to the rest of the country. In all, about 150,000 Union troops from various Ohio Regiments spent time in Camp Chase, including four future Presidents who served as officers in the Union Army: Andrew Johnson, Rutherford B Hayes, James Garfield, and William McKinley. By November, Camp Chase had also added a military prison, where about 300 civilian Confederate sympathizers from Kentucky and West Virginia were held.

In the summer of 1863, about 2,000 captured Confederates, most of them from the surrendered garrison at Fort Donelson, Tennessee, were being confined in the prison at Camp Chase. By February 1865, the POW population there had exploded to 9,400. During the course of the war, about 25,000 Confederate prisoners passed through Camp Chase, most of them on their way to other camps. A total of 2,235 of these died, many of them from a smallpox epidemic that swept through the camp in 1864. At first the dead Confederates were buried in the nearby Columbus City Cemetery, but within a short time they were being buried in an area of the camp that was set aside as a graveyard.

Gravestones at Camp Chase

After the war, relatives reclaimed 126 of the Confederate remains and reburied them in their home states. At the same time, 68 dead Confederate POWs from nearby Camp Dennison and another 31 from the City Cemetery were reburied at Camp Chase. The camp was then closed, abandoned, and neglected. Today all that remains is the cemetery. It's not clear exactly how many people are now buried here: there are 2,260 gravestones currently in the cemetery, but the camp records indicate a total of 2,122 actual graves, some of them containing more than one person, for a total of 2,168 burials.

In 1893, a Civil War veteran from the Union Army named William Knauss took an interest in the old camp, and formed the Camp Chase Memorial Association to protect and maintain the Confederate cemetery and to raise funds for its preservation. A stone wall was built around the grounds and a granite memorial arch was installed in 1902, and two years later the site was purchased by the Federal Government. In 1908, records were found which enabled individual graves to be identified, and the Commission for Marking Graves of Confederate Dead, part of the Arlington National Cemetery, paid for the installation of a headstone on each grave, lettered with the soldier's name, rank, and unit. The vast majority are enlisted soldiers, with a scattering of corporals and sergeants, a handful of lieutenants, and a few captains. (Many captured Confederate officers were temporarily sent to Camp Chase, including General Basil W Duke, but most of the officers were then transferred to Johnson's Island on Lake Erie.)

Today, no trace of Camp Chase remains except for the cemetery and its stone memorials, which is surrounded by suburban Columbus OH. The site is owned and maintained by the Federal Government as a National Cemetery, and is listed on the National Register of Historic Places.

Chickamauga
September 18, 1863
Georgia

In August 1863, the Army of the Cumberland, under the Union General William Rosecrans, was poised to take the important Confederate railroad center of Chattanooga TN, which was defended by the Army of Tennessee under the Confederate General Braxton Bragg. In a deft move, Rosecrans swung his army through the Tennessee mountains and cut off the city's supply lines, forcing Bragg to abandon it without a fight. Bragg in turn made immediate plans to take it back by seizing the Union supply route at Lafayette Road.

Bragg hoped to spring a carefully laid trap. His 70,000 troops outnumbered the Federals by around 10,000—one of the few times during the war when the South had a numerical advantage. He had sent a number of spies to the Union lines to be intentionally captured and pass on the false information that the Confederates were in a confused retreat, hoping to goad the Union forces into attacking before they were ready. Rosecrans took the bait and set off in pursuit, allowing his army to become stretched out and disordered into three separate groups, each too far away to support the others. It was just what Bragg wanted, and he moved his troops to cut off and attack an isolated portion of the Federal army, hoping to engage and defeat Rosecrans' forces one piece at a time. The first fight would take place at Chickamauga Creek, ten miles from Chattanooga.

But things did not happen as Bragg had planned. His subordinate officers were slow in moving into position, and the approaching Union force detected the trap and formed a hasty defensive line.

Memorials mark the position of Federal units along Lafayette Road

On the morning of September 18, the Confederates crossed the Chickamauga at several points in an attempt to outflank the Federals and cut off their route to Chattanooga. At one point, a brigade of Indiana mounted infantry under Colonel John Wilder, armed with new Spencer repeating rifles, held off a much larger Southern force for five hours before being forced to retreat. By nightfall the Federals had formed a stronger defensive line along the Lafayette Road, where the thick forest made it difficult for neighboring units to see each other or any approaching enemy.

The next morning, Union General George Thomas sent one of his brigades forward against what he thought was a single Confederate brigade, but actually concealed in the thick woods was a Southern cavalry division under General Nathan Bedford Forrest and an infantry division commanded by a Confederate General with the wonderfully unlikely name States Rights Gist (yes, that was his actual birth name). Hearing this fighting, two more Confederate units, led by Generals Alexander Stewart and John Bell Hood, also attacked. Fortunately for the Federals, two divisions of reinforcements, under Generals Philip Sheridan and Thomas Wood, entered the fight and broke the assault. The Union line held.

Reinforced by General James Longstreet's forces during the night (Longstreet had accidentally stumbled into a group of Union pickets and had almost been captured), Bragg now ordered an attack at dawn the next day, but due to miscommunication the troops, under John Breckinridge, did not move until 9:30 that morning. Although some of the Federal units suffered 30 percent casualties, the Confederates found themselves crossing an open field into Union positions protected by breastworks, and their assault bogged down.

At this point, around 11am, the Confederates were handed a golden opportunity. During the confused fighting in the thick woods and low visibility, Rosecrans received some incorrect information indicating that there was a gap in his line, and ordered troops under General Wood to move to plug the non-existent hole. Wood was confused by the order—he could see there was no break in the line—but pulled out his troops and moved them anyway (he had already been berated by Rosecrans for moving his troops too slowly in the battle, and apparently didn't want to risk the commander's wrath by asking for clarification). Wood's troop movement then created an actual gap, and as it happened Longstreet was already charging in with 23,000 men, aiming towards a small farmhouse in the Union line known as the Brotherton House.

Under this assault, most of the Union line reeled back in disorder. Only the actions of Union General Thomas staved off complete disaster: forming a defensive line at Snodgrass Hill, Thomas, though under assault by three brigades, held off the Confederates long enough to allow the rest of the Federal Army to regroup and begin an organized retreat back to Chattanooga. His defensive stand earned him the nickname "The Rock of Chickamauga".

Brotherton House

Chickamauga was one of the bloodiest battles of the war: Rosecrans lost 16,000 men and Bragg lost 18,000. It was the last major Confederate victory in the Civil War, but although a tactical win, it was a strategic failure: the Union troops still held Chattanooga, and soon General Ulysses Grant arrived with reinforcements and captured the entire area.

In 1890, Congress formed the Chickamauga and Chattanooga National Military Park to commemorate the two Civil War battle sites. It opened in 1895. During the Spanish-American War, the Military Park was used by the Army as a training ground and a shipping point for troops on their way to Cuba.

Today, most of the 9,000-acre park consists of the Chickamauga battlefield. There is a Visitors Center and a driving tour. The Lookout Mountain area and part of the Missionary Ridge site, from the Battle of Chattanooga, are run as satellite parks.

Chattanooga
November 23, 1863
Tennessee

In the aftermath of Chickamauga, the Union General William Rosecrans was reassigned, and General George Thomas was given command of the Army of the Cumberland. Reinforcements arrived from Vicksburg, and Union troops built up a three-mile defensive line around the city. Chattanooga was of vital strategic importance as a supply and transport base, and Thomas was ordered to hold it at all costs.

The Confederate General Braxton Bragg, meanwhile, had established a strong position just outside of Chattanooga. Deciding that he did not have enough men to attack Thomas's lines directly, Bragg instead decided to occupy a number of positions around the city, threatening to cut off its supply lines and force the Federals to withdraw. Within weeks, the Union army was desperately short of food and supplies. Thomas responded by sending a force to seize Brown's Ferry, which opened up a new supply pathway to Nashville. As fresh supplies of hardtack and coffee began to arrive, it became known as the "Cracker Line".

In October, General Ulysses S Grant, fresh from his win at Vicksburg, arrived in Chattanooga to take command. With the Confederate siege now effectively broken and with Union reinforcements still arriving, the advantage had shifted to the Federals, and the always offensive-minded Grant immediately began planning an attack to drive Bragg back.

Grant divided his forces into three groups, led by General Thomas, General William T Sherman, and General Joseph Hooker. On November 23, Grant received intelligence information that Bragg was pulling troops from the center of his line to reinforce his right flank, and a portion of Thomas's force under General Thomas Wood was sent to make a probing attack on some advance posts at Orchard Knob, near the center of Bragg's lines. His orders were to not engage, but to withdraw as soon as he had made contact and established the strength of the Confederate line there.

Unexpectedly, though, the 600 Confederates on the hill, outnumbered over two to one, broke and retreated to Missionary Ridge, and Grant decided to keep Wood's 14,000 troops there and to launch an attack the next day. On the afternoon of the 24th, while Thomas reinforced Orchard Knob, Hooker attacked the left side of the Confederate lines at Lookout Mountain. During the fighting a heavy fog bank rolled in, filling in the valley while the top of the mountain poked above it. The action became known as "The Battle Above the Clouds". Though the Confederates still held the mountain as darkness fell, their position had become untenable, and they withdrew during the night to join Bragg at Missionary Ridge. Bragg himself considered withdrawing from the Ridge, but in the end concluded that it was the strongest place to make a defensive stand, and decided to stay and await Grant's attack.

And indeed on November 25, with Sherman's troops (who had been delayed in crossing the Tennessee River) now in place, Grant launched an all-out assault. Hooker attacked from Lookout Mountain into the Confederate flank, but was held off: similarly, Sherman's drive onto Tunnel Hill, at the other end of Bragg's lines, also stalled. To force Bragg to withdraw some of the troops from his flanks, Grant ordered Thomas to send a force towards the Confederate center at Missionary Ridge.

"The Battle Above the Clouds"

The Union troops were only supposed to advance as far as the Confederate rifle pits, but once they got there they came under heavy fire from Missionary Ridge. Deciding that they had no choice but to continue the advance to avoid being pinned down and trapped, the Federal units began driving up the hill without orders towards the Confederate lines at the top. The impromptu attack proved to be decisive. Bragg was driven off the ridge, withdrew from the battlefield, and retreated all the way to Georgia. Within months, having lost the confidence of his superiors and his men, he resigned his command.

After the battle of Chattanooga, Tennessee was firmly under Union control, and the way was open for a Union move into the heart of the Confederacy. In March 1864, President Lincoln gave Grant command of the entire Union Army, and Sherman used Chattanooga as the jumping-off point for his march on Atlanta. From now on, the war had only two basic goals: the destruction of General Robert E Lee's army in Virginia by Grant, and the destruction of General Joseph Johnston's army in Georgia by Sherman.

Today, most of the Chattanooga battlefield is gone. An area on the summit of Lookout Mountain, including the Cravens House, is preserved as a part of the Chickamauga and Chattanooga National Military Park.

Confederate Submarine *Hunley*
February 17, 1864
South Carolina

With the successful Federal siege of Vicksburg, the naval "Anaconda" strategy was virtually complete: the Union Navy held nearly all of the major ports along the Atlantic and Caribbean coasts, and controlled access to all of the Mississippi River. The North had also begun building *Monitor*-type ironclads, and could do so at a far faster rate than the South. The Confederate flotilla of blockade-runners, meanwhile, was unable to transport enough supplies past the Federals. In desperation, the South once again sought a technological breakthrough that would allow them to lift the crippling blockade. And one of these concepts was the "submarine".

It was not a new idea. During the Revolutionary War in 1776, George Washington had attempted to break the British blockade of New York harbor with an underwater contraption called "Bushnell's *Turtle*", which made an unsuccessful attack with a black-powder "torpedo" on the Royal Navy flagship *Eagle*. But the *Turtle* had been a crude one-person craft made from wooden planks: the technology of the 19th century allowed for more advanced designs.

The Union Navy had already begun experimenting with submarines. Since they had enough wooden-hull and ironclad ships to seal off all the Southern ports, the primary purpose of the Federal submarines was to help clear the waters of defensive "torpedoes". So most of the Union submarine designs had iron-plate hulls with a hatch for an underwater swimmer to exit, where he could cut the ropes that held the Confederate mines in place and disarm them.

One of the earliest US submarines was the *Alligator*, designed in late 1861 specifically to counter the Confederate ironclads then under construction. She was launched in May 1862. Originally, she was propelled by oars that extended from her sides: this was unworkable, however, and they were quickly replaced with a hand-cranked propeller. President Lincoln himself watched some of the submarine's test runs. But the *Alligator* never saw action. While being towed to South Carolina in April 1862, she sank in bad weather.

Another early submarine was the *Submarine Explorer*. This design, already built privately by Julius Kroehl, was submitted to the US Navy in 1863, but was rejected for some reason. After the war, Kroehl took his submarine to Panama and used it for commercial pearl diving until he and his crew died of disease, when the *Submarine Explorer* was abandoned on a remote beach and sat forgotten until it was rediscovered in 2001.

In October 1863, a Union Army officer identified only as "Major Hunt" died while testing a submarine named the *Sea Miner*. Hunt was reportedly working on a new weapon system that he called an "underwater rocket". Shrouded in secrecy and today mostly unknown, it may have been an early version of what we know today as the torpedo.

Another early Federal submarine was called *Intelligent Whale*. Designed in 1863, she was far advanced for her time, using compressed air to operate the ballast tanks. The *Whale*, however, did not finish construction until after the war ended.

But it was the Confederates who pursued the technology most eagerly. The submarine was viewed as a wonder weapon that could break the Federal blockade and save the South.

In early 1863, a boatbuilder named Horace Lawson Hunley designed an underwater warship made of riveted iron plates. A hand-cranked propeller would move it through the water, and a series of water-ballast tanks would raise and lower it. It would carry a "torpedo" loaded with 135 pounds of black powder at the end of a timber spar: the submarine would approach stealthily underwater, attach the bomb to an enemy ship and then withdraw before detonating it. The entire project would be privately-funded, and the craft would operate as a privateer, a sea-going mercenary that was never officially part of the Confederate Navy. Construction began in Mobile AL, and once the 40-foot cylindrical craft, christened *Hunley*, was finished it was transported to Charleston Harbor for testing.

The submarine Hunley, *a contemporary illustration*

The *Hunley* was, unfortunately, beset by disasters. In one test run, the craft accidentally submerged while its hatch was still open and filled with water, drowning five of its nine crew. Not long after, another mishap sunk the sub and killed all nine aboard, including Hunley himself.

On February 17, 1864, the submarine set out on its first combat mission, with its eight-man crew commanded by Lieutenant George Dixon. Because it was deemed unsafe to run the vessel submerged, the *Hunley* was on the surface, and had intentionally picked a calm moonless night to carry out the attack. Her target was the USS *Housatonic*, a 12-gun wooden-hulled steamer that was part of the Union squadron blockading Charleston Harbor.

One of the *Housatonic's* lookouts spotted the *Hunley* as it approached. The Federals had pretty good intelligence about the submarine and knew what it was, so as soon as it was spotted in the water the ship let loose with her cannons. Small and low in the water, however, the *Hunley* was a difficult target, and, unscathed by cannonballs, made its way up to the *Housatonic*, attached her mine, and backed away.

The explosion tore open the Union ship's hull, and within minutes she had begun to fill with water. The harbor here was only 30 feet deep, so as the *Housatonic* settled on the bottom, the tops of her masts and rigging poked above the surface. Five of her 135-man crew were killed in the explosion, but the rest got away safely, either by climbing the rigging or by launching the rowboats. But the ship was destroyed. The *Housatonic* became the first vessel ever sunk by a submarine.

Confederate military officers on shore saw the explosion and watched the *Housatonic* sink, and waited for the submarine's triumphant return. The wonder weapon had demonstrated that it really could work.

But something was amiss: after several hours, the *Hunley* had not returned. She had been lost, with all eight of her crew.

In 1995, a team of divers from the National Underwater and Marine Agency located the sunken wreck of the *Hunley*, lying intact on the harbor floor. The submarine was raised and sent to the Warren Lasch Conservation Center in North Charleston where it was submerged in a 90,000 gallon tank filled first with a cold freshwater bath to extract the salt from the metal, then with a weak lye solution to remove the ocean concretions and stabilize the hull. She is now on display there, as restoration efforts are expected to continue until the mid-2020's. Fundraising efforts are already underway to construct a permanent museum to house the submarine once the conservation project is completed.

It is still not clear exactly what sunk the *Hunley*. There are indications that the submarine may have been too close to the explosion and was sunk by its own torpedo. The bodies of the crew were still inside and the valves had not been set to pump water out of the hull, indicating that either the sub had sunk too rapidly for the crew to react, or that it had actually made its getaway intact after the explosion, and sunk later. Some have concluded that the crew died of asphyxiation while submerged on the return trip, having used up all their oxygen.

Another Confederate submarine can be seen at the Capitol Park Museum in Baton Rouge LA. Found in 1878 in Lake Pontchartrain near New Orleans, this submarine may have been scuttled when Federal troops captured the city in 1862. For a time, it was believed to be the wreck of the *Pioneer*, another Confederate submarine built by Hunley in New Orleans at around the same time, that is known to have been intentionally sunk to prevent her capture. But drawings of the *Pioneer* do not match this wreck. Today it is something of a mystery: there is no record of who built this submarine or when.

Olustee

February 20, 1864
Florida

When Florida seceded in February 1861, it was a sparsely populated backwater with little military significance. Traded several times between Spain and England and purchased by the United States in 1821, it had only become a state less than 20 years ago, in 1845. During the war, it supplied a few regiments to the Confederate armies, but its primary contribution was its cattle-ranching industry, which, especially after Texas was cut off from the Mississippi River, was the major source of beef for the troops.

As part of its "Anaconda" blockade, the Federals had already landed twice at Jacksonville, leaving gunboats behind in the St Johns River. There was no serious attempt to capture the state or to hold the city, though.

By 1864, however, Florida looked vulnerable. The Union Navy had bottled up all the ports, and only a small militia force defended the state. In February 1864, Lincoln decided that a quick strike into Florida would disrupt the Confederate supply lines and cut off their food stores, and the state's slave population, once freed, could be counted on to join the Union Army. If things went well, an expedition might even be enough to capture Florida and return it to the Union in time for the 1864 elections.

The operation was assigned to General Truman Seymour, who placed 5500 men on boats, including the 54th Massachusetts Volunteer Infantry (made famous in the Hollywood movie "Glory"), the 8th United States Colored Troops, and the 35th United States Colored Troops—all newly-trained African-American regiments composed of former enslaved people. They landed at Jacksonville virtually unopposed.

But then, on his own initiative and without orders, Seymour decided to launch an overland expedition towards Tallahassee. He probably thought it would be an easy conquest: the only force available to oppose him was a collection of Confederate militia under General Joseph Finegan, who had been quickly reinforced by regular troops from South Carolina and Georgia. Now numbering about 5000, Finegan's men gathered at Olustee.

Finegan, knowing he was outnumbered, hoped to fight from behind his defensive works along a railroad embankment. But as Seymour's Federals approached on February 20, they were unexpectedly stopped by the Confederate advance force, and Finegan quickly rushed his men out of their breastworks and formed a skirmish line in the open pinewoods in front of the stalled Federals.

The fighting now grew fierce. Because of the swampy terrain, both forces were hampered in their movements and could only be fed piecemeal onto the battlefield. But the Confederates had the better tactical position and began to push the Federals back, and only a spirited assault by the 35th and 54th African-American regiments prevented a full-scale rout, giving the beaten Federals enough time to withdraw. Seymour, his invasion of Florida a failure, retreated back to Jacksonville.

In terms of the number of troops involved, the Battle of Olustee was one of the bloodiest conflicts in the war: the Confederates lost about 900 of their 5000 troops, almost 20%, and the Federals lost 1800 out of 5500— almost one third of their entire force. But not all of the Federal casualties died during the battle: the three

African-American regiments became the target of Southern vengeance. Confederate policy was to regard any captured Black soldiers as "rebellious slaves", not as enemy combatants. As the Union Army withdrew, leaving its wounded and most of its equipment behind, the Confederates fell upon the injured former slaves and massacred them, summarily executing an estimated 500 disarmed African-American prisoners.

Olustee Battlefield Memorial

In 1909, the state of Florida purchased three acres next to the battlefield and put up a stone memorial to commemorate the battle. In 1912, the state legislature obtained most of the field and established it as Florida's first State Historic Site.

Today, the battleground is preserved as the Olustee Battlefield Historic State Park, located inside the Osceola National Forest. The battleground is maintained in its natural state, much as it was at the time of the fighting. A walking trail winds around the site, with interpretive signs. There is a small Visitors Center with some Civil War artifacts on exhibit: as of 2019 there are plans to replace this with a larger museum.

After the Federals had withdrawn to Jacksonville, the Confederates constructed a three-mile series of fortifications and breastworks near Olustee to defend against a possible second attack. It became known as Camp Milton. Over time the Camp was reduced in size until the Federals overran it in June 1864 as they advanced on Tallahassee and Pensacola.

Today, a small portion of the site is maintained as the Camp Milton Historic Preserve. Although the spot has been eroded and overgrown, about 725 feet of the original trenches and rifle pits are still discernable.

Fort Pillow
April 12, 1864
Tennessee

Within two months of the massacre of surrendered African-American soldiers at Olustee, Confederate cavalry under General Nathan Bedford Forrest carried out another slaughter of Black Federal troops.

At the outbreak of the war in 1861, the Confederates built a small stronghold, named Fort Pillow, on the Mississippi River just north of Memphis. Intended to defend traffic on the river, it was abandoned in June 1862 when the Federals captured the nearby islands as part of the Anaconda campaign to place the entire Mississippi under Union control. By 1864 Fort Pillow was a backwater river checkpoint with not much military value, though it had become a haven for escaped slaves and anti-secession Southerners who fled to the north.

On March 16, 1864, the Confederate General Forrest led a force of 7,000 mounted cavalry on a raid into western Tennessee and southern Kentucky, hoping to disrupt the Federal rear areas and interfere with their supply lines. After several weeks of hit-and-run attacks on Union outposts (including an attack on the town of

Paducah KY), Forrest found himself running low on horses, food and ammunition, and decided to strike the Union garrison at Fort Pillow and take the supplies stored there.

The Fort was defended by about 600 men: half of these were local pro-Union recruits, the other half consisted of former African-American slaves in two Federal artillery units. Forrest took about 1500 Confederate cavalry with him on the raid. They reached the Fort at about 10am on April 12.

As the outnumbered Federals retreated into the Fort, Forrest burned the "contraband camp" where the freed slaves had been gathered, then placed snipers along the high ridges next to the stockade fence. The officers were specifically targeted by the sharpshooters, and one of the first victims was the Fort's commander, Major Lionel F. Booth, who was shot in the chest as he rallied his men. The Confederates were so close to the walls that the Union defenders could not lower their cannon barrels enough to bring them to bear, and a Federal gunship on the river, the USS *New Era*, could not fire on the Southerners for fear of hitting the Union defenders as well.

For the next few hours the Confederate snipers kept up a constant fire, until Forrest sent a message to the defenders demanding that they turn over the fort and threatening "no quarter" if they refused. Major William Bradford, now in command, asked for a one hour truce to consult with his officers: Forrest responded that he had 20 minutes. The message came back, "I will not surrender".

Forrest's troops now assaulted three of the Fort's walls simultaneously, while the snipers continued to pour fire inside. With the outer walls breached, the outnumbered Federal defenders retreated to the river, hoping the gunboat would be able to cover them. But sniper fire now pinned down the *New Era's* crew and forced it to withdraw. Forrest's troops swarmed all over Fort Pillow.

And then the massacre happened. The Federal troops in the Tennessee Regiment were locals who had opposed secession: the Confederates thought of them as traitors, and took their revenge. There are accounts of

Union troops attempting to hide along the riverbank, only to be pulled out and shot. A doctor at the field hospital reported seeing a group of surrendered Federals being lined up and executed. One of those shot after being captured was Major Bradford. In all, about 100 of the white Union troops were killed.

Reconstructed section of Fort Pillow

But it was the African-American artillerymen who were the target of the most intense fury. Forrest's cavalrymen had never faced Black opponents before, and the very sight of a former enslaved man with a gun in his hands enraged them. One Confederate trooper later recalled, "The poor, deluded negroes would run up to our men, fall upon their knees, and with uplifted hand scream for mercy, but were ordered to their feet and then shot down." In one of his official reports describing the battle, Forrest noted, "It is hoped that these facts will demonstrate to the Northern people that negro soldiers cannot cope with Southerners." Of the 300 African-American troops inside the fort, only a few got away and 60 were led off to be re-sold into slavery: the rest were killed as they tried to surrender.

Forrest stayed just long enough to gather up the supplies he needed, then abandoned the Fort and withdrew. He had lost only 14 killed and around 80 wounded.

When word of the Fort Pillow Massacre reached President Lincoln, he asked for a Congressional investigation into the matter. Four days after the slaughter, General Ulysses Grant informed the Confederates by messenger that he would no longer agree to any prisoner exchanges with the South unless the African-American soldiers in the Union Army were given the same rights as POWs that any other soldier could expect. The Confederates balked at this—their policy was to treat captured Black troops as "rebellious slaves"—and Grant consequently suspended all prisoner exchanges for the rest of the war.

In the aftermath of the battle, about 250 Union and Confederate dead were buried at the site, but were later re-interred in Memphis. In the 1970s, the area around the ruins of Fort Pillow was declared a National Historic Landmark and a National Historic Site.

Today, Fort Pillow State Historic Park, established in 1971 near Memphis TN, preserves 1600 acres of the battlefield. There is a section of original earthworks and trenches, and a portion of the Fort has been reconstructed. A museum on the site displays Civil War artifacts.

Wilderness
May 5, 1864
Virginia

In March 1864, General Ulysses S Grant was appointed as Commander in Chief of the Union Army and immediately, in accordance with his aggressive spirit, planned a two-pronged grand strategy to beat the Confederates. In the deep south, General William T Sherman would move from Chattanooga towards Atlanta through the very heart of the Confederacy, and destroy the infrastructure and supply lines that kept the rebel armies alive. Meanwhile, General George Meade would lead the troops through Virginia towards Richmond, in a thrust that would become known as the Overland Campaign. Although Grant was in overall command and accompanied the troops, Meade was in operational control of the Army of the Potomac.

Even though the geographic objective of the Overland drive was Richmond, its real military target was General Robert E Lee's Army of Virginia, the largest of the two remaining Confederate forces (the other was General Joseph Johnston's Army of Tennessee which faced Sherman in the deep south). By the spring of 1864, Lee had mostly made up his losses from Gettysburg, and his army was now about the same size as it had been then. But the strategic picture was no longer the same. Grant's army was twice the size of Lee's, and Grant was not the cautious and plodding general that George McClellan, Ambrose Burnside or Joseph Hooker had been. Lee now faced a commander who was equal to him in aggressiveness and ability. His strengthened army, moreover, had come at the cost of reducing Confederate forces elsewhere; Lee no longer had the advantage of being able to seize the strategic offensive and was now reduced to a defensive stance, forced to react to Grant's actions. Grant, therefore, knowing that he had superior numbers as well as the resources to easily replace his losses, decided on a strategy of attrition: he would, he said, "hammer continuously against the armed force of the enemy and his resources" until the South simply could no longer continue to fight. Both Grant and Lee knew that if the Army of Virginia were destroyed, it would be the end of the Confederacy.

Lee, accordingly, now held his troops in a strong defensive position along the Rapidan River in Virginia, near an area of tangled forest that was known as the Wilderness. With its dense undergrowth and poor roads, the Wilderness made artillery useless and infantry movement difficult, and presented a formidable natural defensive barrier. There were only three decent roads that passed through the area, and Lee reinforced all of them, hoping that their narrow approaches would negate Grant's numerical superiority and allow him to fight the Federals on equal terms.

Meade's Union forces began crossing the Rapidan River on May 3, and by the end of the day had established positions on the other side. Lee, though on the strategic defensive, now took the tactical offensive, sending three columns ahead along each of the three roads, hoping to pin down a part of the Federal army in the tangled Wilderness, while simultaneously sending troops under General James Longstreet in a circular move which would put him on Meade's vulnerable flank. If all went well, Longstreet would be able to cut off and attack the immobilized portion of the Union army and destroy it.

It was a move the Federals did not expect, so it came as a complete shock to them when, on the morning of May 5, a detachment of troops from General Gouverneur Warren's corps ran into a force of Confederates under General Richard Ewell at Saunders' Field, alongside the Orange Turnpike. Fierce fighting developed.

The engagement took both sides by surprise: the Federals thought that Lee was still miles away, while the Confederates did not expect to run into Meade until later that night. Lee now ordered Ewell to hold his ground and pin down as many Federals as he could until Longstreet could arrive in position to make his attack. Ewell's troops threw up an improvised breastwork of logs.

Confederate Battery at Tapp Field

But the terrain now made a mess of both sides' plans, and confusion reigned as each opponent tried to rush in reinforcements through the thick forest. Unable to find their direction, regiments became disorganized and broken into small pieces which then wandered around lost in the woods. Men just yards apart were unable to see each other, and knots of troops fired blindly into the trees wherever they thought the enemy might be. Just before nightfall a wildfire was sparked, and the blaze quickly spread through the dense dry undergrowth. Wounded men either burned in the flames or died when the gunpowder in their belts was ignited. Neither side was able to gain any ground.

The next morning, desperate fighting broke out at Tapp Field. At one point, General Lee himself took up a position to lead a group of troops into battle, prompting cries of "Lee to the rear!" as Confederate soldiers blocked his path and then led his horse behind the lines. By later that morning, Longstreet's detachment was finally in place, and after driving the Federals from Tapp Field, the Confederates followed an unfinished railroad path through the woods and charged into the surprised regiments under General Winfield Scott Hancock. During this fighting, Confederate General Longstreet was accidentally shot in the shoulder by one of his own troops, putting him out of action for the next five months. Hancock was able to hold his ground. When another Confederate assault slammed into the other end of the Federal lines, it too was unsuccessful.

By the morning of May 7, after two days of fighting, both armies were in essentially the same positions they had been when the battle started. The Confederates had successfully halted the Federal advance, and they claimed the tactical victory. But it had come at a high cost: although both sides lost around 20% casualties, the numerically-inferior Confederates could not afford it. And now Grant showed that henceforth it would be a different sort of war. Had McClellan or Hooker suffered such losses, they would have retreated; Grant, however, sent a message to Lincoln that he would "fight it out on this line if it takes all summer". Instead of withdrawing, Grant re-gathered his forces and set out to go around the Wilderness and draw Lee out into the open, at the town of Spotsylvania.

The Wilderness battlefield was incorporated into the Fredericksburg and Spotsylvania National Military Park when it was established in 1927 and became part of the National Park system in 1933. There is no Visitors Center, but a "shelter" presents exhibits giving an overview of the fighting. A driving tour takes visitors to Saunders Field, the Chewning Farm, and Tapp Field.

In the 1970s, the local nonprofit Friends of Wilderness Battlefield obtained the Ellwood House, which had served as Burnside's headquarters during the battle and is also the spot where General Stonewall Jackson's amputated arm is buried. The House is still operated by the Friends.

In 2008, Walmart announced plans to construct a store near the Wilderness site, on historically significant land across the street from the Park entrance. After a multi-year fight by the Friends of Wilderness Battlefield and the Civil War Trust, an agreement was reached to halt the project.

Spotsylvania
May 8, 1864
Virginia

After the inconclusive slaughter at the Battle of the Wilderness, any of the previous Union Generals would have retreated to laboriously rebuild the army back to full strength, and most of the Federal soldiers assumed that General Ulysses S Grant would do the same. But when the Union vanguard reached the crossroads, with one road leading towards Richmond and the other leading back to the Rappahannock River and the safety of Maryland, Grant ordered the columns to turn towards the Confederate capitol. A cheer broke out from the ranks.

Grant's objective was Spotsylvania, where several roads came together. Its real value, however, lay in the fact that if he occupied the town, the Union army would be between the Confederate capitol and General Robert E Lee's army, still entrenched in the Wilderness. It would, Grant knew, force Lee to leave his defensive positions and protect the capitol, allowing Grant to attack him once again on more favorable terrain.

When Lee found out that the Federal Army had taken down all of its pontoon bridges across the

Rappahannock and would not be retreating back to Maryland, he quickly grasped Grant's plan, and raced towards Spotsylvania. Since he had a shorter distance to go, he got there first, and his troops frantically dug in a series of breastworks and trenches stretching for almost four miles. When the Federals arrived on May 8, the Confederates were waiting for them.

The Battle of Spotsylvania would be one of the longest field conflicts of the entire war. For the next 12 days, the two armies stood toe to toe and slugged it out.

Memorial overlooks the Mule Shoe at Bloody Angle

For the first several days, much of the fighting was concentrated around Laurel Hill, along the road into town. In just the first day there were three separate attacks and counter-attacks. The Confederates held firm, then extended their line into a dug-in position that became known, from its shape, as "The Mule Shoe". Projecting forward from the Confederate line, the Mule Shoe was a potential weak spot, but Lee assumed that his cannons would be able to defend it from an assault.

On May 10, Meade sent three Federal Corps against this spot, then added a fourth. All of the attacks failed.

On May 11, after a sharp argument with Meade, General Phillip Sheridan was allowed to take a group of 10,000 cavalry to drive the Confederate cavalry, under General Jeb Stuart, out of Spotsylvania. The two forces clashed at the Yellow Tavern. General Stuart was killed in the fighting, and with General James Longstreet out of action from his wound at the Wilderness, Lee's army had now lost two of its best subordinate commanders. It was a severe blow.

The next day, another assault on the Mule Shoe succeeded in driving the Confederates back, but they quickly re-established new battle lines and stood their ground. In one area of the battleground, known as "Bloody Angle", the assaults and counter-assaults lasted for over twenty hours straight. On May 18, Meade launched yet another unsuccessful attack, followed the next day by a Confederate push towards the Harris and Alsop Farms.

By nightfall on May 20, both armies had been bruised, bloodied, and exhausted. Grant had lost 18,000 in killed/wounded, and another 20,000 who left when their period of enlistment ended during the battle. The effective strength of the Army of the Potomac was down to 56,000 men. But Lee's losses were even heavier: the Confederates had lost 13,000 casualties at Spotsylvania, almost one-fourth of their entire army. Grant, by calling for new reinforcements, was able to make up his losses. Lee was not.

On the morning of May 21, Grant pulled his army back and, in a pattern of action that would be repeated again and again until the end of the war, once more maneuvered around the flank of Lee's army to place itself between the Confederates and Richmond. The next round of fighting would happen at Cold Harbor.

Today, the Spotsylvania site is part of the Fredericksburg and Spotsylvania Battlefield National Military Park. There is no Visitors Center here, but an exhibit gives an overview of the battle. A seven-mile walking path gives access to the major parts of the battlefield including the Mule Shoe and Bloody Angle, along with a paved driving tour. The battlefield is very well-preserved, and remnants of both Confederate and Union trenches and rifle pits can be seen scattered around the area.

Snipers
1864
Virginia

When the American Civil War broke out in 1861, military firearms were undergoing a revolution. Previously, most men in uniform were issued smoothbore muzzle-loading muskets, which were loaded by pouring gunpowder down the mouth of the barrel and then ramming a round lead ball on top of it. It took about twenty seconds to load and fire a single shot, and the smoothbores were notoriously inaccurate beyond 75-100 yards.

But by the time of the First Battle of Manassas, both the Federals and the Confederates were equipped with rifled muskets. These had grooved rifling inside the barrel, and fired conical lead projectiles known as Minié bullets, which were more often referred to as "Minnie balls". This particular invention was made in Europe, and it made the American Civil War more deadly than any war before it. The problem with the smoothbore was that the bullet had to be smaller than the barrel in order to be rammed in, and this allowed the projectile to rattle around in the barrel and let gases escape around it. Then a Frenchman named Minié designed something new: a conical bullet with a hollow base. When fired, the gunpowder gases pushed the hollow part open and forced the sides of the bullet into a series of rifling grooves that ran down the barrel. This had two lethal effects: it prevented any gases from escaping around the bullet, thereby increasing the power and range, and it imparted a spin to the bullet as it left the gun, thereby increasing the accuracy. But these rifled muskets still took a long time to load, and were still most effective when fired in mass volleys by long ranks of troops.

As the exhausted troops from both sides limped away from the Manassas battlefield, they realized that this war would be neither short nor easy. It was then that Hiram Berdan, a New York inventor and champion amateur marksman, made a proposal to the US War Department that he be allowed to raise and train a special unit of sharpshooters, equipped with the very best in firearms technology, to serve as scouts, skirmishers, and snipers. He was allowed to pick the best shots in the entire Union Army, selecting volunteers from as far away as Wisconsin and establishing a training camp in New Jersey. (President Lincoln, himself a skilled marksman, visited the camp and talked with the recruits.) The requirements were stringent: any volunteer recruit had to put ten consecutive shots on a ten-inch target at two hundred yards to qualify. Two regiments were formed, christened the 1st and 2nd United States Sharpshooters. They wore distinctive green uniforms. Unlike other Army units, who fought shoulder-to-shoulder in long lines, the Sharpshooters were trained to conceal themselves in trees, behind logs, in grass, or between rocks, in places that gave them a long-distance overview of the Confederate lines. Their particular targets were enemy officers and artillerymen, but anyone on the Rebel line who poked his head into view was at risk.

At first, the Army supplied the units with new five-shot Colt rifles, which used a revolving chamber similar to that of a pistol. But many of the marksmen weren't satisfied with the Colt's accuracy and preferred to use their own private weapons, particularly the .50-caliber Pennsylvania Long Rifle, which could hit a squirrel at 300 yards. After a time, the War Department began issuing standard Springfield rifled muskets, but these were useless to the snipers; they wanted the newest Sharps rifles instead. The Sharps was a breechloader: to fire the rifle, a lever in the trigger guard was used to lower a metal breech block, and a paper cartridge containing powder and a conical .52-caliber bullet was inserted into the firing chamber. Closing the lever lifted the breech block into place, which sliced the back of the paper cartridge open. A percussion cap was placed on a nipple behind the barrel; when the gun's hammer struck the cap, it ignited a flame which went inside and set off the gunpowder charge, firing the bullet. With its long barrel and rifling, the Sharps was accurate out to over 600 yards. Most Sharps rifles were issued with open iron sights, with the rear sight adjustable for range. But a few were fitted with 14-inch long telescopic sights, fitted onto the left side of the stock to avoid interfering with the breech block. In the hands of a good shot, the Sharps was a lethal weapon.

The War Department, however, decided that not only were the breechloaders too expensive, but their high rate of fire would only encourage the sharpshooters to waste ammunition. They denied the request, prompting Berdan to go over their heads directly to President Lincoln himself. After watching a demonstration by Berdan of the Sharps' range and accuracy, Lincoln personally ordered that the units be equipped with the rifles.

The Confederates, meanwhile, were training sharpshooters of their own. The South did not have the manufacturing capacity that the North did, and throughout the war the Confederates found it difficult to keep their troops equipped. As a result, many Rebel sharpshooters were using their own private hunting or sporting guns. Some of these extra-long rifles weighed as much as thirty pounds and had to be supported by a specially-made forked gunrest (or a substitute such as a rock or tree branch.) The Confederates were also able to produce their own copies of the Sharps rifle in factories in Virginia (known as "Richmond Sharps"), which went to a number of sniping units.

But the weapon that was most favored by the Confederates, and the best sniper rifle of the war, was the British-made Whitworth. Designed in 1850, the Whitworth was a unique solution to a problem that plagued all rifled guns of the time: as the bullet went down the barrel, the rifling grooves cut into the lead, imparting its spin but also measurably slowing the bullet down and reducing its range. Whitworth therefore designed his rifle with a barrel that was hexagonal in cross section—then designed his own special .45-caliber bullet that was also hexagonal and nestled snugly inside the barrel. This ingenious arrangement allowed him to add tighter rifling of one full turn every twenty inches, giving the bullet a greater spin than other barrels of the same length, and at greater speed. The Whitworth rifle was unmatched by any other gun in the world for accuracy and range. With iron sights it was accurate to at least 800 yards; with telescopic sights it was deadly at ranges of almost a mile.

But the Whitworth also had a serious disadvantage—it was a muzzle-loader, and each shot had to be laboriously rammed down the barrel. The British Army decided not to adopt it, and this allowed the Whitworth Company to sell a number of the rifles to the Confederates, smuggling them in past the Union Navy's blockade. The rifles were so valuable that they were only given to the very best of the Southern marksmen.

On both sides, the sharpshooters were elite units; they were excused from all the camp work that the line troops had to do, and spent their off-duty time target practicing. And in combat they quickly became the most hated men on the Civil War battlefield. The favored targets for the snipers were the artillery crews. Many times, an entire gun battery would be silenced because nobody could stand up to load a cannon without immediately attracting a lead bullet to the head. Officers on horseback were vulnerable even in rear areas. In set-piece sieges such as Petersburg, even the ordinary frontline troops were targets for enemy snipers, and both sides took to digging protective trenches for themselves. At the Battle of Fort Stevens near Washington DC, President Lincoln had arrived in person to inspect the fortifications, and came under fire from Confederate snipers. He quickly retreated back to the White House.

The sharpshooters were also the most effective method of dealing with enemy sharpshooters. There were many accounts of snipers on both sides who sat patiently in their concealed spots, often for hours, waiting for the telltale puff of smoke that would reveal an opposing marksman and make him a target.

Some snipers became celebrated for their exploits. On the Union side was "California Joe" Head. According to the legend, Private Head had gone to California during the 1848 Gold Rush and struck it rich, then returned to New York, lied about his age to enlist in the 1st Sharpshooters (he was 52), and carried a Sharps rifle that he had bought himself. In one instance, during the fighting outside Yorktown, Head and a handful of other sharpshooters pinned down an entire company of Confederate cannoneers: by nightfall only 12 of the artillerymen remained un-wounded.

On the Confederate side, there was "Old Jack" Hinson, a 57-year old farmer in Tennessee. He had opposed secession and had avoided involvement in the war until, after the capture of Fort Donelson and the surrender of Nashville, Union soldiers found two of his sons in the woods with hunting rifles and, suspecting them of being guerrillas, executed them both, beheaded them, and stuck the decapitated heads above the gateway to Hinson's farm as a warning to others. From that day on, Hinson waged a one-man war against the Yankees. His favorite tactic was to build a blind on the banks of the Cumberland or Tennessee River, like a duck hunter, and wait for a steamboat to pass by carrying troops or supplies. Any time a Union army or navy officer in uniform would appear on deck, Hinson would pick him off with one shot from his custom-made .50-caliber Pennsylvania Long Rifle, then disappear from the pursuing troops. He is estimated to have killed or wounded somewhere between 80 and 100 Federals.

The most famous sniper shot of the Civil War, however, took place in May 1864, at Spotsylvania Court House. Union Major-General John Sedgwick was watching his troops move some cannon into place on Laurel Hill for the impending battle. A number of Confederate sharpshooters were also watching, at distances up to 1,000 yards, and soon the distinctive whistle of the hexagonal bullets from Whitworth rifles was heard. With each shot, all the Federal cannoneers dropped to the ground, prompting Sedgwick to chastise them, declaring, "I am ashamed of you. They couldn't hit an elephant at this distance." A moment later, a bullet struck the General in the face below the left eye, and he crumpled to the ground. He was the highest-ranking Union officer to be killed in action during the war.

Sedgwick memorial at Spotsylvania

Today, the Virginia Museum of History and Culture in Richmond and the Tennessee State Museum in Nashville both have Whitworth rifles with scope on exhibit, and interpretive displays explaining the role of the Civil War sniper. At the Fredericksburg and Spotsylvania Battlefield National Military Park, a stone memorial marks the spot where General Sedgwick was killed.

Resaca
May 13, 1864
Georgia

While Grant and Meade were hammering Lee's army in Virginia, General William T Sherman had launched his campaign from Chattanooga towards Atlanta. Sherman's March would become one of the most famous (or notorious) campaigns of the Civil War. It had two aims: to destroy the Confederate economic infrastructure, and to cripple General Joseph Johnston's Army of Tennessee. Sherman declared that he would "make Georgia howl".

Sherman had almost 100,000 men, far outnumbering Johnston's 60,000. But Johnston had the advantage of terrain, which he used skillfully. In the hilly Georgia landscape, it was difficult for Sherman to concentrate his forces, while Johnston was able to gather his men on high ground where it would be costly and dangerous for Sherman to assault him. Sherman, in turn, would attempt to go around Johnston's entrenched position, leading the Confederates to deftly retreat to a new hill and start the process again. Johnston's tactics of avoiding combat were dubbed "Fabian" by the Southern press, after the famous campaign waged against Hannibal by the Roman General Fabius, "The Delayer", who, like Johnston, hoped he could wear down a superior opponent through constant retreat, impeding the enemy by tiring his troops and using up his supplies. It was a strategy of giving up "ground" in exchange for "time".

By May 7, Sherman had gotten only as far as the town of Dalton, in northern Georgia. Confederate troops set up a defensive line at nearby Resaca to once again block the Federal progress.

By now, Sherman was desperate to draw Johnston's army into a pitched battle so it could be destroyed. But the Confederate position at Resaca was a strong one, so Sherman planned an action to draw the troops out into a more open area: he would hold the railroad and telegraph centers at Dalton, and send two detachments to try to surround the Confederates.

The site of General William Carlin's unsuccessful attack

The battle began on May 13 when two cavalry scout units clashed. When the Confederate cavalry withdrew, Sherman launched an attack at Camp Creek, but was beaten back by an artillery battery. For the next two days, the Federals launched a series of assaults on the Confederate lines, but were not able to break through. Things were at a stalemate.

On May 15, realizing that he could not break through the Confederate lines, Sherman once again went around them. Using pontoon bridges, he sent a force over the Oostanaula River at Lay's Ferry and advanced towards the railroad tracks that were keeping Johnston's troops supplied. The Confederates once again withdrew and retreated to a new position, where they once again blocked Sherman's advance.

Johnston's "Fabian" tactics were working. The fighting around Resaca had cost the Federals around 3,500 casualties and the Confederates 2,600, and it would take Sherman almost two full months to cross Georgia and approach Atlanta. In the meantime, Grant began to worry that Sherman's seeming inability to bring Johnston's army to bay would not only allow the Confederates to move more of their troops to Virginia, but might bring the entire Union thrust through Georgia to a grinding halt.

After the war, a Confederate cemetery was placed at the Resaca battle site, containing the graves of almost 500 Southerners who were killed in the Atlanta Campaign.

Over the decades, the suburbs of Atlanta grew to cover most of the place. Much of the remaining battleground was then destroyed when Interstate Highway I-75 was built through it. As a result, in 2001, the state of Georgia announced plans to obtain a 500-acre tract of the battlefield and convert it into a State Historic Site. A local nonprofit group, the Friends of Resaca Battlefield, was formed to help raise money. In 2002, several pieces of land were purchased, but state budget cuts meant that work did not begin on the park until 2008, which was then turned over to the local county government. The Resaca Battlefield Historic Site officially opened in May 2016. It consists of four pieces of the battleground totaling about 1100 acres.

There are two walking trails, about five miles total, with interpretive signs, covering a part of the battlefield and running along the Federal and Confederate positions. In some places, the faint traces of rifle pits and breastwork trenches can still be seen.

Cold Harbor
May 31, 1864
Virginia

The Confederates had taken a considerable pounding during the fighting at the Wilderness and Spotsylvania, and were now, General Grant thought, on the verge of collapse. "Lee's army," he confidently told President Lincoln, "is really whipped." The battle at Cold Harbor would prove him wrong.

After Spotsylvania, Grant's army resumed its move towards Richmond, and once again Lee was forced into a defensive position to block the Union advance. This time, the battle began when a Federal cavalry unit under General Phillip Sheridan captured the little town of Cold Harbor, named after a traveler's tavern.

Both sides, exhausted from the previous fights, now called for reinforcements. Lee received 7,000 veteran troops from General Pierre Beauregard in Richmond; Grant's reinforcements were mostly inexperienced new recruits taken away from garrison duty. But the 100,000 Federals greatly outnumbered the 59,000 Confederates. The battle lines stretched for over seven miles, and Lee struggled to prevent the Union troops from extending their lines beyond his and outflanking him. At one point a message arrived from Richmond asking Lee how many regiments he had in reserve. Lee answered emphatically, "Not a regiment, and that has been my condition ever since the fighting commenced on the Rappahannock. If I shorten my lines to provide a reserve, he will turn me; if I weaken my lines to provide a reserve, he will break them." The Confederacy was down to its last manpower.

After a few days of back and forth fighting, while reinforcements were still arriving, Grant made what was, in retrospect, a series of bad decisions. First, rather than the flanking maneuvers he had been using up to now in the campaign, he decided to make an all-out frontal assault on the Confederates, along the whole line. This would, he thought, break the back of what he presumed to be Lee's demoralized and crippled army, allowing him to surround it and bring the war to an end.

Then, when a corps of troops under General Winfield Hancock arrived at the battlefield in the middle of the night after a long forced march, Grant made another bad decision and delayed the planned attack for 24 hours to give these troops a chance to rest. It allowed the Confederates another full day to dig in their defenses. To the Federal troops who had been ordered to attack the next morning, it was already apparent what the result would be: they could see their opponent excavating trenches and putting up breastworks. Many of them fatalistically pinned pieces of paper with their name and hometown into the insides of their shirts so their bodies could be identified.

The frontline soldiers had recognized, as the generals had not, that the entire face of war had changed. At the beginning of the Civil War, both sides were still practicing the field tactics that had been used by Napoleon in 1812—massed ranks of troops formed lines in the open, shoulder to shoulder, and blasted at each other until one side broke and ran. But the development of the rifled musket and the exploding artillery shell had made this suicidal, and the troops quickly learned that safety lay in cover—they protected themselves with low earthen and log breastworks, and as the war went on these turned into deep trenches and rifle pits. But although the troops understood the enormous advantage that these fortifications gave to the defenders, the generals on both sides had not caught up, and continued to order units to make frontal assaults on these positions. It was a recipe for disaster.

So when Grant launched his attack at Cold Harbor on June 1, it was a debacle. From their well-protected rifle pits and trenches, the Confederates poured volley after volley into the Union ranks. The Federals lost over 7000 casualties in the first hour. When Grant issued orders for another assault later that afternoon, several of his subordinate generals simply refused to carry them out, calling it a "wanton waste of life". After the war, Grant himself would write, "I have always regretted that the last assault at Cold Harbor was ever made... no advantage whatever was gained to compensate for the heavy loss we sustained."

Remains of trenches at Cold Harbor

Two more days of inconclusive fighting followed. When Grant sent a messenger to Lee asking for a temporary truce so that both sides could go retrieve their wounded, Lee replied defiantly that he didn't *have* any wounded: it was another two days before Grant sent another message asking for a truce to recover *his* wounded, thereby tacitly acknowledging that he had lost the battle. The Federals had suffered 13,000 casualties at Cold Harbor; the Confederates 2,500. It was one of the most lopsided battles of the war.

On June 12, Grant disengaged and once again turned Lee's flank to force him into another fight, this time crossing the James River and moving towards the railroad center at Petersburg. Richmond was now less than ten miles away.

But now there was rumbling in Washington. In his move from the Wilderness to Cold Harbor, Grant had lost some 55,000 casualties—an amount almost as much as the size of Lee's entire army at the beginning of the campaign. Politicians began referring to him as "The Butcher" and there were calls for him to be fired and replaced. These were all resisted by President Lincoln, who seemed to be alone in understanding that Grant's actions, while costly, were steadily wearing down the Confederates in an attrition which they could not sustain. "I begin to see it," he wrote to Grant. "You will succeed. God bless you all."

In the aftermath of the battle, the retreating Union Army left most of its dead where they had fallen, and bones remained strewn across the ground for months before burial details could gather them and place them in mass graves. After the war, some 2,000 Union troops, most of them unidentified, were buried at the Cold Harbor National Cemetery.

Today, however, most of the Cold Harbor battlefield has been lost. Of the seven-mile long battleground, about 300 acres is preserved as part of the Richmond National Battlefield Park. A walking trail takes visitors around the battle site, including the Garthwright House, which was used as a field hospital. There is also a small county park next to the battle site which holds another 50 acres. The Civil War Trust lists Cold Harbor as one of the "ten most endangered Civil War battlefields".

Petersburg
June 15, 1864
Virginia

The heavy loss at Cold Harbor had tarnished Grant's reputation, reduced Union morale, and given a much-needed boost of hope to the Confederates, but in the end its military effect was minimal. The Federals, with their far larger army and virtually unlimited ability to supply and reinforce them, simply pulled away from Lee's army and continued to march towards Richmond. Grant's immediate target was Petersburg, an important railroad hub less than a day's march from the Confederate capitol. Lee, knowing that if Petersburg were captured then Richmond could not be defended, desperately raced to reach the town before Grant did.

He didn't make it. On June 15, Union General General William F. Smith reached Petersburg with 10,000 troops. Confederate General Pierre Beauregard, who had sent most of his troops to reinforce Lee at Cold Harbor, now had only a few thousand armed men, mostly convalescents and garrison troops, to defend the town. But the Confederates had surrounded Petersburg with an extensive belt of trenches, rifle pits, and fortifications, and when Smith attacked, he was unable to break through. Both sides now rushed troops to Petersburg, with the Union continuing to launch attacks against the Confederates and the entrenched defenders always managing to hold out. Grant's forces reached 120,000, and Lee's arrival gave the Confederates a total of 52,000. Within days, both sides had dug in, and the city was surrounded by ten miles of extensive trenches, breastworks, cannon redoubts, and rifle pits, several layers deep. It was eerily prescient of the trench warfare that would characterize the First World War some fifty years later.

Reconstructed siege works at Petersburg

The fighting here, Lee knew, would be decisive. While Grant had succeeded in continuously driving the Confederates back towards Richmond, Lee understood that the real point of the entire Federal campaign was to destroy his Army of Virginia, and although Grant had inflicted crippling losses on him, Lee's army was still intact—and with it the hopes of the Confederacy. But now, trapped with his back to Richmond, Lee could retreat no further. This would be his last stand.

On June 18, General George Meade sent an attack by two Union Army corps against a section of Confederate trenches. The Federals broke their way through the first line of defenses, but did not know that Lee's troops had already constructed a new series of defensive positions further back, and Meade's men were halted when they ran into these new Confederate lines. That afternoon another attack followed at Rives's Salient, and then a third assault that evening, in which the 1st Maine Artillery Regiment lost 632 of its 900 men. In four days of futile assaults, the Federals had lost over 11,000 men. Although the Confederates were heavily outnumbered, their multiple layers of defensive fortifications were too strong to take by storm.

Reluctantly, as he had at Vicksburg, Grant decided that the only way to take Petersburg would be by siege. As his troops began surrounding the Confederates with their own extensive belt of trenches and gun positions, Grant sent out a series of cavalry raids to both secure his own railroad supply lines and to cut off those of the enemy. In almost two weeks of skirmishing, however, the Federal cavalrymen were driven back and were unable to cut off the railroads. Nevertheless, the Confederates' only source of supplies was from Wilmington NC and they were continuously short of food and ammunition.

For the next four weeks, Grant moved artillery into place, and began shelling the Confederates every day. Using his own railroads, he brought in a number of massive siege mortars mounted on flatcars, one of which became famously named "Dictator". With these huge guns, the Federals were able to reach the outskirts of Richmond itself. At one point President Lincoln traveled to Petersburg to meet with Grant and discuss the situation. It was apparent that Lee's army, though still not defeated, was trapped inside its trenches, and the end of the war was now in sight.

Near the end of July, Grant decided once again to strike at the Confederate railroad lines. He sent cavalry under General Philip Sheridan to cross the Appomattox River, circle around behind Richmond and destroy the tracks—and carry out a raid on the city itself if possible. It was hoped that this action would not only cut off

Confederate supplies and weaken Southern morale, but also force Lee to pull troops out of his trenches to defend the railroad depots. But Sheridan's cavalry was stopped by a Confederate force at Bailey's Creek.

Things had reached a stalemate.

Today, portions of the original siege lines are preserved in the Petersburg National Battlefield. Established in 1926 as a National Military Park, it was transferred to the National Park Service in 1933 and designated a National Battlefield Park in 1962.

The Visitors Center is located at the site of Battery 5, the scene of heavy fighting. It contains walking paths and a driving tour as well as exhibits about the siege.

Other portions of the siege lines are preserved in the nearby Richmond National Battlefield Park.

CSS *Alabama*
June 19, 1864
England

Although the American Civil War is not often thought of as a naval conflict, the Confederates did have a Navy which operated across the globe. Many of these were "commerce raiders" who attacked Federal merchant shipping, and the most successful of these raiders was the CSS *Alabama*.

As the Union fleet began blockading Southern ports in 1861, the Confederates realized that they could never match the naval strength of the industrialized North, and that if they wanted to wage a war at sea, it would have to consist of scattered raiders and marauders. It was hoped that these sea-going guerrillas would inflict enough damage on Federal overseas trade to force the US Navy to divert resources from its blockades into a long and grinding hunt on the open seas.

The Richmond government placed James Bulloch, a cotton trader, in charge of producing a fleet of Confederate commerce raiders. Since the South had only a limited capacity for ship-building, Bulloch was forced to look overseas. The ideal choice would be Britain, with its long-established maritime tradition, but

England was officially neutral in the war, and British law banned any company from building military ships for the Confederate government.

And so, to get around these laws, Bulloch recruited the English firm of Fraser, Trenholm & Company, a shipping line which had carried much of Bulloch's pre-war cotton trade. Now, he used his connections to convince the company to act as his go-between: they would order a series of ships to be built in Britain which would be secretly paid for by Bulloch, and once the ships were launched they would be turned over to the Confederates and armed for war.

In early 1862, Fraser, Trenholm and Co, acting on Bulloch's behalf, placed an order with the John Laird Sons and Company shipbuilding firm for a steam-bark, a sleek fast ship that carried a full set of sails as well as a two-cylinder steam engine and a retractable screw propeller. She was named the *Enrica*, and although she carried no obvious military equipment, she was carefully built with an extra-thick upper deck and heavy-walled reinforced compartments below decks. The *Enrica* was launched on May 15.

The Federal intelligence services, meanwhile, had learned about the new Confederate ship, and lodged a protest asking the British Government to confiscate the vessel and halt its delivery. Partly because of bureaucratic blunders and partly because of reluctance to get involved in the war, London dragged its feet, leading to diplomatic tensions with Washington. Some hotheads in Congress called for another war with England. The US Navy dispatched one of its ships, the USS *Tuscarora*, to wait outside the harbor and intercept the ship as she sailed out, but when the *Enrica* left her dock on July 29, the *Tuscarora* failed to find her.

The *Enrica* sailed for the island of Terceira in the Azores, in international waters where England no longer held any jurisdiction. Here she was met by her new captain, Raphael Semmes, who oversaw her conversion into a warship. The reinforced upper deck was fitted with six 36-pounder cannons along the sides, plus a 7-inch rifled gun and 8-inch smoothbore cannon mounted on center pivots to allow them to fire to either side. The bunkers below decks were filled with ammunition. On August 24, 1862, the *Enrica* was officially redesignated the CSS *Alabama* and commissioned into the Confederate Navy.

Semmes's first task was to recruit a crew, since at this point he had only about half as many sailors as he needed. By offering a pay rate twice as high as other ships (to be paid in gold) and a share in any captured prizes, he managed to entice some of Liverpool's sailors to join him. When the *Alabama* left the Azores, over half of her crew consisted of British seamen.

For the next two months, the *Alabama* prowled the area around the Azores, looking for the Northern whaling ships which regularly hunted in that area. Her first capture came on September 5—the whaler *Ocumlgee*. By the end of the month she had boarded nine more Union merchant ships, burned them, and set their crew ashore.

After crossing the Atlantic, Semmes sailed up and down the East Coast, from Virginia down to Bermuda, capturing a total of 13 commercial ships. Ten of these were burned, and the rest were loaded with prisoners and set free.

To avoid the Federal blockade, the *Alabama* never entered any Confederate ports, but depended on small fast resupply ships to keep her stocked with food and ammunition. There was also a coaling ship, the CSS *Agrippina*, specifically dedicated to supporting the *Alabama*, meeting up with her at neutral ports to periodically refuel the ship.

In January 1863, after one of these rendezvous in Martinique, the *Alabama* briefly stopped in Mexico for some repairs and maintenance, then set its course for Galveston TX, where a Federal fleet had gathered in support of a landing operation. Here the *Alabama* had its first encounter with a Union Navy ship—in a short firefight she sank the sidewheeler USS *Hatteras*.

The next six months marked the pinnacle of the *Alabama's* career. Operating off the coast of Brazil, Semmes boarded and captured a total of 29 Union ships, burning most of them, releasing a few with his accumulated prisoners, and keeping one, the bark USS *Conrad*, rechristening her CSS *Tuscaloosa*. By this time the *Alabama* had become one of the most successful and famous of the Confederate commerce raiders, and the US Navy began an all-out effort to find and destroy her.

Re-crossing the Atlantic, the *Alabama* and *Tuscaloosa* arrived at Cape Town, South Africa, in August 1863. Here Semmes became something of a local legend, and a popular song was written about his ship, in Afrikaans, titled "*Daar Kom Die Alibama*".

After making a few captures, US Navy ships began to arrive looking for him, and Semmes sailed all the way to Singapore in January 1864. Here his ship underwent an overhaul, but the two years of nearly constant cruising had fouled her hull and worn out her engines, and the *Alabama* now needed a full refit. She left Singapore and headed to Europe. On the way, Semmes overtook and captured a merchant ship in the Java Sea. The HMS *Martaban* had a British captain and registry, but the ship's papers showed that she had only been purchased just two weeks before, and was previously an American ship named the USS *Texas Star*. Semmes suspected that the papers were a forgery and that the Americans were using a false British identity to protect themselves, so he burned the ship. He then crossed the Indian Ocean to South Africa before setting course for Europe.

He hoped to travel to England for a drydock and a refit of his engines, but the British, already under pressure from the Americans to refuse entry to Confederate ships, were now also angered by the *Martaban* incident. Semmes was forced to go to France instead, and docked the *Alabama* in Cherbourg.

But the only drydocks in Cherbourg belonged to the French Navy, and France had also declared its neutrality. As Semmes waited in port for a decision, US diplomats sent word back to Washington DC that the *Alabama* was here. On June 14, 1863, the US Navy ship *Kearsarge*, under Captain John Winslow, arrived and took up a position just outside the harbor.

Semmes was now trapped. Realizing that the longer he waited the more US ships would arrive, he decided that his best option was to fight the *Kearsarge* one on one. So, in an act of bravado, he sent a message to Winslow reading, "My intention is to fight the *Kearsarge* as soon as I can make the necessary arrangements. I hope these will not detain me more than until to-morrow or the morrow morning at farthest. I beg she will not depart until I am ready to go out." It was to be a duel on the high seas.

On June 19, the *Alabama* sailed out of Cherbourg to meet the *Kearsarge*. She was shadowed by the French ironclad *Couronne*, who was there to insure that neither ship entered France's territorial waters. Also nearby was an English private yacht called the *Deerhound*.

It was a lopsided battle. The *Alabama's* shells had deteriorated from her long time at sea, and several of her hits failed to explode. The *Kearsarge* had also been armored by lengths of iron chain bolted to the outside of the hull. Within an hour, the *Alabama* was sinking. Most of the crew was captured. Captain Semmes and other officers managed to escape in a longboat, were picked up by the *Deerhound,* and taken to England and released. Making his way back to America, he became the Confederate naval commander in Virginia.

CSS Alabama, *a contemporary illustration*

Although other Confederate commerce raiders, including the CSS *Florida* and CSS *Shenandoah*, continued to operate for the rest of the war, their military achievement was minor. The Union Navy did not divert any significant effort away from its blockade, and eventually it was able to strangle all of the Southern ports into submission. Despite the impressive feats of the *Alabama* (she had burned or captured a total of 65 Union ships), the raiders ultimately had little effect.

In 1984, a French Navy minesweeper detected a shipwreck near the mouth of Cherbourg harbor, which was identified by divers as the CSS *Alabama*. A joint French-American effort was organized to explore the wreck, and a nonprofit group was founded to run the effort. Since 2002, a number of artifacts have been archaeologically excavated and raised from the site.

Today, several of these relics from the CSS *Alabama*, including one of her 32-pounder cannons, are on display at the History Museum in Mobile AL. In addition, flags that were flown on the *Alabama* are on display at museums in Newport News VA, Nashville TN, Pensacola FL, and Cape Town, South Africa.

Kennesaw Mountain
June 27, 1864
Georgia

After the inconclusive fighting at Resaca, Union General William T Sherman and Confederate General Joseph Johnston continued their "two-step", with Johnston moving to block the Federal Army's path in a way that avoided a pitched battle, and Sherman attempting to go around him and find a way to attack. "As fast as we gain one position," Sherman complained to Grant, "the enemy has another all ready." After six weeks of this, Sherman was still 20 miles away from Atlanta.

Johnston had now formed a strong defensive line on Kennesaw Mountain, and was once again blocking the Union advance. On June 21, after eleven days of rain, Sherman made preparations for a maneuver around the left end of the Confederate lines which would force Johnston into a retreat off the mountain. But Johnston detected the signs of the impending move and placed a corps of troops under General John Bell Hood to extend his left flank.

Hood's orders had been to simply block any attempt by the Federals to advance and turn Johnston's flank. But Hood was an impetuous and aggressive commander with a reputation for undue haste, and on June 22, acting on his own without orders from Johnston, he launched an assault at the Federal lines around Kolb's Farm held by troops under Generals Joseph Hooker and John Schofield. It was a disaster. The Confederates marched across an open field straight into at least 40 Federal guns, which cut them to pieces. But although Hood's impulsive attack had cost the Southerners over 1,000 casualties, it had succeeded in disrupting Sherman's attempt to outflank Johnston. Both sides now held their ground.

But now Sherman thought he saw an opportunity. By moving Hood's troops, he concluded, Johnston had overextended his lines—now stretched out in an arc over seven miles long—which he did not have enough men to defend. By launching feints at both ends of the Confederate lines, Sherman reasoned, he could force Johnston to move some of his troops to reinforce them, thereby weakening his own center and making it vulnerable. And so, despite the dangers of assaulting uphill against an entrenched enemy, Sherman decided on a full-out attack. After weeks of fruitless maneuvering, it would, he concluded, allow the Federals to finally force the Confederates into an open fight, and, after their defeat, lay open the way to Atlanta.

The carefully-planned attack began on the morning of June 27. General Schofield's troops were sent to take Pigeon Hill on the Confederate left flank, while General James McPherson was sent towards Cheatham Hill on the Confederate right. General George Thomas would then follow up with a crushing assault on Johnston's center.

But Sherman had miscalculated. Johnston's men had constructed an extensive series of fortifications which made up for their weakness in numbers. The Union troops, in turn, made the mistake of attacking across open fields with little cover. The Confederates stopped the Federal advances and inflicted some 3,000 casualties. At Cheatham Hill, one regiment from Illinois became trapped in front of the Confederate lines, in a position that became known as the "Dead Angle". As the rest of the Federals retreated, the Illinois regiment was pinned down by rifle and cannon fire. For the next five days, they were unable to either retreat or advance.

Federal positions

Finally a truce was called to allow both sides to collect their wounded. Sherman was making plans to renew the assault, but General Thomas convinced him that it would be a futile waste of life. The battle came to an end.

The Confederates had won a tactical victory and had inflicted 3500 casualties while losing only 500 of their own. But Sherman, with his much larger army, still held the strategic offensive, and on July 8 he was able to send a corps of troops across the Chattahoochee River, the last geographic barrier between the Union Army and Atlanta. The Confederates were forced to withdraw from Kennesaw Mountain and Johnston established a new defensive line at Smyrna.

But the most important effect of the fighting was political. The Confederate General Johnston, despite being heavily outnumbered and chronically short of supplies and replacements, had done a masterful tactical job of giving ground to Sherman's Federals while at the same time delaying and blocking their advance as much as possible, and he had won a morale-boosting victory at Kennesaw Mountain. But now Confederate President Jefferson Davis decided that Johnston's delaying tactics were not working. Declaring, "You have failed to arrest the advance of the enemy to the vicinity of Atlanta," Davis fired Johnston and placed General Hood in command of the Confederate forces in Atlanta. Sherman, meanwhile, was planning his assault on the city.

In 1899, a native of Illinois named Lansing J. Dawdy, who had participated in the fighting at the Dead Angle, purchased 60 acres of the Kennesaw Mountain battlefield, centered on the site, as a memorial to his fallen friends. Five years later he donated the land to the Kennesaw Mountain Battlefield Association, a local citizens group which was lobbying Congress to preserve the battleground, and in 1914 the Association put up a stone memorial to the Illinois troops.

In 1916, the land was donated to the Federal government as part of a planned Kennesaw Mountain National Battlefield Park, but various difficulties meant that the park was not established until 1935.

Today, the protected area has grown to around 3,000 acres, and it is the largest green area inside the city. The Visitors Center has a small museum display, and walking trails give access to Kennesaw Mountain and Pigeon Hill. Cheatham Hill, some two miles away, is accessible by county roads that run through the park.

However, some areas of the park are being limited by the encroachment of suburban Atlanta, and some historically significant areas still lie outside the park boundaries. The Civil War Trust has placed Kennesaw Mountain on its list of "Ten Most Endangered Battlefields".

Monocacy
July 9, 1864
Maryland

The heavy fighting in Virginia had forced General Ulysses S Grant to pull more and more troops from around Washington DC to reinforce his positions there, and in the summer of 1864 General Robert E Lee decided to make use of that. He sent 15,000 troops under General Jubal Early to cross into Maryland and threaten Washington DC. This would, Lee hoped, force Grant to withdraw some of the Union troops from Petersburg in order to defend the capitol. Early's troops reached their staging area at Harper's Ferry on July 4 and entered Maryland.

The Union commander in the area was General Lew Wallace, based in Baltimore. From his fragmentary information, Wallace was unsure how many troops Early had and whether he intended to move towards Washington DC or Baltimore. Wallace himself had only 3200 local troops and could not afford to divide his forces, so he chose a defensive position that would cover both the routes to Washington and Baltimore—at the little railroad and roadway hub of Monocacy. Grant, meanwhile, sent a force of 3400 troops to reinforce him there.

As Early moved from Frederick MD towards Monocacy, Wallace knew he was outnumbered over two to one, but hoped he could delay the Confederate advance long enough for more Federal troops to arrive in DC from Grant's army at Petersburg. Early's troops reached Monocacy on the morning of July 9. A small force was sent to attempt (unsuccessfully) to raid a Union POW camp nearby and free the several thousand Confederate prisoners there. The rest of the Confederate forces formed their initial line near where the Visitors Center sits today.

Monuments overlooking the Best Farmhouse

The Federals were formed into a defensive position where two railroad lines met and two bridges crossed the Monocacy River. Early's first move was to capture the Best farmhouse, which stood between the two armies. Concluding that a direct attack across the bridges would be too risky, Early sent a detachment of artillery to the Best farm to shell the Federals, then moved some of his troops down the Monocacy River to find a ford to cross. In response, Wallace burned the river bridges and turned his troops to meet the Confederates. For the rest of the day, heavy fighting raged around the Thomas and Worthington farmhouses. The Union forces stood firm, but by the time darkness fell, they had enough. Wallace's troops withdrew and retreated back towards Baltimore. Early's Confederates camped on the battlefield, and continued their advance towards Washington DC the next morning.

But Wallace's outnumbered force had accomplished its purpose: it had delayed the Confederates for 24 hours. By the time Early's troops reached Fort Stevens on the edge of Washington DC, Grant had been able to move two entire divisions from Petersburg into place, and now it was Early who was outnumbered. After a brief probing clash at Fort Stevens (with President Abraham Lincoln watching the fight from a nearby hill and at one point coming under sniper fire), Early withdrew his troops and marched all the way back to Virginia. Although Wallace's soldiers had lost the tactical battle at Monocacy, they had fulfilled the larger strategic purpose of defending Washington DC, and in the North it became known as "the battle that saved the capitol". General Early summed up the result in his message to Lee: "We haven't taken Washington, but we scared Abe Lincoln like hell."

As Early's forces retreated, Grant was already moving his own troops back to Petersburg, where they would soon score a significant win over Robert E Lee.

After the war, the Monocacy site remained in private hands, much of it with the Worthington family. They petitioned Congress to obtain the land as a memorial, and in 1934 a bill was passed authorizing the US to purchase the area for a national park, but no land was actually bought until the 1970s, with the first purchase in 1976. A part of the battlefield had already been lost when the I-270 Highway was built through the area and later widened.

The Monocacy National Battlefield Park was finally established in 1991, covering 1600 acres, including the Best farmhouse. Today, a Visitors Center displays artifacts, and a series of trails with interpretive signs gives access to the battle location, leading to the site of the railroad yard, the bridges, and the Best House and Worthington Farm. There are plans to obtain further sections of the battlefield once funds become available, but the Monocacy site is considered by the Civil War Trust as one of the ten most endangered battlefields in the country.

Tupelo
July 14, 1864
Mississippi

By the summer of 1864, Union General William T Sherman had already crossed much of the South and was approaching Atlanta. But before Sherman could assault the city itself, he had to insure the safety of his rear supply lines, particularly the railroad from Memphis—and that meant cornering the Confederate cavalry raider General Nathan Bedford Forrest.

Forrest had already defeated a Union cavalry force that had been sent to capture him, in June at the Battle of Brice's Crossroads. On July 1, Union General Andrew Jackson Smith was sent from Memphis with 14,000 more men and 20 guns, with the sole mission of defeating Forrest. (Sherman reportedly declared that he would bring Forrest to bay "if it costs 10,000 lives and breaks the Treasury".) Forrest, meanwhile, was reinforced by troops under General Stephen Dill Lee (no relation to Robert E Lee). Both sides were planning on establishing a strong defensive position and allowing the other to beat itself against it.

After some skirmishes (during which the Union supply train came under attack and was partially destroyed), Smith approached the Confederate force at its position near Okolona MS. Deciding that the Southern line was too strong for a frontal attack, Smith went around it, heading for the city of Tupelo instead. (Many of the troops defending Tupelo had been withdrawn to join Lee at Okolona.) This forced Lee and Forrest to leave their defensive works and meet him in open battle.

By the morning of July 14, both armies were drawn up facing each other at Harrisburg, just outside Tupelo. Smith had a strong position along a ridge that straddled the road into town. Lee and Forrest were outnumbered. There was now some disagreement, as both Lee and Forrest insisted that the other should take overall command: Lee was the ranking officer, but Forrest the more experienced. (And it may be that neither one wanted responsibility for what they both thought would be an impending defeat by a superior force.)

Lee finally took charge and planned an assault on the Union left flank at 7am. But before it could begin, the battle started somewhat accidentally. A group of Kentucky troops had been ordered to push back some Federal pickets, but in their zeal they advanced all the way to the Union lines, sparking off the fighting. The Confederates were stopped by a devastating fire, then driven back by a counter-attack. Of the 800 troops in the advance, 300 were killed or wounded.

Two more Confederate charges followed, and both were repelled with heavy losses. Then at 10:30am the Federals launched an attack of their own but made no headway. At 10 that night, the Union troops opened up with an intense fire, but in the dark they could not see their targets and casualties on both sides were light.

The next morning, the Federals, running low on food and ammo, began to withdraw towards their supply base. When Smith noticed that the Union troops were retreating, he sent in an attack with two brigades, but they failed to gain any ground and were pushed off the battlefield by a Federal counter-attack. Both sides now withdrew.

The fighting at Tupelo had cost the Confederates 1,300 of their 6,000 troops: five Southern regimental commanders had been killed, three brigade commanders wounded, and General Forrest himself had been shot in the foot, which would put him out of action for almost a month. Against this the Federals had lost only 600 casualties. More importantly in the strategic sense, although Forrest's force managed to escape without being destroyed it was now unable to interfere with Sherman's march towards Atlanta.

Tupelo National Battlefield

Today, most of the Tupelo battlefield has been lost. In 1929, a one-acre tract of the battle site, at the ridge where the initial attack occurred on the right flank of the Union line, was obtained by the War Department and preserved as the Tupelo National Battlefield Park. It was transferred to the National Park Service in 1933, and three years later the concrete memorial was destroyed in a tornado and rebuilt.

The one-acre site is located along Main Street in the town of Tupelo, and virtually all of the rest of the battleground has been lost to development. There is no Visitors Center: the park contains only the rebuilt memorial, some commemorative cannons, and a few interpretive signs.

The Brice's Crossroads National Battlefield is not far away. Most of that battlefield has also been lost, and the Park there consists only of a one-acre field with cannons and a memorial stone.

Atlanta
July 22, 1864
Georgia

By the time Confederate General John Bell Hood assumed command of the forces defending Atlanta, he was already in trouble. Union forces under William T Sherman had already dug in northeast of the city. On July 20 they seized a ridge near Peachtree Creek known locally as "Bald Hill" and placed a battery of cannons there. Now renamed Leggett's Hill after the Federal artillery commander, this position allowed the Union troops to pour cannon fire into Atlanta.

Although his Confederate troops were firmly entrenched inside the city in a ring of fortifications built by engineer Lemuel Grant, General Hood by temperament disdained the defensive and was always eager to attack. Now, he formed a plan to dislodge Sherman. General William Hardee would be sent to circle around the city and approach the Union Army along their left flank: once Hardee was in position, General Benjamin Cheatham would simultaneously attack the center to break Sherman's lines and drive him back.

Sherman could see Hardee's troops being pulled out of their fortifications and moving to the other side of town. But with his own troops heavily outnumbering the Confederates and his artillery blasting them constantly, Sherman assumed that Hood was abandoning the city and withdrawing to keep his army intact. He didn't know that the Confederates were actually moving towards him.

Hardee's march around Atlanta, however, was too slow. Before the Confederates could reach the Union lines, Federal General James Birdseye McPherson had decided that his left flank was too exposed, and moved his reserve corps into position to reinforce it. On July 22, not knowing that the Union lines had been extended, Hardee ran right into them.

Confederate General W.H.T. Walker now moved up in an effort to examine the Federal position in front of him. He was picked off by a sniper. When the Confederates launched their charge, several Union regiments were pushed back, creating a hole in the Federal line, and as General McPherson rode forward to inspect the situation, he mistakenly passed through this gap and into the Confederate line. Realizing his blunder, he gallantly tipped his hat at the Southerners and wheeled his horse around to ride off, but was hit in the chest by a Minnie ball and fell to the ground. He died later that day.

At about 4pm, as the Federals began to reorganize their lines and hold their ground, Confederate General Cheatham launched his assault, focusing on Leggett's Hill. In heavy fighting, the Southerners bent the Federal lines and captured two Parrot rifled cannons, but the Union forces held, and a counter-assault soon recaptured the guns. When the Union troops were able to move up another 20 cannons at Copen Hill, the Confederates were forced to withdraw.

The battle had cost the Southerners 5500 casualties, to the Union's 3400. But Hood still had a substantial force firmly entrenched inside the city. Sherman, not wanting to risk a frontal attack on such a strong position, now began laying siege. For the next four weeks Union cannons continuously shelled Atlanta. Twice, Sherman sent large cavalry raids around the city to cut off the vital railroad lines from Macon that were keeping Hood's troops supplied with food and ammunition: both attempts failed. Sherman then began to systematically advance his entire Army towards the railroad stations.

Finally, on August 31, he captured the depot at Jonesborough, severing the last of Hood's supply lines. The Confederates began withdrawing the next day, after setting fire to all of their storage warehouses and over 80 fully-loaded trains to prevent their supplies from being captured by the Federals. Whether intentionally or simply because the occupying Union troops lacked enough means to fight them, these fires spread and burned for days afterwards, consuming much of the city.

General McPherson Memorial

On September 2, the Mayor of Atlanta formally surrendered the city. Sherman sent a triumphant telegraph to Lincoln, "Atlanta is ours, and fairly won." The effect was immediate: the fall of Atlanta convinced most in the North that the war was coming to a conclusion. In the Presidential elections held shortly later between Lincoln and George McClellan, the former

Union Commander's platform of seeking a negotiated peace with the Confederacy fell on deaf ears, and Lincoln was re-elected by a substantial margin. Sherman established his new headquarters in Atlanta, and immediately began planning his next campaign— towards Savannah.

Over the years, Atlanta grew rapidly, and its expanding suburbia soon overtook and covered the battlefield. Today, virtually all of it is gone except for random bits and pieces. Leggett's Hill is now an exit ramp for I-20, and the Jimmy Carter Presidential Library now occupies the location of Sherman's headquarters.

There are a number of historical markers scattered through the city, and a memorial at the spot where General McPherson was killed. In Grant Park (named after Lemuel Grant who designed the city's defenses, not after that other guy), there is a small remaining portion of bank and ditch earthworks from Fort Walker.

Crater

July 30, 1864
Virginia

By the time Atlanta surrendered to the Federals, the armies of General Ulysses S Grant and Robert E Lee had been locked in a bloody stalemate at Petersburg for over a month. Grant knew that it was just a matter of time before the Confederate army, worn out from lack of supplies and reinforcements, would collapse, Petersburg would fall and Richmond shortly after, and the war would essentially be over. But Grant was by nature aggressive and prone to attack, and the long dull job of siege warfare held no appeal for him. So he formulated a bold plan to force his way through the Confederate lines and quickly bring the war to an end.

Actually the plan came from Lt Col Henry Pleasants, a regimental commander in General Ambrose Burnside's Ninth Corps. Pleasants commanded the 48th Pennsylvania Infantry Regiment, which had been recruited from miners in that state's anthracite coal belt. As the ex-miners studied the Confederate redoubts across from them, they concluded that they should be able to tunnel their way underneath them, plant an explosives charge and destroy the fortresses, opening up a gap in the lines. Pleasants submitted the plan to his superiors, but Burnside's engineers decided that the required tunnel would be too long and they would not be able to give it sufficient ventilation to allow for safe digging. Pleasants and his miners disagreed and, on June 25, began digging on their own, installing a separate ventilation shaft as they went and shoring up the tunnel with scraps of wood that they were able to scrounge up.

By the last week of July, they were approaching the Confederate lines, 20 feet above them. The tunnel was 586 feet long and ended with a cavity directly underneath a cannon redoubt held by troops from Virginia and South Carolina. On July 28, the miners began packing the chamber with 4 tons of black powder, held in 320 barrels.

Once Burnside saw that the tunnel would successfully reach underneath the Confederate lines, he formed a plan to use it as a surprise prelude to an attack. By packing the tunnel full of black powder, he would trigger an explosion that would destroy the redoubts and blow a huge gap in the enemy position. Burnside would then send Union troops from his Fourth Division, consisting of 4,000 ex-slaves in the United States Colored Troops, through this breach towards a ridge of hills. Once the ridge had been captured, the Federals could move up a number of cannon batteries and begin bombarding the center of Richmond. The African-American troops began rehearsing for the assault about two weeks before the mine was completed.

When the plan was presented to General Grant, he in turn consulted with General George Meade. Meade and Burnside had both previously been Commander of the Army of the Potomac, and both hated each other. While Burnside had seniority and technically outranked him, Meade had been retained in command of the Army of the Potomac by General Grant, and to smooth their ruffled feathers he always gave each of them separate instructions so neither would have to take orders from the other.

Now, the day before the attack was set to launch, Grant and Meade made some last-minute changes to Burnside's plan. Burnside had intended to use the

Fourth Division, which had just arrived and was the freshest body of troops he had available, for the attack. But Meade now argued to Grant that, never having been in combat before, that unit was too inexperienced to lead the planned assault. Meade also made the political argument that placing African-American soldiers at the front of what could be a risky attack might be taken to indicate that the Union Army valued their lives less—he suggested one of the other divisions be placed in the lead instead, with the ex-slaves to follow behind them. When none of Burnside's other division commanders volunteered to lead the charge (none of them thought the mine tunnel would work), Burnside had them draw straws. The lot fell to General James Ledlie of the First Division. His troops now had less than a day to get ready. The African-American troops, under General Edward Ferrero, would follow them.

An hour before dawn on July 30, the fuse was lit on the explosives. And nothing happened. After a half-hour wait, two ex-miners volunteered to go into the tunnel to see what was wrong: they found that the fuse had gone out. Re-lighting it, they scrambled out and, at 4:44am, over an hour late and just as the morning sky was lightening, the black powder detonated.

It was one of the largest manmade explosions ever made up to that time. The blast ripped a crater that was 170 feet long, 60 feet wide and 30 feet deep. Some 300 Confederate troops, most of them asleep, are estimated to have been killed in the explosion: their body parts were scattered over the area.

Burnside's troops poured into the gap. But things went wrong almost immediately. The orders given to the First Division men were unclear, and many of them, rather than running around the rim of the Crater towards the ridge beyond, instead assumed that their goal was to capture the Crater itself, and they climbed down inside. The confusion was increased by the fact that neither General Ledlie nor General Ferrero were there: they were both in a tent back at headquarters, sharing a bottle of rum.

Once Burnside and Meade realized that the attack had stalled, they traded angry telegraph messages accusing each other of messing up the plan. After an hour, the other supporting troops, including the African-American Fourth Division, were sent in to try to capture the ridge. But by this time the Confederates had recovered from the shock of the explosion and had begun to re-form their defensive lines. The attacking Federals were driven back, and many of them now too sought shelter inside the Crater.

Entrance to the mine tunnel, which ran to the top of the hill

As the Union troops crowded into the hole, they probably thought it was a safe position, akin to a giant foxhole. In reality, it was a deathtrap. The sides of the Crater were steep and loose, and once in, most troops found that they couldn't climb back out. At about 9:30am, it became apparent that the attack had failed, and Burnside was ordered to withdraw. Instead he delayed, arguing first that he should make another assault, and then that he should wait for dark to pull his troops back under cover.

By 2pm, the remaining Confederates in the area were able to move right up to the edge of the Crater and fire unimpeded down into the mass of Federals trapped inside. Then a force of Southerners entered the Crater itself, and fierce hand to hand fighting broke out. It became a slaughter. The African-American troops became the special target of the Confederates. Many were killed as they tried to retreat, and even after the trapped Federals inside the crater surrendered, the former slaves were summarily executed. The Union troops suffered almost 4000 casualties—about half of which were from the African-American division, and most of these inflicted after the surrender. One of the Confederate officers present, General Edward Porter Alexander, later reported, "Some of the Negro prisoners who were originally allowed to surrender ... were afterward shot by others, and there was, without doubt, a great deal of unnecessary killing of them."

The slaughter had been so great that General Grant launched an official court of inquiry into the disaster. Most of the blame fell on Ledlie, Ferrero, and Burnside for their lack of leadership during the attack, but the ultimate cause of the fiasco, the investigation concluded, was Meade's decision to change the plan less than a day before the attack. Burnside and Ledlie were placed on indefinite leave, in effect relieved of command. Burnside resigned from the Army shortly later.

Grant bemoaned the failure of what had been his best chance to break the stalemate and move upon Richmond to end the war. "Such an opportunity for carrying fortifications I have never seen," he reported to the War Department, "and do not expect again to have."

The siege of Petersburg would drag on for another eight months. After the failure at the Crater, President Lincoln encouraged Grant with a telegram which read, "I have seen your dispatch expressing your unwillingness to break your hold where you are. Neither am I willing. Hold on with a bulldog grip, and chew and choke as much as possible." A few weeks later, Grant launched assaults towards Deep Bottom and the Weldon Railroad, seizing and destroying a portion of track near the Globe Tavern. By the end of August the Federals had occupied the Reams Station. In September the Confederates managed to raid a Union supply depot and capture 2500 head of cattle. But Lee knew that his supply situation was critical—just one railroad line remained unbroken.

For the next several months, Grant systematically tightened his noose around Petersburg, while raids and counter-raids steadily drained Lee's army of irreplaceable manpower. On March 25, 1865, Lee made a last desperate assault at Fort Stedman to try to break out, and failed. Grant countered with an attack of his own at Five Forks on April 1, which broke through the Confederate lines at Boydton Plank Road.

Lee pulled his entire army back into Petersburg and, with his supply routes gone, the Confederates abandoned both Petersburg and Richmond. As Grant's troops entered the two cities, Lee fled towards the supply station at nearby Appomattox Courthouse, hoping to reorganize his troops and head south to join together with General Joseph Johnston's army in North Carolina.

Today, the Crater is a part of the Petersburg National Battlefield Park and is a stop on the park's driving tour.

Mobile Bay
August 5, 1864
Alabama

By 1864, as the siege dragged on at Petersburg, the Federal "Anaconda" blockade of Southern ports was already effectively strangling the Confederacy of supplies. Only one major port in the Gulf of Mexico remained relatively open—Mobile AL. Although the Union Navy had a blockading force just outside the harbor entrance, the port itself was defended by three cannon positions—Fort Morgan, Fort Gaines and Fort Powell—which prevented the Federals from sealing it off completely. As a result, Confederate blockade runners were still able to slip in and out and carry on trade with Havana and the rest of the Caribbean.

The task of eliminating Mobile Bay as a Southern trading port had been assigned to Admiral David Farragut after he had captured New Orleans and Baton Rouge. But more pressing matters intervened and Farragut's ships were kept busy in the siege of Vicksburg through much of 1863. It wasn't until 1864 that planning could begin for an assault on Mobile Bay.

Farragut had a fleet of 18 ships available. Eleven of these were conventional wooden-hulled steam frigates and gunships. Three more were experimental designs called "double-ends"; they were designed with a bow at each end to allow them to sail either forwards or backwards in narrow river channels. The remaining four ships were "monitors", ironclads with one or two revolving turrets, of basically the same design as the USS *Monitor*. There were also a number of troopships: the intent was not to capture or occupy the city, however, but to knock out the Forts and allow the Federal fleet to enter and control the harbor.

To oppose Farragut's fleet, the Confederates had 90 guns in the three Forts, including 11 long-range rifled cannons. There were a handful of small wooden gunships, but the primary naval force in the harbor consisted of just one ship, the ironclad CSS *Tennessee*. Built under the command of the former captain of the first Confederate ironclad CSS *Virginia,* who was now an Admiral overseeing the naval defenses at Mobile, the *Tennessee* had some of the strongest armor in the world at that time, as well as 6 long-range guns. Plans called for a number of additional ironclads to join her at Mobile, but Farragut struck in August 1864 before they were completed.

At dawn on August 5, some 1500 Union troops were landed near Fort Gaines and advanced upon it. Simultaneously, Farragut's fleet entered Mobile Bay with the intention of providing covering fire for the troops. The Federal ships were tied together side by side in pairs, an odd configuration which Farragut had used successfully before: the theory was that if one ship suffered damage, the engines on the other ship could maintain them both in motion and keep all their guns in play.

The Federal ships, however, were entering a carefully-laid Confederate trap. In the middle of the channel, a large area had been seeded with what were known as "torpedoes"—barrels of explosive that were tethered to the bottom and functioned like modern naval mines. The edges of the minefield were clearly marked by buoys (so Confederate blockade runners would not hit them), and this had the effect of forcing any enemy fleet to the sides of the channel—within gun range of the Forts. And behind the minefield lay the CSS *Tennessee* and several smaller gunships.

Fort Gaines, at the entrance to Mobile Harbor

Just minutes after entering the harbor, the Union ironclad *Tecumseh* hit one of the mines and sank. One by one, the rest of the fleet slowed down, reluctant to enter the area. But Farragut knew that if he slowed or stopped here, the Forts around him would batter his ships to bits. So he issued what must be the most famous order in US Navy history: "Damn the torpedoes! Full speed ahead!" The fleet charged in. Fortunately, most of the torpedoes had been submerged for so long that they leaked and their explosives failed to detonate.

The smaller Confederate gunships were quickly knocked out, and Farragut expected that the *Tennessee* would retreat to the cover of the inner harbor. Instead, he was shocked to see the *Tennessee* move in to attack the entire Union fleet, single-handedly. It was a brave move, but a futile one—outnumbered, the Confederate ironclad was pounded by the Federals, especially the 15-inch guns on the monitors. After three hours, the *Tennessee* was dead in the water and surrendered.

With free reign inside the Bay, Farragut now concentrated a bombardment against the Confederate forts. Within two weeks, under fire from the water and siege by landed Federal troops, all three had surrendered. The Union fleet would control Mobile Bay for the rest of the war, and the city itself would finally be captured in April 1865 just as the war ended.

Today, the forts still stand at the harbor entrance. The two biggest, Fort Morgan and Fort Gaines, were expanded during the Spanish-American War by the addition of new batteries of "hiding guns", which could be loaded behind the walls and then briefly raised to fire. Fort Morgan is now a State Historical Park. The museum inside the Visitors Center has relics on display from the sunken ironclad *Tecumseh*. Fort Gaines, on the other side of the harbor mouth, is run as a local park by the city of Dauphin Island. The museum there also has a display of artifacts from the battle, including the anchor from Admiral Farragut's flagship *Hartford*. Damage from Union cannons can still be seen on the Fort's walls.

Memphis
August 21, 1864
Tennessee

Although the Confederate General Nathan Bedford Forrest had been defeated and wounded at Tupelo, his cavalry unit was still a danger to the Federals, operating in the Union Army's rear areas and raiding supply centers, railroad stations and isolated garrisons. A month after his unsuccessful battle at Tupelo, Forrest planned another daring raid against the Federals. This time his target was Memphis.

When the Union Army captured Nashville in February 1862, the Confederate state's capitol was moved to Memphis, which was an important river port as well as Tennessee's largest city. In June 1862, the Union Navy moved against the port as part of the Anaconda blockade. On June 6, a Federal fleet of 18 ships with 80 guns faced off against a Confederate flotilla of 8 ships and 18 guns. The Battle of Memphis was over in just 90 minutes, with 7 of the 8 Southern ships sunk. A force of Union troops came ashore and occupied the city, hanging the US flag from the roof of the Post Office building. Within a short time, Fort Pickering had been built, and the city became a hospital center, with beds for over 5,000 wounded or sick soldiers. General Ulysses S Grant and General William T Sherman both had their headquarters here.

One building in Memphis, however, quickly became notorious. The Irving Block office building had been constructed just before the outbreak of war. The Confederates had used it as a hospital, but when the Federals occupied Memphis they decided that the building—with its iron-slatted windows—was better suited for another purpose; it became a prison, used to hold both captured Confederate troopers and civilian secessionists, including the city's former Mayor.

However, under the occupation government of General Stephen Hurlbut, the Irving Block Prison became the center of a vast extortion racket. One of Hurlbut's duties was to root out the underground market for contraband Confederate cotton, which was being illegally sold in the city and the profits smuggled back to the Confederacy. But Hurlbut quickly turned the anti-smuggling campaign into a crooked and corrupt scam. At first, he simply arrested the city's most wealthy traders, accused them (without evidence) of smuggling, and demanding exorbitant bribes for their release. Many were held anyway even if they paid.

When Hurlbut appointed Union Army Captain George Williams as the commandant at the prison, things got worse. Not only did Williams also begin extorting bribes from the family members of prisoners, but much of the money slated towards caring for the POWs and detainees disappeared into corrupt pockets, and conditions inside the prison soon turned wretched. There were about 1200 Confederate POWs (and a handful of Federal troops who were awaiting court-martial) inside the prison, as well as 100 or so civilians who were deemed "dangerous". They received little food or medical care, and many were chained in their cells 24 hours a day, denied even trips to the bathroom. City residents began calling it "The Bastille".

By April 1864 the corruption and horrible conditions inside the Irving Block Prison had become so widely-known that an investigation was launched by the Union Army's Office of the Judge Advocate General, which reported to President Lincoln that, "The prison ... is represented as the filthiest place the inspector ever saw occupied by human beings. The whole management and government of the prison could not be worse." The Secretary of War, Edwin Stanton, removed Captain Williams as commandant, but soon afterwards General Grant intervened on his behalf, and Williams was reinstated.

Meanwhile, rumors of the conditions inside the prison had spread throughout the Confederacy, and in August 1864 Confederate General Forrest decided to act. With 1500 cavalry, Forrest moved stealthily towards Memphis. Outnumbered four to one by the 6,000 Federal occupation troops there, he could not hope to capture the city, but he did have the goals of attacking the prison and releasing the prisoners there, and raiding the headquarters buildings used by Hurlbut and by the Union General Cadwallader Washburn, in an attempt to capture them. He also hoped that a raid on Memphis would force the Union to withdraw troops from Petersburg or Atlanta to reinforce the city.

The raid, which would become known as the "Second Battle of Memphis", began at 4 in the morning on August 21. It was a foggy night, and Forrest's troops took advantage by calling out to the Federal sentries that they were a patrol that was bringing in new Confederate POWs. Once they overpowered the pickets and entered the city, Forrest's cavalry split into three groups.

One detachment headed for the Irving Block prison, hoping to storm the building, release the prisoners, and burn it. But they were stopped by the armed prison guards, who were quickly reinforced by nearby Union troops.

A second group made its way to the building where General Hurlbut was billeted—the Gayoso House Hotel—but the military governor was not there.

The final squadron, led by the General's brother Lt Colonel Jesse Forrest, rode to another hotel where General Washburn had his quarters, but Washburn had already been warned and had fled on horseback, in his nightclothes, to nearby Fort Pickering. The Confederates captured only his dress uniform.

For the next two hours, while knots of soldiers fought each other in the streets of Memphis, the Confederates cut the city's telegraph lines, burned a few buildings, and searched for the missing Union Generals. Then, as the sun came up, Forrest and his troops mounted up and left, taking 600 horses and about 500 Union prisoners along with them.

They also took General Washburn's captured uniform coat, which Forrest mockingly returned to him the next day by messenger, after having it cleaned and pressed. When General Hurlbut was told about the raid, he was reported to have exclaimed, "They replaced me with General Washburn because I couldn't keep Forrest out of west Tennessee—and Washburn couldn't keep Forrest out of his own bedroom!"

General Stephen Hurlbut

After the raid, Hurlbut was removed as military governor of Memphis. Captain Williams remained in command of the prison, but now he had a change of heart and began trying to clean up the corruption and improve the conditions inside. Despite his efforts, the

Irving Block Prison was ordered closed by President Lincoln in early 1865.

Today, none of the buildings that were the focus of Forrest's raid still exist. There is a display of naval artifacts from the period at the Mississippi River Museum. When he died after the war, the Confederate General Forrest was buried in Memphis, his home town, and a gravestone was erected at Forrest Park.

In 2013, while the state legislature considered a bill to prevent any city in Tennessee from removing its Civil War monuments, the Memphis city government voted to change the name of the park to "Health Sciences Park"; nearby Confederate Park was renamed "Memphis Park", and Jefferson Davis Park was rechristened "Mississippi River Park". The city also removed a statue of Jefferson Davis, some cannon memorials, and a statue of Forrest that had been put up by the Sons of Confederate Veterans. Since Forrest is still buried there, it is not clear what will happen to his body.

St Albans
October 19, 1864
Vermont

One of the oddest events in the Civil War happened in 1864 when a group of Confederate partisans crossed the border from Canada and occupied a small Vermont town for a short time.

When the war started to turn against the Confederates in 1863, they began to desperately search for ways to distract the Federals, draw away their troops, and harass their supply lines. In particular, Richmond wanted to "take the war to the North", and create havoc and panic among the Yankees.

To do this, the Confederate Secretary of War at the time, Stephen Mallory, proposed to utilize a partisan network that had already been put into place in Canada. The Union had established a number of POW camps in Ohio and New York, near the border with Canada, and the Confederates had shipped a number of volunteers to attempt to carry out cross-border raids to free the captured prisoners. All of these attempts were botched, succeeding only in provoking an official diplomatic protest from the US to Canada about the "enemy forces" sheltering along the border.

But in October 1864, one of the members of this network, an escaped POW named Bennett Young, contacted the Confederate War Department with a scheme to gather a force of partisans in Canada and begin a series of hit-and-run raids into Vermont and New York to destroy infrastructure, to weaken the morale of the civilian population, and to gain some measure of revenge for General Sherman's march through the south.

The Confederate Congress had already passed a "Secret Service Bill" and appropriated $1 million for the use of partisans in Canada (under the command of Jacob Thompson). And so, with the approval of President Jefferson Davis and Secretary of War James Seddon, it was agreed to begin cross-border raids into Union territory. Young, along with several dozen others, was assigned to lead the group, under Thompson's direction.

After slipping into the US and reconnoitering several potential targets, Young settled on the little town of St Albans VT as his first target. Although St Albans had only 2,000 residents, it was the location of a farm-machinery factory. More importantly, it was the hometown of Vermont Governor John G Smith.

The raid was planned for October 18. For several days, around 20 Confederate partisans infiltrated individually into Vermont and made their way to the little town, posing as Canadian vacationers, hunters, or traders, and obtaining rooms in local boardinghouses. (Young even managed to get inside the Governor's manor house by joining a tour.) They then met to plan their actions.

Immediately, they ran into a difficulty: the planned day of the attack happened to be Tuesday—the local market day, when hundreds of people from the surrounding countryside would be crowded in for their periodic supply trips. It was decided that there would be too much chaos to carry out a coordinated action, and so the attack was postponed till the next day. The raiders also dropped plans to set the Governor's house on fire, concluding that it would be too difficult to carry out. Instead, they settled on three local banks as their targets: the St. Albans Bank, the First National Bank and the Franklin County Bank. At three o'clock, each of the teams would make their move on their assigned bank.

Bennett Young, a contemporary illustration

And so, as the village clock tolled on the afternoon of October 19, 1864, Lieutenant Young, accompanied by a number of others, stepped onto the front veranda of the American Hotel, drew a pair of Colt Navy pistols, and loudly announced, "In the name of the Confederate States, I take possession of the town of St. Albans." Immediately, the raiders began rounding up the townspeople and escorting them to the village green, where they were kept under guard. One of the residents, named Collins Huntington, refused to cooperate and was shot and wounded. Another citizen, Union Army Captain George P. Conger, ran into the hotel, slipped out the back door, and dashed to the other side of town and raised the alarm, gathering a ragtag group of armed vigilantes.

Simultaneously, three other groups of Confederates occupied the three banks. Within fifteen minutes, all three had been robbed for a total of around $220,000 (over $3 million in today's money). The bank robbers all made speeches declaring that they represented the

Confederate States of America and that the raid was in retaliation for General Sherman. They then left and gathered with the others in the town green, setting several buildings afire as they went.

By this time, Captain Conger had returned with a group of armed citizens, and in the subsequent gunfight one of the raiders was wounded and a building worker from New Hampshire was shot and killed. As the raiders all rode away on stolen horses, the local telegraph operator dashed off a message to the state capitol: "Southern raiders are in town, robbing banks, shooting citizens and burning houses." By the time evening fell, there were militiamen and cannons stationed in St Albans. For months afterwards, there were regular patrols and garrisons in towns across the northeast who feared another Confederate attack.

All of the raiders made it back to Canada. But as word of the "battle" spread and American militia crossed the border in pursuit, the Canadians arrested 13 of the Confederates, including Lt Young. But the Canadian Government was reluctant to get involved in the American Civil War, and, concluding that they were belligerent combatants rather than common criminals, it refused to extradite the arrested prisoners to the US for trial. After a court hearing in Montreal the raiders were all released. When the US protested, the Confederates were re-arrested and new court proceedings begun in Canada. Once the war ended, before the trials were complete, the charges were dropped and the prisoners were again let go.

Today there is a historical marker in St Albans which commemorates the raid. Although modern banks now stand today where two of the Confederate targets once were, none of the original structures from the time survives.

Westport

October 22, 1864
Missouri

By 1864, the Confederacy was in deep trouble. They had lost key battles at Gettysburg and Vicksburg, Atlanta had been captured, and Lee's army was being pinned down in Petersburg. And Federal gunboats controlled the entire length of the Mississippi River, cutting the Confederacy in two.

So General Sterling Price, a Missouri native who was in command of Confederate troops in Arkansas, formed a plan that, while it seemed desperate, was really the last option that the Confederates in the west had. Price had already tried to invade Missouri in 1862 along with General Earl Van Dorn, and had been stopped at Pea Ridge. Now, he decided to try again.

In consultation with General Edmund Kirby Smith, the Confederate commander in charge of the Trans-Mississippi Department, Price decided that he would take his "Army of Missouri" and move north to capture St Louis, thereby breaking the Federal grip on the Mississippi and forcing Grant to draw troops away from Petersburg and move them west, allowing Lee to break out. And, by placing the secessionist "state government in exile" back in power, Price and Kirby hoped to officially remove Missouri from the Union—perhaps upsetting the political picture enough to lead to Lincoln's defeat in the 1864 elections and a negotiated end to the war.

The expedition began at the end of August 1864. Price had three divisions under his command, with about 12,000 troops and 14 field guns. His orders were to capture St Louis, recruit as many local volunteers as possible and use the weapons in its arsenal to arm them, move on to Jefferson City and install the pro-Southern government, then move to cross the border into Kansas to capture the supplies at Fort Leavenworth and destroy as much Federal infrastructure as possible.

It was an unrealistically ambitious plan, and it fell apart almost from the start. Contrary to his hope, there was no wave of volunteers to join Price's army, and he was not treated as a liberator. Most of the troops he took into Missouri were raw militia, and they were undisciplined and slow, spending much of their time plundering the local towns.

The Federals, meanwhile, knew that Price and his troops were on the way. The Union General in command at St Louis was William Rosecrans, who had been transferred there by Lincoln after his unimpressive performance at Chickamauga. The Confederates' slow advance gave Rosecrans time to bring in more troops by diverting a unit that was traveling down the Mississippi to join Sherman's force in Atlanta, and by the time Price reached St Louis he found that the Federals had reinforced their garrison and thrown up a belt of fortifications.

Price knew his army wasn't strong enough to deal with this, so he turned west and headed towards the state capitol in Jefferson City, now pursued by a Federal cavalry force from St Louis under General Alfred Pleasonton, who fought a series of skirmishes with the Confederate rearguard. Once again, Price took too long, and finding Jefferson City also reinforced and too strong for him to attack, he now headed for Kansas City.

That in turn caught the attention of General Samuel Curtis, who commanded the Federal forces in Kansas. Knowing that he would also be a target for Price, Curtis called up the Kansas militia. This provoked a controversy, since most of the militiamen refused to fight anywhere outside of their own state, but a force of several thousand men, called the "Army of the Border", entered Missouri and skirmished with Price's army near Independence, just enough to slow it down, before forming up in a line along the Big Blue River just east of Westport. (Today Westport is a suburb of Kansas City, but back then it was an important transport hub.) Price's troops, in turn, accompanied by 400 wagons loaded with plunder and civilian sympathizers and herding along some 5,000 captured cattle, took up positions near the town of Independence.

Realizing that his grand expedition in Missouri was a failure, Price's priority now became a matter of reaching Kansas with his troops, exacting vengeance with a trail of burning and destruction.

But with Curtis's entrenched line of troops in front of him and Pleasonton's cavalry force closing in behind him, Price was now in a desperate position. Pinned between two forces, he decided that his only hope of escape lay in attacking Curtis's army in Westport and defeating it before Pleasonton's forces could reach him, then turn and beat Pleasonton too.

The Union forces were lined up on the far bank of the Big Blue River, at a crossing known locally as Byram's Ford. Price's force was outnumbered, but he knew that these Federal troops were mostly green and untested, so he was confident he could beat them.

The Battle of Westport began on the morning of October 22, 1864, when a unit of Confederates attacked the Union lines head-on across Byram's Ford. Meanwhile, two more groups crossed the Big Blue River north and south of the Ford and attacked, outflanking the Union troops and forcing them to withdraw to the northwest and form a line along Brush Creek. Price moved his force across Byram's Ford and that night dug his troops in, making use of the Federal breastworks they had just captured.

Shortly after dawn the next morning, Confederate forces crossed Brush Creek and attacked Curtis's positions. At first, the fight was stalemated, but then a local farmer pointed Union troops to a dry streambed that led behind the Confederate lines, and a group of infantry and a battery of artillery attacked, forcing Price to retreat.

Confederate position at Bloody Hill

Just after 8 that morning, moreover, the Union cavalry under Pleasonton reached Byram's Ford, fought their way across, and attacked the lower half of Price's lines. Price's army was now caught between two forces which outnumbered him almost three to one. After several hours of back and forth fighting, Pleasonton's troops broke through the Confederate line at a place which was known locally as Potato Hill, but which after the battle was christened Bloody Hill. While the Confederate General Joseph Shelby's units fought a desperate rear-guard action, the bulk of Price's army (and his wagon train) managed to escape the trap and fled into Kansas.

The Battle of Westport was decisive. It ended any hope of attacking Grant's army from the west, and because most of the Confederate sympathizers and guerrillas had fled along with Price's troops, it left Missouri and Kansas securely in the hands of the Union.

Today, most of the battlefield has been lost to Kansas City's suburbia. Two key areas, several miles apart, are still accessible, however—the area around Byram's Ford and Bloody Hill, and the area around Brush Creek where Curtis's troops drove the Confederates back from Westport. A portion of the Brush Creek area is protected by Loose Park, which has a historical display about the battle.

The Battle of Westport Visitors Center, containing a small museum with relics from the battlefield, is located about a mile from the Byram's Ford site, and near that is the Adams House, which served as Price's headquarters during the fighting. Most of this portion of the battlefield is now covered with factories and warehouses and much of it is fenced off and inaccessible. (There is a local nonprofit group raising money to buy back portions of the site and restore it to its original condition.) The Byram's Ford site, though unmarked, is accessible by a bicycle path on the far side of the Big Blue River. A historical marker and a cannon mark the location of Bloody Hill, where the Confederate lines were broken.

Scattered around Kansas City are 20-some additional historical markers, indicating the position of field hospitals, troop units, and other points of interest. Pamphlets are available allowing visitors to take a "driving tour" from each of these markers to the next.

Mine Creek
October 25, 1864
Kansas

After the Confederate army under General Sterling Price was surrounded and barely escaped at Westport, he crossed the border over into Kansas, intending to capture as many supplies as he could and destroy the infrastructure in pro-Union areas. Most important, he wanted to get his 400-wagon train to safety, since the captured plunder and supplies they carried were the only things that made his raid worth the while.

That meant he had to cross Mine Creek at a particular place, a ford with a rocky streambed that could support his heavy wagons. He reached it on October 25, 1864, hotly pursued by the Union cavalry under General Alfred Pleasonton, who had followed him from Westport.

About a third of Price's forces made it across the Creek. But the ford couldn't handle the number or weight of his wagons, and within a short time the banks of Mine Creek began to crumble and turn into thick mud, which bogged down the wagons and created a huge bottleneck at the crossing. And just then, a Union Cavalry force appeared on the horizon. It consisted of two brigades under the command of Colonel John Philips and Colonel Frederick Benteen.

The Confederate units that hadn't yet crossed Mine Creek were now trapped—although they could have ridden away and escaped, their orders were to protect the wagon train. They had no choice but to turn and fight. And although they had always been trained to dismount and meet an enemy charge on foot behind cover, they now realized that their only hope in these circumstances was mobility, so they remained on their horses. As a result, the Battle of Mine Creek became one of the largest cavalry vs cavalry engagements of the Civil War. The Federals had around 2,500 troopers, and the Confederates had around 7,000.

But the Federals, though outnumbered, had far better weaponry than the Southerners: they were armed with Spencer and Sharps repeating rifles, while the Confederates had single-shot Enfield rifled muskets. (Repeating firearms were for the most part limited to the Union cavalry, and awed infantrymen remarked that one could "load it on Sunday and shoot it all week.") As the Confederates were still organizing their defenses along the creek banks, Benteen ordered an immediate charge.

The fight almost came to a quick end, however. Benteen's 10th Missouri cavalrymen, when they saw how many opposing troops they faced, pulled up and halted. It was only quick action by Major Abial Pierce, who took his 4th Iowa Regiment through the stalled Missourians and directly at the Confederate lines, which saved the day. The other Union regiments followed.

The fighting lasted only half an hour. The Confederates were routed: they lost 1200 troops, and had two Generals captured. The Federals lost only 100 men. Price was forced to burn all of his wagon train to lighten his load and allow the surviving cavalry to escape into Oklahoma. In the end, his entire Missouri venture had accomplished nothing.

The most controversial part of the action, however, happened after the battle was over. Many of Price's ill-equipped troops were wearing captured Union Army overcoats against the cold. The Union's 10th Missouri Regiment, which had been fighting against Confederate irregulars for years, had a standing policy that any enemy they captured in Union uniform was to be considered as a spy or guerrilla and summarily shot rather than taken prisoner. In the aftermath of the fighting, then, the Missourians executed dozens of Price's men.

Today the Battle of Mine Creek is mostly forgotten. At the time, it was considered to be just another skirmish in a long running battle, which took place at an unnamed place with no towns or landmarks nearby. Also, there were no newspaper reporters accompanying the troopers, so nobody to dispatch a telegraph report of the fight, and in any case it was overshadowed by the far larger and better-covered contests back East.

Visitor Center at Mine Creek Battlefield

The battlefield is now run by the Kansas Historical Society and is preserved in pretty much the same condition it was in at the time of the fighting. The Visitor

Center has a film about the battle and a replica cannon on display, and the grounds offer a self-guided walking tour of the battlefield and a nearby nature trail. There is a stone memorial to the troops located on private land just outside the park's boundaries.

Franklin
November 30, 1864
Tennessee

In 1864, General William T Sherman led a Union army through the very heart of the Confederacy, and his march took him all the way to Atlanta. In September 1864, Confederate General John Bell Hood withdrew his troops and abandoned the city to Sherman.

But Hood wasn't ready to give up yet. He had developed a reputation for being reckless, and now he was also being driven by desperation. So he formulated a plan that he hoped would pull a victory out of his hat. Marching north from Atlanta, he planned to attack the Union forces in Nashville. This would cut off Sherman's supply lines and, Hood hoped, force the Federals to leave Atlanta.

Hood's plan was never realistic. He had only 30,000 men; the heavily-fortified Federals in Nashville already outnumbered him. The Union forces were also being reinforced by General George Thomas and his detachment from Atlanta, consisting mostly of rear-area garrison soldiers and a number of "Colored Regiments" made up of African-American volunteers. Hood was outnumbered by over two to one. Nevertheless, he set off for Tennessee. (Hood hoped that he could recruit another 20,000 or so new volunteers as he marched along—which never happened.)

On November 29, Hood reached the town of Franklin, just south of Nashville. Here he was approached by a Union force of 15,000 under General John Schofield, who was moving to join Thomas in Nashville. Slowed down by its large baggage and supply train, Schofield's outnumbered column made a tempting target for Hood, but a series of miscommunications and mistakes allowed Schofield to march right past the Confederates and reach the town of Franklin. Here, the Federals stopped and formed a defensive position, occupying and improving an old series of trenches that had been dug in around Fort Granger during the Union's occupation. By November 30, Schofield's men were arranged in a formidable defensive line of ditches and gun pits that stretched around the town.

Eastern Flank Battlefield Park

At around noon on November 30, Hood's force arrived and formed a line centered on Winstead Hill. Against the advice of all his subordinates, who thought the Union position too strong, Hood decided to attack. At 4pm, just before dark, he launched a frontal assault by six divisions, almost his entire force. He intended to overwhelm Schofield's defenses and destroy the Federal army.

Hood paid the price for his rashness, in what was almost a replay of "Pickett's Charge". The Confederates had to advance almost two miles over open ground into a line of Federal guns and riflemen who were protected by extensive fortifications. Schofield was shocked: he had assumed that Hood would try to go around him and force his withdrawal, and did not expect the Confederates to attack such a strong defensive position. In the initial wave, the Southerners overran some Union positions at the Carter House, but a Federal counter-attack quickly closed the breach.

The fighting continued into the night. In some areas, the Confederates made as many as six separate charges against the Federal positions, and were driven back each time. On the Union right, an attack by Confederate General Nathan Bedford Forrest's cavalry was halted. At around 10pm, the Confederates finally drew back to their lines. They had lost 14 Generals, 55 Regimental Commanders, and 7,000 men as casualties—almost a third of their entire army.

Hood, however, refused to withdraw, and began making plans for a new assault in the morning. He never got the chance: Schofield retreated overnight and entered Nashville.

Hood sent a request for reinforcements, but there were none available. Nevertheless, incredibly, Hood did not abandon his plans, and continued on to Nashville with the battered remnant of his troops, intending to attack the Union General Thomas and his army there.

Today, most of the battleground has been developed and lies underneath the town of Franklin, but some sites still remain. Much of the fighting actually occurred in the town itself.

In 2007 the city, in partnership with the Franklin Battlefield Trust and other preservationist groups, made plans to purchase several tracts of land and form a battlefield park. So far about 180 acres have been obtained, and are being preserved as the Eastern Flank

Battlefield Park, run by the city of Franklin. The park preserves the extreme right end of the Confederate lines, including the Carnton House which served as a field hospital (and still bears bullet scars from the fighting). A Confederate Cemetery holds about 1500 graves. Nearby, the eroded remains of trenches can still be seen at the Fort Granger site.

Nashville

December 15, 1864
Tennessee

The Battle of Nashville, in December 1864, destroyed an
entire Confederate Army and ended the Civil War in
what was then the western part of the United States.
But today the battle has been largely forgotten.

In February 1862, in one of its first major successes
of the Civil War, the Union forces managed to capture
Fort Donelson in Tennessee. This left the way open to
Nashville, and Federal gunboats sailed up the
Cumberland River to capture the city without a shot.
Nashville became the first Confederate capitol to
surrender. It quickly became an important Union supply
center, and the occupying Federal forces constructed a
number of defensive positions around the city, including
a large cannon fortress at Fort Negley.

By the time the Confederates under Gen John Bell
Hood reached Nashville in December 1864, after the
Battle of Franklin, they were already battered and
disorganized. Hood hastily dug in a defensive line just
south of Nashville, anchored on a series of cannon
positions known as "redoubts". Hood had about 15,000

men. The Union General George Thomas, inside the Union fortifications, had about 70,000 men.

Hood, even after the beating he had just taken at Franklin, was still confident of victory. His plan was to build a strong defensive line and goad Thomas into attacking him. It would be a re-play of the Battle of Franklin, but this time, Hood expected, it would be the Union forces that wore themselves out attacking his fortified positions, allowing him to then counter-attack and take the city. But as the Confederates were digging in, a severe winter storm descended. The snow and ice halted everything.

Meanwhile, the Union commander Ulysses S Grant, seeing that the Union forces heavily out-numbered the Confederates, was sending frantic orders to Thomas to attack immediately. After almost two weeks, Grant, who was unaware of the weather conditions in Nashville, concluded that Thomas was needlessly delaying things, and dispatched one of his own subordinate generals with instructions ordering Thomas to attack, and relieving him of command if he didn't. Grant made plans to leave for Nashville himself to take personal command.

Grant's dispatch was still en route when the weather finally broke on December 15, and Thomas launched his assault against the right end of Hood's lines, beginning with a cannon barrage from Fort Negley. One by one the Confederate redoubts were taken, and by the time the fighting temporarily stopped at nightfall, the Confederates had been pushed back about two miles.

In the morning the assaults began again, and at about 4pm on December 16, a Union regiment from Minnesota broke through the Confederate strongpoint at Shy's Hill and rolled behind the lines.

Hood's entire army collapsed. Almost 6,000 Confederates were killed, wounded or captured; the rest retreated all the way to Mississippi, where General Hood resigned his command in disgrace. It was one of the most lopsided Union victories of the war; the Confederate Army of Tennessee had been destroyed as an effective force, and the Civil War in the "western theater" had essentially ended.

Shy's Hill

Today, although the Battle of Nashville occurred over a huge area, almost all of the actual battlefield has disappeared under the suburbs of Nashville. Only a few key places have been preserved as isolated pieces surrounded by the modern city. Fort Negley was abandoned after the war and allowed to fall into ruin. In 2000 a restoration project was undertaken and seven years later a Visitors Center was constructed, and today the remaining ruins of Fort Negley are part of a park located next to the science museum.

Confederate Redoubt Number One is in an empty suburban lot, and Shy's Hill is accessible by a walking path in a city park. Both of these sites are owned by the Nashville Preservation Association. The city's downtown area also has a walking tour with historical markers pointing out various buildings that were used by Federal forces during the war, and a Confederate Cemetery is located at Mount Olivet.

Fort Fisher

December 24, 1864
North Carolina

During the siege of Petersburg, General Robert E Lee's lifeline was the port of Wilmington NC, one of the only remaining Confederate ports that had not already been closed down by the Federal blockades. Supplies from the port were carried along several railroad lines to Richmond and Petersburg and provided the vital link that kept Lee's army in the field.

The critical harbor was protected by Fort Fisher, one of the strongest citadels in the entire South. In the summer of 1862, as the Union Navy began imposing its Anaconda blockade along the Atlantic, Col. William Lamb arrived in Wilmington NC and, recognizing the importance of the port, supervised construction of a massive defensive fort at the mouth of the Cape Fear River. Since traditional brick and mortar forts had already demonstrated their vulnerability to rifled cannon fire, Lamb built Fort Fisher using earth and sand instead, which could absorb the impact of even the largest explosive shells. The seaward side of the fortress was protected by 22 cannons, while the landward side bristled with 25. Inside each earthen mound was a reinforced chamber for ammunition and bombproof shelters, connected to the others by underground tunnels. The fort was virtually impregnable, and under its guns the Confederates were able to keep the port open for a fleet of blockade runners who delivered vital supplies imported from the Caribbean. It became known as "The Gibraltar of the South".

When Lee and the Army of Virginia became holed up at Petersburg, Wilmington turned into his lifeline. During the siege, General Ulysses S Grant expended considerable effort towards cutting the railroad tracks and interrupting the flow of Confederate supplies, but at first he was simply not strong enough to strike at the port itself and close off the source of Lee's lifeblood.

It wasn't until December 1864 that Grant felt himself at enough of an advantage to spare the resources for an attack on Wilmington. Mobile Bay had just been captured and that freed up a significant Federal naval force, and the Confederate General Braxton Bragg had left Wilmington to join General Joseph Johnston's army in Georgia against Union General William T Sherman's march across Georgia, taking 2,000 troops with him and thereby weakening Fort Fisher's garrison. Only about 2,000 Confederates remained.

Grant decided to take the opportunity. A joint army and navy expedition was assembled under General Benjamin Butler and Admiral David Porter to attack and capture Wilmington. In Richmond, General Lee learned of the impending attack and sent 6,000 troops under General Robert Hoke to reinforce Fort Fisher.

The Federals arrived on Christmas Eve and opened up a massive naval bombardment. Although they managed to blow up an ammunition reserve and destroy several guns, most of the shells either missed their target or were absorbed by the earthen walls. Around 1,000 Union troops were then landed as an advance force, but they were stopped by Hoke's Confederates.

With his attack stalled, Butler concluded that the Fort was too strong to take, and on December 27 he pulled his soldiers off the beach and back to the boats, then withdrew the fleet. This was contrary to the instructions he had received from Grant, who had told him to lay siege to the Fort if the assault failed.

When Grant learned that his orders had been disobeyed, he angrily relieved Butler of command, placed General Alfred Terry in charge, and planned a second assault. On January 12, 1865, Admiral Porter began a naval bombardment with 56 ships, which continued for three days. During this time, 8,000 Federals, including a division of US Colored Troops, landed north of the Fort, intending to attack the landward side; at the same time, another force of 1600 armed sailors and 400 Marines landed at the seaward side as a diversion.

Fort Fisher

After six hours of fierce fighting, the Federals managed to break into the Fort at Shepherd Battery, and the Confederates retreated to Battery Buchanan on the other side of the parade ground. But the Union troops moved outside the Fort and around its walls to attack Battery Buchanan from the rear. At 10:00pm the Confederates surrendered.

Elated by their victory, the Federal troops began a drunken celebration that lasted all night. But it had a tragic ending: around dawn, someone, probably a drunken Union trooper, accidentally set off an explosion in one of the powder magazines which demolished a portion of the Fort and killed over 200 Federal soldiers and Confederate prisoners.

The loss of Fort Fisher was a crippling blow to General Lee at Petersburg, who was now forced to move whatever supplies he could from the railroad center at Danville VA. It was not enough. Within two months, the Union Army would seize his last remaining railroad supply line, and force the Confederates to withdraw from Petersburg and abandon Richmond.

Today, most of the original Fort Fisher has been lost. During the Second World War a grass airfield was built on the Fort's location, used by coastal patrol airplanes. Later, US Highway 421 was constructed through the location. By the time the Fort was declared a National Historical Landmark in 1960, only about ten percent of the original sand berms and wooden walls remained. In 1999 a seawall was put up to help control wave erosion at the Fort's location.

The 300 acres surrounding the Fort are now protected in the Fort Fisher State Recreation Area. The remaining portion of the Fort itself is included in the Fort Fisher State Historic Site. There is a Visitors Center with maps and displays, and a walking trail that winds through some of the original sand berms and a reconstructed portion of palisade wall. A reconstruction of Shepherd Battery contains a replica 32-pound sea gun.

The North Carolina Underwater Archaeology department, which has carried out excavations offshore, has its headquarters at the Fort site, and some of the exhibits in the museum display artifacts recovered from wrecked Civil War warships and blockade runners. The Cape Fear Museum in Wilmington also has an interpretive exhibit about the fighting at Fort Fisher, with a display of artifacts and dioramas.

Selma
April 2, 1865
Alabama

After his raid on Memphis, the Confederate cavalry commander General Nathan Bedford Forrest retreated to Alabama. With the crushing Southern defeat at Nashville and the withdrawal from Petersburg and Richmond, it was becoming apparent that the war was almost over, but Forrest now took charge in northern Alabama, where he had about 5,000 troops, scattered in several locations.

The Federals, meanwhile, had also set their sights on Alabama—particularly the city of Selma. Located on the Alabama River, Selma was the largest remaining industrial center in the Confederacy: the Ordnance and Naval Foundry was the second-largest ironworks in the South, and the city contained another ten iron foundries as well as a gunpowder factory and nitrate plant, lumberyards, cotton warehouses, and coal storage. Two previous Union cavalry raids, in 1863 and 1864, had failed to reach the city.

Now, knowing that the city had only minimal defenses, the Union General James Wilson decided to lead another large-scale cavalry raid, with almost 15,000 troopers, to capture Selma and destroy its industrial facilities. Because his pickets had captured a Confederate courier who was delivering orders to the Alabama troops, Wilson knew where all of Forrest's men were located.

And so, entering Alabama on March 22, the raiders were able to strike several towns along the way before approaching Selma on April 1. At Ebenezer Church they ran into a detachment of about 2,000 of Forrest's cavalry, and in the ensuing skirmish Forrest was wounded, and he and his men were forced to retreat to Selma.

Confederate General Nathan Bedford Forrest and Union General James Wilson, in contemporary photographs

The city was protected by two layers of defensive trenches and redoubts, each almost three miles long, but the inner layer was unfinished. The fortifications had also been designed to hold 20,000 troops, and Forrest only had about 4,000, mostly old men and boys who were unfit for frontline service, to man them. The approaching Federals outnumbered them over two to one.

Wilson arrived at about 2pm that afternoon. He planned to launch an assault after dark, but when a skirmish broke out after a Confederate patrol stumbled into the Union baggage train, it sparked immediate fighting. The Federal cavalry was armed with repeating Spencer carbines, and the Confederates, outnumbered and outgunned, lasted just 30 minutes before withdrawing to the inner fortifications. As the attacks continued, the Union forces drove through at several spots, and the Confederate defenders broke apart.

By 7pm Wilson's troops were swarming through the city's streets, and while General Forrest and his staff escaped on horseback, the rest of the garrison surrendered. The Union cavalry spent the next seven days burning everything in the city that was of military use.

Today, nearly nothing remains of the battleground. Much of the heaviest fighting took place along what is now Broad Street. The badly-eroded remnants of some of the Confederate earthworks can still be seen along the banks of the Alabama River. The Old Depot Museum exhibits some artifacts from the battle, and there is a self-guided driving tour around the city which features a number of ante-bellum plantation houses and buildings that were used during the war.

Sailor's Creek
April 6, 1865
Virginia

After abandoning Petersburg, General Robert E Lee's Army of Virginia was desperately in need of food and supplies. At first, Lee directed his troops to move towards the nearby town of Amelia Courthouse, where he thought there was a food depot. When they got there, however, they found it empty. After waiting a day for his straggling men to catch up, Lee now tried to move towards the railroad center at Danville VA, where he could receive supplies—but this route had already been blocked by General Ulysses S Grant's forces. That left Lee with no alternative but to try to make his way to Lynchburg VA. To get there, he would have to cross Sailor's Creek (also sometimes spelled as Sayler's Creek) at the Danville Road.

As the Confederates marched, they became more and more disorganized. The column was led by General James Longstreet's division, with General Richard Ewell behind him accompanying the baggage and supply wagons. As they marched, the slower baggage train fell behind, opening a gap between Longstreet and Ewell.

When Ewell crossed the Little Sailors Creek, he was blocked by Union forces under General Philip Sheridan. Behind Ewell, Confederate General Richard Anderson was also forced into a defensive line along Sailor's Creek.

The Hillsman Farm

At about 5pm, a Federal unit commanded by General Horatio Wright opened fire with 20 cannons: Ewell, lacking artillery of his own, was unable to retaliate. As Ewell was pinned down by cannon fire, the Union General Wesley Merritt charged into Anderson's position at Marshall's Crossroads and succeeded in breaking the Confederate lines and routing Anderson's troops. Among the cavalry officers involved in this fighting was General George Custer. With their horses exhausted by the previous fighting, some of the Federal cavalry were mounted upon Confederate mules taken from the captured baggage train.

During the fighting at the Crossroads, General Custer's brother Captain Thomas Custer managed to capture a Confederate regimental flag. In this pre-radio era, the only way commanders in the field could keep track of where their units were was by visually tracking their flags, so the regimental flag was heavily protected, and the act of capturing one was viewed as a spectacular feat of prowess. Tom Custer won a Medal of Honor for his actions here at Sailor's Creek. Just four days earlier, moreover, he had won that same honor for capturing another regimental flag during the fighting at Namozine Church. He remains today one of the few people who have won two Congressional Medals of Honor—and the only one to have done so in less than a week—making him the most highly decorated soldier in the Civil War.

At about 6pm on April 6, Wright launched an assault on Ewell's lines at Hillsman Farm which, after heavy fighting, was driven back. After regrouping, the Federals attacked again, and this time broke through. Ewell was unaware that Anderson had already been driven off the field by Merritt, and when he tried to withdraw he ran into Merritt's troops and found himself surrounded. Most of Ewell's 3,000 troops surrendered; six Confederate Generals, including Ewell himself, were captured in this action.

During this time, in a separate action, the Confederate General John Gordon was trying to move the remaining supply wagons across two bridges near the Lockett Farm. The bridges were unable to handle the traffic, however, and baggage carts were backed up for miles when cavalry troops under Union General Andrew Humphrey arrived at the scene and attacked. Gordon was unable to hold them off and withdrew, losing 1700 casualties (mostly captured) and 200 supply wagons.

It was a crushing defeat. In total, the Confederates had lost at least 8,000 men and ten Generals at Sailor's Creek, most of them as prisoners. In addition, much of the supply train was lost. When General Robert E Lee was told about the fighting, he rode to the top of a nearby bluff to see for himself—and was shocked when the shattered remnants of Ewell and Anderson's divisions began to straggle past him. "My God," he exclaimed, "has the army dissolved?"

Only later did General Lee learn that his son Major General George Washington Custis Lee had been captured during the fighting.

Although the fighting at Sailor's Creek was spread out over several square miles, only 800 acres have been designated a National Historic Landmark, and of this only 321 acres are preserved in the Sailors Creek Battlefield State Park. A series of walking trails cover the battlefield, and a driving tour takes visitors to nearby places which are not part of the actual park. The Hillsman Farm House, which was used as a hospital during the battle, is preserved as it was in 1865—bloodstains can still be seen on the wooden floors. The Lockett Farm House, the scene of heavy fighting, is also preserved.

Appomattox
April 8, 1865
Virginia

After the blow at Sailor's Creek, General Ulysses S Grant knew that the Confederate Army of Virginia was beaten, and sent a message to General Robert E Lee asking if perhaps it was not time to begin discussing a surrender. Lee, however, was not ready to give up yet, though he realized that his only remaining chance was to reach the railroad station at Appomattox Courthouse, where loaded supply trains were waiting for him. Gathering what was left of the Army of Virginia (now reduced to around 28,000 men), he set off for the train station, hoping to resupply his troops, move south, and join up with General Joseph Johnston's army.

Just after dawn on the morning of April 8, the Confederate advance force of cavalry, under General John Gordon, reached Appomattox Courthouse—and discovered that the Federals had marched all night to beat him there. A unit of Federal cavalry under General George Custer had already burned the three trains carrying the Confederate supplies, and more Union cavalry had formed up in a defensive line along a ridge nearby. Gordon charged the Federals and managed to seize part of the ridge—but from this vantage point he was able to see the entire Union Army of the Potomac stretched out before him. He sent back a message to General Lee: "I have fought my corps to a frazzle, and I fear I can do nothing unless I am heavily supported by Longstreet's corps." Gordon knew there could be no reinforcement.

Robert E Lee knew it too. When he saw Gordon's message, he realized that it was the end of his army—they were surrounded on all sides and cut off from any possible source of food or supplies. "There is nothing left for me to do," he told his aides, "but to go and see General Grant. And I would rather die a thousand deaths."

By messenger, Lee sent a note to Grant asking for a meeting. In response, Grant requested him to find a suitable place where they could convene and to send word to him. After sending aides to scour the village of Appomattox Courthouse, Lee and his staff chose the little cottage where Wilmer McLean, a sugar speculator, lived.

After further exchanges, a ceasefire went into effect and the meeting was arranged for the next afternoon. Lee was the first to arrive, clothed immaculately in full dress uniform and sash. Grant was late, and when he finally arrived he was, characteristically, clad in an old service uniform, wet with mud, with his pant legs tucked into his boot-tops. Only the dirt-splattered star insignia on his shoulders gave any clue to his rank as commander in chief.

The two had met before, twenty years ago as young officers in the Mexican-American War, and for a few minutes they chatted about old times. It was Lee who brought them back to the business at hand.

Grant then handed a written summary of the surrender terms: "I propose to receive the surrender of the Army of N. Va. on the following terms, to wit: Rolls of all the officers and men to be made in duplicate. One copy to be given to an officer designated by me, the other to be retained by such officer or officers as you may designate. The officers to give their individual paroles not to take up arms against the Government of the United States until properly exchanged, and each company or regimental commander sign a like parole for the men of their commands. The arms, artillery and public property to be parked and stacked, and turned over to the officer appointed by me to receive them. This will not embrace the side-arms of the officers, nor their private horses or baggage. This done, each officer and man will be allowed to return to their homes, not to be disturbed by United States authority so long as they observe their paroles and the laws in force where they may reside."

In addition, Grant added, he would provide the starving Confederate troops with rations from his own commissary. Lee thanked him for the gesture, saying that it would go far towards reconciling the country.

The McLean House at Appomattox, where Lee surrendered

The terms were then formally written down by one of Grant's aides, Ely S Parker. When Lee learned that Parker was a member of the Seneca Native American nation, he remarked, "It is good to have one real American here." "Sir," Parker replied, "we are all Americans."

After the surrender document was signed, Lee stepped outside and was met by a crowd of Union soldiers cheering their victory over the Confederacy. Hearing this, Grant immediately sent an aide outside to silence them, declaring, "The war is over; these are our countrymen now."

With Lee's surrender, however, there were still well over 100,000 armed Confederate troops in the field. But as word of the Army of Virginia's capitulation spread across the South, everyone realized that further resistance was pointless. On April 26, General Joseph Johnston and his men in North Carolina submitted to General William T Sherman. On May 9, General Nathan Bedford Forrest disbanded his cavalry force in Alabama. General Edmund Kirby Smith, though hearing about the surrender, stubbornly refused at first to give up, and did not surrender his forces in Louisiana until May 26. The last Confederate land force, led by the Cherokee General Stand Watie in what is now Oklahoma, did not capitulate until June 23, and the last surrender to take place, of the sea raider CSS *Shenandoah*, happened at Liverpool in Great Britain on November 6. But after Lee's surrender the fighting was not yet quite over....

Wilmer McLean and his family occupied the McLean House until 1869. It passed through several buyers and then stood vacant and neglected, until it was purchased by a group of investors who disassembled it brick by brick, planning to relocate it in Washington DC as a museum. That plan was halted by the Great Depression, and instead the National Park Service bought the property in 1949, reassembled the house, and incorporated it into the Appomattox Court House National Historical Park, which had been established in 1935.

Today the house has been restored and reconstructed to the condition it was in at the time of the surrender. The rest of the 1800 acre park contains historical buildings from the town of Appomattox, including a jail, a tavern, and the old courthouse. There are also interpretive signs and monuments at the ridge area where Gordon's last attack took place.

Fort Blakely
April 9, 1865
Alabama

After the Battle of Mobile Bay, the Union occupied Forts Morgan and Gaines to control the flow of shipping in and out of the harbor, but did not move on the city of Mobile itself. Both sides, however, knew that an eventual assault on the city was inevitable. The Confederates poured what resources they could into strengthening their defenses: a three-mile arc of trenches and redoubts protected Mobile with 30,000 troops and 300 guns, centered on Fort Blakely. They were commanded by General Dabney Maury.

By the spring of 1865, however, the majority of the Confederate troops in Alabama had been siphoned off to more important areas like Virginia. Maury was now down to around 9000 troops, most of them veterans of the disastrous fighting at Franklin and Nashville. The Federals were also desperately moving troops into Virginia to deal with Robert E Lee.

It wasn't until it became apparent that Lee was trapped at Petersburg that the Union was finally able to spare enough resources to launch a campaign against Mobile, which was now one of the largest remaining

Confederate-held cities. The task was assigned to General Edward Canby, who was given 30,000 troops that were landed at Forts Morgan and Gaines, and another 12,000 who marched overland from Pensacola under General Frederick Steele, including 5,000 former African-American slaves in the "US Colored Regiments". The Navy provided a fleet of gunships and ironclads. Canby marched his troops up the east coast of Mobile Bay, covered by the Navy's ironclads, and laid siege to the "Spanish Fort", a Confederate defensive position built at the site of an old colonial redoubt. Meanwhile, Steele's troops moved to Fort Blakely to prevent Maury from moving reinforcements against Canby. Both Union Generals were in position by March 27, 1865.

Since both of the forts were too strong to fall to a direct frontal attack, the Federal troops began digging siege trenches. These were placed as a series of rings: while one ring gave protection to the troops, they would dig a number of zigzag trenches towards the fort's walls, then dig another circle. The process was slowly repeated until the Union forces were within cannon range, and then within rifle range. Inside the Spanish Fort were 1800 defenders and 40 guns commanded by General Randall Gibson; the Federals surrounded him with 100 guns and mortars. Canby's plan was to take the Spanish Fort first, then concentrate all of his forces against Fort Blakely.

For the next week, Federal siege mortars and howitzers lobbed explosive shells at the two forts. As his defenses began to crumble, Gibson expected a Union assault against his walls any time now and, realizing that he would not be able to hold out, began laying an escape plan. After scouting out a retreat route through the surrounding swamps, he sent work parties out at night to lay roadways made from cut logs, and arranged for Maury, back in Mobile, to dispatch boats across the Bay to pick his men up at a given signal.

Meanwhile, the Federals continued to pound the fort. By the morning of April 8, most of Gibson's cannons had been destroyed. That afternoon, the Union guns punched a hole in one of his outer walls. The final assault would probably come the next morning.

Gibson decided to pull out before Canby could attack. That night, he sent word to Maury and began withdrawing along the homemade swamp road. Maury's boats took about 1000 of the defenders back to Mobile, and moved another 800 to Fort Blakely. When Canby's troops entered the Spanish Fort on the morning of April 9, they found only 100 wounded Confederates, who had been left behind.

Confederate Redoubt Number 4 at Fort Blakely

At Fort Blakely, siege operations had also been started, and General Steele's troops were already within cannon range of the fort. The Confederate defenders under General John Liddell fought back with over 40 guns, at one point destroying an entire Union battery with a barrage of cannon fire, but the Federals had overwhelming force. By the time the Spanish Fort was taken, Steele's trenches were already within 75 yards of the Confederate walls and in position to start an assault on Fort Blakely.

The attack was launched at 6pm on April 9, as some 2000 troops led by the 83rd Ohio Regiment headed directly for Confederate Redoubt Number 4. Liddell's troops broke and ran, retreating all the way back to Mobile. After just 20 minutes of combat, the Federals entered Fort Blakely. General Lidell was captured along with 3000 of his troops.

The first thing Canby did was assemble the captured Confederate soldiers. As part of their defenses, they had buried hundreds of artillery shells with pressure-sensitive triggers as "torpedoes" (today known as "mines"), and Canby now ordered the prisoners to dig them all up.

As the captured Confederates worked under Federal guard, neither side was aware that General Robert E Lee had just surrendered to General Ulysses S Grant at Appomattox, and the war was essentially over. In Mobile, Maury still had about 4000 troops, but not wanting to have the city destroyed in a fight he knew he could not win, he decided to withdraw, marching north. The day after he left, city officials approached the Federals to arrange a surrender. Canby entered Mobile on April 12. For the next two weeks Federal cavalry patrols would fight a series of small skirmishes with Maury's troops, until word finally reached Alabama of Lee's surrender. Maury then capitulated on May 5, the last major Confederate force to surrender east of the Mississippi River.

Today, the battlefield is contained within the 1500-acre Historic Blakely State Park, formed as a privately-owned park in 1976 and obtained by the state in 1981. In 2011 state funding was ended, and the park is now privately-run and funded through gate admissions.

The battle site is extraordinarily well-preserved, with many of the original trench lines, embankments, zigzags, rifle pits and cannon positions still mostly intact. Almost 4000 acres of the battlefield are protected, and there are walking trails that wind around the Confederate and Union positions.

Ford's Theater
April 14, 1865
Washington DC

Everyone knows that stage actor and Southern sympathizer John Wilkes Booth shot and killed President Abraham Lincoln at Ford's Theater on April 14, 1865. Less well-known, however, is the rest of the plot: Booth's co-conspirators had planned to assassinate Vice President Andrew Johnson and Secretary of State William Seward at the same time. There is also debate among some historians about the extent of Confederate Government involvement in the assassination, and even whether the plot included Lincoln's own Secretary of War.

On April 11, 1865, President Abraham Lincoln gave a speech from the balcony of the White House to a throng of cheering people outside. Just two days before, Confederate General Robert E Lee had surrendered in Virginia and, although other Confederate armies would still fight on for a short while, the end of the Civil War was now in sight. Lincoln looked forward to healing the wounds that had torn the country in two.

Unknown to either Lincoln or the crowd, however, two of the men who had joined the gathering were not celebrating. John Wilkes Booth was one of the most famous actors in the US, and though he lived and worked in Washington DC, he had long been a supporter of the secessionist South. With him in the crowd was Lewis Thornton Powell, a former Confederate soldier and a relative of a Confederate General. The two were already planning an action that, they hoped, would still win independence for the South.

At first, the Confederates had won an impressive string of victories on the battlefield, and it appeared as if the South would be able to force the North to grant independence. But after the Battle of Gettysburg and the surrender of Vicksburg in 1863, the Confederacy's fortunes turned. By 1864, it was becoming apparent that there would be no military victory.

It was sometime in late 1864 that the conspiracy began which would eventually assassinate the President. John Wilkes Booth, as a well-known theater actor, had numerous political connections, and one of these led him to a Maryland doctor named Samuel Mudd, who was part of an underground Confederate network that carried out spy work and sabotage. Mudd in turn introduced Booth to John Surratt. The 21-year old Surratt was an agent for the Confederate intelligence service, and had acted as a courier to carry messages and information between Washington DC and Confederate territory in Virginia. Now, Booth and Surratt, meeting in the DC roominghouse owned by Surratt's mother Mary, began an audacious plan: they would kidnap President Lincoln and exchange him for a release of Confederate prisoners of war. In 1864, security precautions were lax: not only was the White House unguarded and open, but Lincoln often walked or rode, sometimes alone, through the streets of the city.

Over the next few months, more Southern sympathizers were recruited for the plan. David Herold was a former schoolmate of John Surratt who worked as a pharmacist. George Atzerodt, who ran a coach-painting business, lived in northern Virginia and served the Confederacy as a spy and a courier for Surratt. Samuel Arnold and Michael O'Laughlen were both former schoolmates of Booth: Arnold was an ex-

Confederate soldier, and O'Laughlen was part of a Confederate sabotage ring. The final plotter was Lewis Thornton Powell—using the alias "Lewis Payne"—a Confederate soldier who had been captured as a POW, escaped, and now was fighting as a guerrilla in Maryland.

On March 17, 1865, the group was ready to put their plan into action. President Lincoln was scheduled to visit a group of wounded Union soldiers in a hospital in DC, and Booth, Surratt and the others positioned themselves along the route, planning to ambush him, kill any escorts, and spirit him away to Richmond. At the last minute, though, Lincoln changed his schedule and did not make the trip. Less than a month later General Lee surrendered, and Booth and Powell found themselves on the White House lawn listening to Abraham Lincoln.

Lincoln's theater box

Now, the goals of the plot changed: instead of kidnapping President Lincoln, the group would kill him. Originally, the plan seems to have been to use explosives to blow up the White House. When there seemed to be no good way to accomplish that, the plan turned to shooting Lincoln instead. At the same time, the plotters would kill Vice President Johnson and Secretary Seward as well, decapitating the Union Government in one stroke and, they hoped, giving the South an opportunity to rise up again, continue the war, and win its independence from a crippled and confused US Government. Over the next three days, once again meeting in Mary Surratt's boardinghouse, the plan took shape: Booth would kill Lincoln at the Ford Theater, just a few blocks from the White House. Atzerodt would kill Vice President Johnson at the Kirkwood House hotel, and Powell and Herold would kill Secretary Seward at his home on Pennsylvania Avenue. The others would then help the assassins escape into Confederate-held Virginia. It was decided that all three assassinations would take place at 10:15pm.

On the evening of April 14, all three assassins took their positions. Booth spent some time in a nearby tavern, then went into Ford's Theater, entered the second floor balcony, and fired one fatal shot before leaping to the stage and limping away with a broken leg.

Booth's pistol

Atzerodt checked into the Kirkwood House, taking room 126, one floor above Johnson's room. At about 8pm, he decided to calm his nerves with a trip to the bar, where he asked the bartender whether the Vice President regularly left his room. Unfortunately for the plotters, Atzerodt was an alcoholic, and within a short time he was not only thoroughly drunk, but had gotten cold feet and decided not to go through with the plan. Instead, he spent hours drinking, then walked aimlessly around Washington DC.

Secretary of State William Seward had, just a few days before, been in a carriage accident and had broken his jaw, and now on the night of April 14 he was in bed recovering. At around 10pm, Powell and Herold arrived at the house. With Herold staying behind to act as a lookout, Powell, armed with a Whitney Navy revolver and a Bowie knife, entered the house by telling the doorkeeper that he was delivering medicine. Once inside, Powell started up the stairs, but was stopped by Seward's son Frederick, who said Seward was sleeping and he would take the medicine to the Secretary himself. Powell pulled his revolver and tried to shoot the younger Seward, but the gun misfired, and Powell pistol-whipped him instead, fracturing his skull. Entering Secretary Seward's room and drawing his knife, Powell was then confronted by the Secretary's daughter Fanny, and threw her to the floor before making his way to the bed where Seward was stretched out. Jumping on Seward, Powell slashed at his face and neck, stabbing him five times. At this point Seward's male Army nurse, George Robinson, entered the room and pulled Powell off the bed.

Powell slashed at him too, and, thinking Seward was dead (in fact the wounds were mostly superficial), ran down the stairs, where he engaged in a fight first with Seward's other son Augustus and then with a messenger from the State Department named Emerick Hansell, who just happened to be there. After stabbing both of them too, Powell ran outside–only to find that Herold, upon hearing all the commotion inside the house, had panicked and run away with both of the horses. In desperation, Powell ran off into the night. For the next several days, he hid in a nearby cemetery, sleeping in a tree, until he was discovered and arrested.

Booth, meanwhile, had ridden his horse to the Surratt boardinghouse, where he met with Herold, but no Powell or Atzerodt. Booth and Herold fled to Mudd's house in Maryland, where the doctor set Booth's broken leg, then both of them went on horseback to the banks of the Potomac River. For twelve days, the two hid out in the woods and waited for a chance to cross into Virginia while avoiding Union patrols. They finally managed to cross, only to be found by a Federal cavalry unit. Booth was killed in the shootout, and Herold was captured. The Union Army, meanwhile, had already identified most of the conspirators and arrested them. Only John Surratt, who had left for Richmond after the kidnapping plot had fallen through, managed to escape to Canada, then to England and Italy.

In all, eight people were put on trial for conspiring to kill Lincoln, Johnson and Seward. (One of these was Edmund Spangler, a Ford Theater employee who hadn't actually been part of the plot but had been tricked into helping Booth.) Because the war had not yet officially ended on April 14, Secretary of War Edwin Stanton tried them in a military court rather than on civilian criminal charges, on the grounds that they had attacked the military Commander in Chief. Four of the defendants– Lewis Thornton Powell, Mary Surratt, David Herold and George Atzerodt–were sentenced to death. They were hanged in July 1865. John Surratt, meanwhile, was finally arrested in Egypt in 1866, returned to the US, and went on trial (this time in a civilian court) in 1867. Surratt was set free by a hung jury, and eventually died in 1916.

Since then, two branches of conspiracy theory have surrounded the Lincoln assassination. The first, that Secretary of War Stanton was somehow a part of the conspiracy and hoped to take over control of the government himself in the assassination's aftermath, has virtually no supporting evidence. The other theory, however, that Booth and his cohorts were actually recruited by the Confederate intelligence service for the plot with the full knowledge of the Richmond government, has never been demonstrated with actual documentary evidence, but is supported by some circumstantial evidence. Several of the people involved in the assassination did indeed have ties to the Confederate intelligence service, including a spy ring operating in Canada. But no solid proof has been found linking the Confederate Government to the Lincoln assassination plot.

After the assassination, the Federal Government purchased Ford's Theater, using it for records storage. In 1893 part of the front façade collapsed and was repaired. In 1928, the now-empty building was converted into a museum run by the city's parks department before being turned over to the National Park Service in 1933. In 1966 the building was completely restored.

Today, Ford's Theater and the Petersen House across the street, where Lincoln died, are jointly run as a National Historical Site by the National Park Service. The Visitors Center contains a museum managed by the nonprofit Ford's Theater Society, which exhibits artifacts from the assassination and from Lincoln's life.

Irwinville

May 9, 1865
Georgia

On April 2, 1865, as Federal troops poured into his broken lines at Petersburg, General Robert E Lee told Confederate President Jefferson Davis that his army could no longer defend Richmond, and recommended that the Confederate Government flee its capitol city. Davis, a handful of his Cabinet members and a military guard retreated to Danville VA.

General Lee's surrender at Appomattox sealed the fate of the Confederacy, and by now Jefferson Davis was the most wanted man in the world: not only was the Federal Army convinced that his capture would end all remaining Confederate resistance, but many in the War Department believed that the Richmond government had been involved in John Wilkes Booth's conspiracy to kill Lincoln. The War Department offered a $100,000 reward (an immense sum at that time) for Davis's capture, and he was being pursued by several different Federal cavalry units.

But Davis obstinately refused to accept defeat. With various plans to either form another Army out in the western states to continue the war or to flee to Europe and form a government-in-exile, he left Danville and headed south, reaching the Savannah River and crossing into Georgia on May 3. The next day, in the town of Washington GA, the Government of the Confederate States of America held its last cabinet meeting: Davis paid them with gold from the remains of the Treasury, then officially disbanded the Cabinet.

Moving on to Sandersville GA, Davis, in his last official act as President, released the Confederate Government's remaining gold supplies to Treasurer Captain Micajah Clark for safekeeping, then met up with his wife Varina and their children.

Monument at Jefferson Davis State Historical Site

On the evening of May 9, the little group made camp near a streambed at Irwinville GA. Early the next morning, two Union cavalry patrols, one from the 4th Michigan Regiment and the other from the 1st Wisconsin, independently stumbled onto Davis's camp. Not knowing that the other was there and not recognizing each other at first, the two Union patrols briefly opened fire on each other, killing two of their own soldiers. Davis and his wife tried to take advantage of the chaos by hiding under the stream bank, but they were found by a Michigan cavalry trooper. It was raining that morning and Davis had been sick, and to keep dry he had wrapped himself in his wife's shawl: this was later exaggerated by the press into the story that he had tried to escape by disguising himself in women's clothing.

The streamside meadow where Jefferson Davis had been captured was turned into a state park, today known as the Jefferson Davis Memorial State Historical Site. In 1939, during the Great Depression, the New Deal jobs program known as the Works Progress Administration constructed a stone museum in the park, exhibiting a collection of Civil War artifacts and interpreting the story of Davis's capture. A granite bust stands at the capture spot. In 1980, the 13-acre site was designated as a National Historical Landmark.

Palmito Ranch
May 12, 1865
Texas

The last organized battle of the Civil War was fought after the war was already over. And in a historical irony, the battle ended in a Confederate victory.

In the first years of the Civil War, Texas was important to the Union for three reasons. The state's beef supplies were a major source of rations for the Confederate Army. The Confederacy was circumventing the Federal blockade and obtaining weapons by trading cotton, smuggled into Brownsville TX, across the border to Mexico. And the French Government had sent its troops into northern Mexico to prop up its puppet Emperor Maximilian, which presented a serious danger of a French-Mexican alliance with the Confederacy. The US had already fought a war with Mexico just 20 years previously, and now it looked like it might happen again.

To deal with all of this, the Union General Nathaniel Banks was sent into Texas in 1863 with 6,000 troops. Overwhelming the small Confederate force there, Banks occupied the Rio Grande valley from Corpus Christi to Laredo, cutting off the Mexican border from the Confederacy.

As the war went on, however, Union troops were pulled out of Texas and sent elsewhere where they were needed. In 1864, a force of 1500 Confederate cavalry commanded by former Texas Ranger Colonel John "Old Rip" Ford managed to push the remaining Federals out of the Rio Grande Valley, and they fled to tiny Brazos Santiago Island. For the rest of the war, four Union regiments—the 34th Indiana Infantry, the 2nd Texas Cavalry, and the 87th and 62nd US Colored Troops, around 2000 men in total—remained on the island, under the command of General Lew Wallace. Meanwhile, Ford's Confederate cavalry and some Texas infantry, about 1200 in all, stayed in Brownsville under the command of General James Slaughter. By 1865, with each marooned in their backwater assignment, Wallace and Slaughter had decided that any combat here would be pointless, and reached an informal agreement not to attack each other.

Then in May 1865, things changed rapidly. News came of General Robert E Lee's surrender in Virginia, followed by the assassination of President Lincoln. In Louisiana, Confederate General Edmund Kirby Smith, Slaughter's commanding officer, was still vowing to fight on. And on Brazos Santiago Island, Colonel Robert Jones of the 34th Indiana resigned from the Army and went home, turning command of the garrison over to Colonel Theodore Barrett of the 62nd US Colored Troops.

Barrett was an ambitious 30-year old who had joined the Union Army in 1862 but had never been in combat. Anxious to rise in rank, he had volunteered to command the 1st Missouri Colored Infantry Regiment in 1863, which later became the 62nd USCT. Now, with the Confederate commanders sounding belligerent and the war coming to a rapid end, Barrett apparently decided to take advantage of his unexpected position of command to see a little action and gain some fame before the war was over.

On May 11, using a fleet of small boats, Barrett took 300 troops with him and crossed the water from Brazos Santiago to Brownsville, where the next morning he seized a small post called Palmito Ranch that was held by a handful of Confederates. The Confederate General Slaughter, angered that the Federals had broken their unofficial truce, responded in force, sending a detachment of 150 cavalry and six cannons under Colonel Ford.

Private John Williams

At about 4pm on May 12, Ford's Confederates arrived at Palmito Ranch. Opening fire with his cannons, he took the Federals by surprise—they had not expected artillery and they did not have any cannon of their own. The result was a rout as Barrett's troops turned and ran. Ford's troops chased them all the way back to Brazos Santiago Island.

The Battle of Palmito Ranch is now considered to be the last combat of the Civil War. Fought apparently to feed one man's ambitious ego, it was not much of a fight, and it accomplished nothing at all. The Confederates reported five men wounded, Barrett's Union troops had lost 103 men captured, nine men wounded, and one man—Private John Jefferson Williams of the 34th Indiana Regiment—killed. He was the last man to die in the Civil War.

Two weeks later, General Kirby Smith surrendered all the Confederate forces under his command. Barrett, stung by the loss of the only battle he ever fought, tried to court-martial one of his subordinates for disobeying orders, but the charges were dismissed. After the war, the Rio Grande Valley was occupied by units of General Philip Sheridan's cavalry, as a show of force and a warning to the French soldiers in Mexico to stay on their own side of the river.

Today, the Palmito Ranch battleground is a patch of empty desert near Brownsville. Although it has been designated a National Historic Landmark, the battlefield is mostly forgotten. There is no Visitors Center, and only an interpretive sign marks the location.

Andersonville
May 1865
Georgia

When the Civil War began, both the Union and the Confederacy were unprepared for a long conflict, and often lacked enough resources to properly provide for their own troops, much less for taking care of captured enemies. As a useful expedient, therefore, both sides avoided the need to care for large numbers of prisoners by subjecting their captured enemy soldiers to "parole", an arrangement in which the captured prisoner gave his name and residence, and was then released after signing a promise that he would stay at home and not fight again in the war. It may seem to be a shockingly naive system to us today, but it actually worked pretty well—military men of that time prided themselves on their honor, and in any case the parole was enforced by the practice of checking all new prisoners against the list of previous parolees, and if a paroled prisoner was captured again, he would be summarily executed.

To hold captured enemy officers (and their own local civilians who were arrested for aiding the enemy), both sides converted military prisons into makeshift POW camps. In 1861, the Confederacy held a few hundred captured Federals at Salisbury Prison in North Carolina, while the Union held its Confederate prisoners at Elmyra Prison in New York and Alton Prison in Illinois.

During the first years of the war, both the Union and the Confederate Armies were all-volunteer, with each Regiment being made up of members from a particular county, town, or area. Many Volunteer Regiments were privately raised and paid for by some wealthy local town official, who then usually appointed himself as "Colonel" and assumed command of the unit.

As the war dragged on, however, and losses mounted, many regiments were in the field at sometimes less than half strength, and a method was sought to replenish the ranks without resorting to the politically-undesirable option of conscription. As a result, officers from both armies would regularly meet to arrange "prisoner exchanges", in which the paroles of a certain number of troops from each side were revoked, allowing them to once again re-join their units. (Even this, it turned out, wasn't enough, and both the Union and the Confederacy were forced to resort to drafting conscripts—which provoked vicious draft riots.)

Because the agrarian-based Confederacy had a much smaller population than the industrialized North, the battlefield losses that it suffered had a much greater impact on the Southern armies. The Union recognized this too, and, to weaken the Confederate armies as much as possible, in 1864 General Ulysses S Grant stopped the practice of "prisoner paroles", and began keeping captured Confederate prisoners as POWs for the duration of the war—a tactic which the Confederacy was then also forced to adopt. (The Union also ceased prisoner exchanges in retaliation for the Confederacy's refusal to parole or exchange any of the African-American soldiers it captured, instead often selling them into slavery or shooting them out of hand as at Olustee and Fort Pillow.)

The end of the parole system, however, turned out to be a humanitarian disaster. Neither side was prepared to take care of the tens of thousands of prisoners that it was suddenly stuck with. In April 1864, the Confederates decided to build a new POW camp near the little town of Andersonville GA, which was conveniently near a railroad but was isolated enough to be safe from

Federal cavalry raids. The camp was assembled quickly by slave labor: it consisted of a 17-acre open field surrounded by a palisade fence. It was planned to hold 10,000 POWs. By June, it was already overcrowded with 20,000, and an extension was added to increase the camp's size. This too was quickly overwhelmed, though, as the prison population peaked in August at 35,000. In all, about 45,000 captured Union troops passed through "Andyville's" gates during the war.

Reconstructed "shebang" shelters used by prisoners

The South, crippled by the Union Navy's economic blockade, was particularly short on resources, and with its own people on the verge of starvation, little effort was made to care for Federal POWs. At Andersonville, no buildings were provided for shelter: the Union prisoners lived in crude cloth lean-to's known as "shebangs", and had only a small running stream as a water source (which doubled as the toilet facility). Dysentery, cholera, and other diseases ran rampant. Almost 13,000 prisoners died in Andersonville over 14 months—more than one-fourth of all the prisoners held here, and over one-third of all the Union POWs who died during the entire war.

The North had more economic resources available to care for POWs, but didn't have any greater inclination to do so. In all, at least 56,000 POWs from both sides died in the prison camps—about ten percent of all the total deaths in the war.

When Union troops entered Georgia and proceeded to Atlanta, the Confederate government built a series of cannon emplacements around the prison fence at Andersonville to protect it from raiders, then transferred most of the prisoners elsewhere, only to later bring about 5,000 of them back.

Although rumors had reached northern ears about the horrible conditions in Andersonville, Union officers were not able to enter the camp until after the war ended—but when they did, they were appalled at what they saw. The emaciated prisoners were living in the open air with no food and little water. The camp commandant, Major Henry Wirz, was arrested and tried for murder. He argued that the conditions in the camp were not his fault, but that the Confederate Government had simply not given him enough resources to properly care for the prisoners. Wirz was hanged in November 1865.

In the summer of 1865, Red Cross representative Clara Barton and former POW Dorence Atwater returned to the prison site. During his incarceration, Atwater had been assigned by the Confederates to keep a list of names of all the POWs who died in the camp, and he secretly kept a copy of the list. Because of this, he and Barton were able to identify the graves of all but 460 of the 12,913 prisoners buried in the cemetery.

After the Civil War, the Andersonville campsite was purchased by the Grand Army of the Republic, a nationwide nonprofit organization of Union veterans. The GAR donated the Andersonville site to the Federal Government in 1910. Today, it is a National Historical Site. The 27-acre camp is surrounded by a reconstructed stockade fence. There is a walking trail around the prison field and the nearby National

Cemetery, and a Visitors Center. In 1998, the National Prisoner of War Museum was opened inside the Andersonville Visitors Center. It contains artifacts and exhibits depicting the history of American POWs from the Revolutionary War to the present.

Reconstruction

After the end of the Civil War in 1865, the Confederacy lay beaten and prostrate on the ground. Its armies had been crushed, its government collapsed, and its territory occupied by Federal troops. Yet even in the ashes of this defeat, the embers of the old Confederacy still survived. In a sense, the South never really surrendered, and we still live today with its effects.

As the end of the war came into view in 1864, Lincoln began preparing for the peace. Realizing that a reconciliation had to be worked out that would bring the southern states back into the Union and that old resentments could not be allowed to smolder, Lincoln proposed that the prodigal states be welcomed back and treated with respect. In his second inaugural address, Lincoln pledged to follow a policy towards the defeated Confederates of "malice toward none, charity toward all".

At the same time, however, Lincoln recognized that the end of slavery would alter the entire social structure of the Old South. In all, some 3 million formerly enslaved people—180,000 of which had already enlisted in the Federal Army—were now to be freed. To help integrate them into their new social structures, Lincoln had Congress establish a Freedmen's Bureau which would help the former slaves with land, funding, education, and whatever else they needed to make new lives as free citizens. And, in a speech he gave on April 11, 1865, Lincoln announced that this would also include the right to vote as citizens of the US.

Unfortunately, we will never know what process Lincoln had in mind to accomplish this—he was assassinated just four days later. The task of Reconstruction fell to the Vice President, Andrew Johnson. Johnson, a Democrat, had been the only southern Senator to oppose secession, and had been appointed as the Federal military governor of Tennessee. As the 1864 elections approached, the Republican Lincoln sought to win Democratic votes by choosing Johnson as his running mate.

President Andrew Johnson

After the assassination, Johnson accepted Lincoln's basic approach of reconciliation rather than iron-fisted punishment, and wanted to return the Southern states to the fold as quickly as possible. But unlike Lincoln, Johnson also continued to hold a strong belief in "states rights", and, disregarding the fact that the United States had just fought a long and bloody war against the Southern elite to destroy slavery, Johnson now allowed the occupied states to decide for themselves what social structure they would have, and issued pardons to prominent former Confederates. Under this policy of "Presidential Reconstruction", the former Confederates were given free reign to rule their re-admitted states as they saw fit.

The result was predictable. As Reconstruction began, the same group of interests that had always dominated Southern society—based on class aristocracy, agrarian economic structures, and, most of all, race—quickly regained control. With Johnson's acquiescence, state legislatures passed so-called "Black Codes" which in effect forced African-Americans into second-class citizenship, restricting their rights to vote and to hold property. When Congress passed a Civil Rights Bill in 1866 which pledged the Federal Government to guarantee equal treatment under the law of all US citizens regardless of race, Johnson vetoed it—then Congress promptly overrode the veto. It was one of the first salvos in what would become a bitter political battle between Congress and the President.

Public opinion in the North was outraged. Although the war had begun with the aim of holding the Union together, it had been transformed into a crusade to abolish the institution of human slavery and to live up to the country's pledge of "liberty and justice for all". In the 1866 Congressional elections, a wave of abolitionists was elected, with the clear policy of providing full and equal citizenship for the newly-freed slaves—whether the South liked it or not. It became known as the "Radical Reconstruction".

The result was political war. The former Confederates fought bitterly against what they called "carpetbaggers" (northern politicians who favored equal rights and who often moved to the South to seek political office) and "scalawags" (southern politicians who supported racial equality). The abolitionist-dominated Congress passed laws requiring the Southern states to adopt the 13th, 14th and 15th Amendments—freeing all of their enslaved people and granting them full citizenship rights—as a precondition for readmission to the Union. Another law specified the structure of all the new state governments including provisions for protecting voting rights for all citizens, and divided the former Confederacy into five military zones, with the Federal Army assigned the task of enforcing those rights. Johnson vetoed all of this, and in retaliation, after overriding all his vetoes, Congress passed the "Tenure of Office Act", forbidding the President from replacing any cabinet official without a Senate vote. Johnson defiantly tried to fire Secretary of War Edwin Stanton, and Congress filed articles of impeachment against him over the violation of the Act. In the resulting impeachment trial, the verdict fell just one vote shy in the Senate of removing the President from office.

By 1870, all of the former Confederate states had been re-admitted to the Union, under state constitutions that were specified by Congress and enforced by Federal troops. The results were immediate. In many areas, African-Americans now made up the majority of the population, and they elected former slaves to offices in state government and to Congress. Publicly-funded schools (open to all races) were established, progressive tax codes were passed, and subsidies were given to badly-needed industries and infrastructure such as railroads and bridges. It was the largest and most successful attempt at social reform and racial integration that had ever been attempted up to that time.

The reaction of the former Confederate states, however, was swift. In addition to political foot-dragging, Southern politicians resorted to full-out terrorism. The Ku Klux Klan, originally formed by former Confederate General Nathan Bedford Forrest as a fraternal society, carried out clandestine attacks on African-Americans, abolitionist politicians, and anyone else who challenged white supremacism. By 1871 the Klan had become so powerful in the former Confederacy that newly-elected President Ulysses S Grant had a law passed specifically outlawing the organization and authorizing him to use the Federal Army to combat it by force.

But now public opinion began to change. In 1874, the US suffered an economic depression that left thousands in poverty. Facing struggles of their own, the victors of the Civil War now lost interest in helping those newly-freed slaves on whose behalf they had fought on the battlefields. In addition, Grant and Congress realized that the terrorist violence in the South would require a substantial and prolonged military effort to uproot, and that breaking the power of the white aristocracy in the South would require an economic power shift—including land reform to break up the large plantations and provide farms to newly-freed slaves as well as landless poor whites, which neither the public nor the government was prepared to carry through.

In 1875, when a new wave of Klan violence broke out during elections in Mississippi, President Grant declined to send Federal troops to deal with the situation. The message was clear—the Federal Government no longer could or would use its power to defend its African-American citizens against the depredations of neo-Confederate state governments. In 1876, the decision was formalized when, during a contested Presidential election, the Southern states threw their electoral votes to Rutherford B Hayes in exchange for a pledge to withdraw all the Union troops from the occupied South. The former Confederates once again had free reign. All of the previous social gains were lost, and segregation would rule in the South for the next 100 years until the civil rights movement appeared in the 1950s. The abolitionist North had won the war, but lost the peace.

Since that time, moreover, the United States has continued to struggle with the issues of racial equality, white supremacy, voting rights, and cultural diversity. The Civil War, it could be argued, has still not really ended.

One symbol of this continuing fight is the Beauvoir Estate in Biloxi MS.

After being captured in Georgia at the close of the fighting in 1865, Confederate President Jefferson Davis was taken to Fort Monroe in Virginia, where he would be held for the next two years. President Johnson, despite his preference for leniency towards the South, had planned to put him on trial for treason, but eventually, as the hot emotions over the war began to cool and the Federal Government became bogged down with the difficulties of Reconstruction instead, the charges were dropped and Davis was released in May 1867.

Davis retired with his wife and children to Beauvoir, a seaside estate in Biloxi that had been given to him by admirers. Here, he spent the next several years writing a 1,000-page two volume history of the war, titled *The Rise and Fall of the Confederate Government*. In it, he remained stubbornly unrepentant, defending slavery, white supremacy, secession, the war, and "the Southern way of life". When Davis died in 1889, he was buried in New Orleans. Four years later he was moved and reburied in the former Confederate capitol of Richmond.

The Beauvoir estate house where Davis lived out his last years is now a museum, and there are guided tours of the house and the grounds. It remains today a symbol of the ambiguities and argument which the Civil War still provokes in the US. After a series of racially-motivated attacks and shootings during the presidency of Barrack Obama, many states moved to outlaw the practice of flying Confederate battle flags on their monuments to the "Lost Cause", or even decided to remove such monuments completely, arguing that by honoring the Confederacy they were glorifying and commemorating racial hatred, slavery, segregation, and divisiveness. In response, the Sons of Confederate Veterans organization—which owns the former Jefferson Davis house—announced plans to buy as many of these discarded Confederate monuments as it could, and relocate them to Beauvoir where they will be displayed and celebrated.

Preservation

The Civil War is now over 150 years old. In that stretch of time, the ways in which we have remembered and memorialized it have changed, and those changes have reflected the way our own views of our past have evolved over the years.

The first of the Civil War commemorations were cemeteries. The fighting produced thousands of dead, which littered the battlefield. The art of mortuary embalming had just appeared, and some of the remains, especially the officers, were embalmed and sent home for burial on their family plots. But most of the dead from both sides were simply gathered up and buried near where they fell on the battlefield, often in unmarked mass graves.

These cemeteries were then designated as national memorials, and became the setting for orations and commemorations. The most well-known of these was at Gettysburg, which in November 1863 became the site of the most famous speech in history when President Abraham Lincoln delivered the Gettysburg Address on the occasion of the cemetery's official dedication. National cemeteries were also established at Antietam, Shiloh, Vicksburg, and Chickamauga.

After the war ended, veterans on both sides formed national organizations: the Grand Army of the Republic contained former Union soldiers, and the South had the United Confederate Veterans. In 1868, the Commander of the GAR named May 30 as "Decoration Day", when the graves of fallen Civil War soldiers would be set with flowers. The Confederate veterans had their own "Heroes Day", which was celebrated on different dates by different states. In 1919, after the end of World War One, both organizations agreed to celebrate a joint "Decoration Day" as a memorial to the fallen in all US wars, not just the Civil War, and in 1971 Congress established "Memorial Day" as an official holiday.

By the 1890s, the passionate emotions over the Civil War and Reconstruction had begun to fade as the country reunited. With both the Confederate and Union troopers now growing old and dying, attention turned to commemoration. Veterans' organizations from both sides, as well as state governments, began to take an interest in memorializing the battles that their soldiers had fought rather than just honoring their dead, and battlefields began to be viewed as historical sites to be preserved for future generations. At the major battlegrounds, the US War Department began establishing National Military Parks, which combined the cemeteries with preserved areas of the hills and fields at which the soldiers had fought.

It became common for veterans groups and state governments to raise money to put up ornate memorial stone markers on these battlefields, locating them at the positions that each of their regiments had held during the fighting. Soon more of these monuments appeared, honoring fallen commanders and famous participants. By 1922, the Gettysburg battlefield alone had over 800 stone monuments, cannon displays, memorial statues, and commemorative plaques and tablets, marking out the original battle lines and signifying crucial events.

In 1916, the National Park Service was established, and the United States began the process of setting up one of the largest national park systems in the world. This helped to establish the idea of "public lands", which soon spilled over into historical preservation. By the

1930s, Civil War sites, along with other historically significant locations, began to be viewed as a public resource to be shared and used by everyone for the common good. Across the country the Federal Government set up National Parks, National Monuments, and National Historic Sites, either purchasing the land from its private owners or exercising its power of eminent domain to obtain the sites for public use. In 1933, the War Memorials and Military Parks being run by the War Department were transferred to the National Parks Service. At smaller battlefields and historic sites, this process was echoed by state or local governments.

Confederate Redoubt Number One, on a roadside suburban lot in Nashville TN

But already there were problems. Much of the Civil War fighting had taken place near what were then small towns, often on rivers or near railroad junctions. In the decades after the War, however, many of these small towns had grown into major cities, and their relentless outward expansion had already overrun many of the old battlefields, covering them with factories, homes, and roads. In some areas, such as Gettysburg, Vicksburg, and Franklin, the town itself had formed part of the battleground.

Few cities or states had given any thought to protecting and preserving these historic sites—especially in areas of the old Confederacy, where nobody was particularly interested in keeping the memory of battles that they had lost in a disastrous war. So, unfortunately, many significant battlegrounds (including Nashville, Westport, Atlanta, and others) were lost before they could be preserved.

In many of the still-remaining areas, moreover, practical problems multiplied. During the four years of Civil War there had been over 10,000 battles, skirmishes, raids and encounters of all sizes, and it would be simply impossible to obtain this many sites and commemorate them all. So priorities had to be set about which locations were important enough to be protected, and which would be abandoned to their fate.

Even at the major battlefields, choices had to be made. Many of these clashes had involved more than a hundred thousand men and stretched out over several miles, and there were not enough resources to obtain and preserve such large areas. As a result, the Federal Government decided on what was called the "Antietam Plan", in which only the most significant and important segments of the total battleground would be obtained as a memorial park. In many cases, the National Park would consist of only a thin ribbon of land marking a portion of the actual battle line: the rest of the site, such as rear areas, headquarters, hospitals and artillery sites, would be left in private hands. A significant landmark was reached when the Supreme Court ruled in the 1890s, in a case involving a proposed railroad through the Gettysburg Battlefield, that the Federal Government had the legal right to take land under eminent domain in order to safeguard historical sites of national importance.

Today, however, only about 20% of all the historically-significant Civil War areas are held by the public (only about half of the Gettysburg battlefield is actually inside the borders of the National Park, for example, and less than a third of the Vicksburg battlefield). This policy would have disastrous effects in later years, as areas that were once rural farmland became part of suburbia, and houses and roads began encroaching upon the borders of the battlefield parks.

Tupelo Battlefield, on downtown Main Street

After the Bicentennial celebrations in 1976, Americans took a renewed interest in their national history, including the Civil War, and this sparked a rekindled attention to the protection and preservation of historical sites. It came at just the right time. In 1980, plans were announced by a real-estate developer to build a shopping mall at the Manassas battlefield, on privately-owned land that was historically significant but was not actually part of the National Park. Over the years, other conflicts soon followed: a Walmart was planned at the Wilderness battlefield, a Disney theme park was proposed at the Manassas site, a casino was intended near the Gettysburg National Park, and a motor racetrack was being considered at the Brandy

Station battleground in Virginia. At Gettysburg, a large observation tower was erected on privately-owned land next to the park.

All of this sparked a massive backlash. In 1987, the Association for the Preservation of Civil War Sites, a nonprofit citizens group containing Civil War buffs, professional historians, and educators, was formed to both file legal challenges to the proposed developments and to raise money to buy and permanently protect historically significant tracts of land. In 1991, the Civil War Trust, another nonprofit organization, was formed with the same goals—it was intended to focus more on soliciting corporate donations. For several years the two groups clashed with each other over priorities, credit for successes, and personality-driven conflicts, but even though they had trouble getting along with each other, they scored a number of major successes that saved important areas from destruction. In 1999, the two groups finally worked out their differences and merged as the Civil War Trust Inc.

Since 1987, as the Federal national park system came under political assault with budget cuts and ideological attacks, private preservation efforts have safeguarded over 140,000 acres at 130 different Civil War battlefields. Using private donations and government matching funds, the Trust purchases historically-significant pieces of land from private owners, paying market-value prices. Where possible, these tracts are then turned over to a "public steward", either the National Park Service or a state or local park system: if this is not feasible, the Trust holds the land itself to protect it from commercial or residential development, and raises money to install walkways and interpretive signs at the site. The Trust has been so successful that in 2014 the National Park Service requested that the organization expand its scope to also help preserve and protect historical sites from the Revolutionary War and the War of 1812, many of which were also under imminent threat from encroaching suburbia (including a proposed housing development at the Brandywine battlefield and a dormitory house at the Princeton battleground).

Our national history is worth saving, not only because it holds lessons for our present and warnings for our future, but because it is unique and irreplaceable. A shopping center or a highway or an apartment building can be put anywhere else without affecting its functionality. We have our choice of places where such things can be located.

But historical events are exceptional precisely because they are tied inextricably to a specific time and place. The Battle of Gettysburg or the raid on Harpers Ferry, for instance, through the contingencies and accidents of history, happened in a particular spot. We cannot relocate them elsewhere, nor can we rebuild the places where they happened if those locations are destroyed. Like history itself, once made, historical sites cannot be unmade. The "place" cannot be separated from the "event". And that is why the "places" of our Civil War history must be protected, conserved, and remembered. History cannot be undone—but by remembering it, we can perhaps prevent ourselves from doing it all over again.

www.ingramcontent.com/pod-product-compliance
Lightning Source LLC
Chambersburg PA
CBHW060454090426
42735CB00011B/1986